Groh's paper

P. 29

MALCOLM X

BOOKS BY JOHN HENRIK CLARKE

Rebellion in Rhyme (poetry) 1948
Edited
Harlem, a Community in Transition (1964)
Harlem U.S.A. (1964)
American Negro Short Stories (1966)
William Styron's Nat Turner:
    Ten Black Writers Respond (1968)
Malcolm X: The Man and His Times (1969)

MALCOLM X

THE MAN AND HIS TIMES

Edited, with an introduction and commentary, by

John Henrik Clarke

ASSISTED BY A. PETER BAILEY AND EARL GRANT

THE MACMILLAN COMPANY

Library of Congress Catalog Card Number: 77-75902
FIRST PRINTING
The Macmillan Company
Collier-Macmillan Canada Ltd., Toronto, Ontario
Printed in the United States of America

ACKNOWLEDGMENTS

The editors of this book gratefully acknowledge permission to use the
material in this book.

The following by Malcolm X is used with the permission of Betty
Shabazz (Mrs. Malcolm X), who is the administrator of the estate of
Malcolm X: "A Visit from the FBI"; "Telephone Conversation"; "Defini-
tion of a Revolution"; "God's Judgment of White America"; "Speech to
African Summit Conference—Cairo, Egypt"; "The Second African Summit
Conference"; "Racism: The Cancer That Is Destroying America"; "Com-
munication and Reality"; "Some Reflections on Negro History Week"; "The
Role of the Black People in History." "Our Shining Black Prince" and
"Why I Eulogized Malcolm X" is used with the permission of Ossie Davis.
"The Meaning of Malcolm X" by C. Eric Lincoln, published in The
Christian Century Magazine, April 7, 1965, is used with the author's per-
mission. "The Myths about Malcolm X" by Rev. Albert Cleage, published
in 1968 by Merit Publishers, is used with the author's permission. "Nothing
But a Man" by Wyatt Tee Walker, published in Negro Digest, August 1965,
is used with permission of the author and Negro Digest. "Malcolm X: The
Minutes of Our Last Meeting" by Gordon Parks, published in Life maga-
zine, March 5, 1965, under the title "The Violent End of the Man Called
Malcolm X," is used with the permission of the Robert Lantz Literary
Agency. "Where Is the American Negro Headed," copyright © 1961 by the
National Broadcasting Company and the individual participants on this
program. "Malcolm X Talks with Kenneth B. Clark," copyright by Kenneth
B. Clark, used with the permission of Kenneth Clark and the Beacon Press.
All other material was written especially for this book.

DEDICATION

*To the Children of Malcolm X
with the Hope That They Will
See the Tomorrow of His Dreams*

ATTALLAH

QUBILAH

ILYASAH

GAMILAH LAMUMBAH

MALIKAH SABAN

MALAAK SABAN

And to Betty Shabazz

(MRS. MALCOLM X)

CONTENTS

OUR SHINING BLACK PRINCE

——————— EULOGY DELIVERED BY *Ossie Davis*
AT THE FUNERAL OF MALCOLM X
FAITH TEMPLE CHURCH OF GOD *

Here—at this final hour, in this quiet place—Harlem has come to bid farewell to one of its brightest hopes—extinguished now, and gone from us forever.

For Harlem is where he worked and where he struggled and fought—his home of homes, where his heart was, and where his people are—and it is, therefore, most fitting that we meet once again—in Harlem—to share these last moments with him.

For Harlem has ever been gracious to those who have loved her, have fought for her, and have defended her honor even to the death. It is not in the memory of man that this beleaguered, unfortunate but nonetheless proud community has found a braver, more gallant young champion than this Afro-American who lies before us—unconquered still.

I say the word again, as he would want me to: Afro-American—Afro-American Malcolm, who was a master, was most meticulous in his use of words. Nobody knew better than he the power words have over the minds of men. Malcolm had stopped being a "Negro" years ago.

It had become too small, too puny, too weak a word for him. Malcolm was bigger than that. Malcolm had become an Afro-American and he wanted—so desperately—that we, that all his people, would become Afro-Americans too.

There are those who will consider it their duty, as friends of the Negro people, to tell us to revile him, to flee, even from the presence of his memory, to save ourselves

* February 27, 1965.

by writing him out of the history of our turbulent times.

Many will ask what Harlem finds to honor in this stormy, controversial and bold young captain—and we will smile.

Many will say turn away—away from this man, for he is not a man but a demon, a monster, a subverter and an enemy of the black man—and we will smile.

They will say that he is of hate—a fanatic, a racist—who can only bring evil to the cause for which you struggle!

And we will answer and say unto them: Did you ever talk to Brother Malcolm? Did you ever touch him, or have him smile at you? Did you ever really listen to him? Did he ever do a mean thing? Was he ever himself associated with violence or any public disturbance? For if you did you would know him. And if you knew him you would know why we must honor him: Malcolm was our manhood, our living, black manhood! This was his meaning to his people. And, in honoring him, we honor the best in ourselves.

Last year, from Africa, he wrote these words to a friend: "My journey," he says, "is almost ended, and I have a much broader scope than when I started out, which I believe will add new life and dimension to our struggle for freedom and honor and dignity in the States. I am writing these things so that you will know for a fact the tremendous sympathy and support we have among the African States for our Human Rights struggle. The main thing is that we keep a United Front wherein our most valuable time and energy will not be wasted fighting each other."

However much we may have differed with him—or with each other about him and his value as a man—let his going from us serve only to bring us together, now. Consigning these mortal remains to earth, the common mother of all, secure in the knowledge that what we place in the ground is no more now a man—but a seed—which, after the winter of our discontent, will come forth again to meet us. And we will know him then for what he was and is—a Prince—our own black shining Prince!—who didn't hesitate to die, because he loved us so.

INTRODUCTION

THE man best known as Malcolm X lived three distinct and interrelated lives under the respective names Malcolm Little, Malcolm X, and El-Hajj Malik El-Shabazz. Any honest attempt to understand the total man must begin with some understanding of the significant components that went into his making.

The racist society that produced and killed Malcolm X is responsible for what he was and for destroying what he could have been. He had the greatest leadership potential of any person to emerge directly from the black proletariat in this century. In another time under different circumstances he might have been a king—and a good one. He might have made a nation and he might have destroyed one.

He was a creation of the interplay of powerful and conflicting forces in mid-century America. No other country or combination of forces could have shaped him the way he was and ultimately destroyed him with such unique ruthlessness.

Malcolm X knew, before he could explain it to himself and others, that he was living in a society that was engaged in the systematic destruction of his people's self-respect. His first memories are of conflict. In this respect his early life was no different than that of most black Americans, where conflict comes early and stays late. In his own words:

When my mother was pregnant with me, she told me later, a party of hooded Ku Klux Klan raiders galloped up to our home in Omaha, Nebraska, one night. Surrounding the house, brandishing their shotguns and rifles, they shouted for my father to come out. My mother went to the front door and opened it. Standing where they could see her pregnant condition, she told them that she was alone with her three small children and that my father was away, preaching, in Milwaukee. The Klansmen shouted threats and warnings at her that we had better get out of town because "The good Christian white people" were not going to stand for my father's "spreading trouble" among the "good" Negroes of Omaha with the "back to Africa" preachings of Marcus Garvey.

This was how he remembered his father, an ambitious dreamer attempting to maintain himself and his family while bigoted white policemen, Ku Klux Klansmen, and Black Legionnaires were determined to teach him to stay in "his place." The father of Malcolm X was killed while fighting against the restricted place that was assigned to his people in this country. Much later, and in many different ways, Malcolm X continued the same fight and was subsequently killed for the same reason.

Every major event in Malcolm's life brought him into conflict with the society that still thrives on the oppression of his people.

His mother was born as a result of her mother being raped by a white man in the West Indies. When he was four the house where he and his family lived was burned down by members of the Ku Klux Klan. When he was six his father met a violent death that his family always believed was a lynching.

After the death of his father, who was a follower of the black nationalist Marcus Garvey, his family was broken up and for a number of years he lived in state institutions and boarding homes. When he finally went to school he made good marks, but lost interest and was a dropout at the age of fifteen. He went to live with his sister in Boston and went to work at the kinds of jobs available to Negro youth—mainly the jobs not wanted by white people, like: shoeshine boy, soda jerk, hotel busboy, member of a dining car crew on trains traveling to New York, and a waiter in a Harlem nightclub.

From these jobs, he found his way into the underworld and thought, at the time, that his position in life was advancing. In the jungle of the underworld, where the fiercest survive by fleecing the weak and the defenseless, he became a master manipulator, skilled in gambling, selling drugs, burglary, and hustling. A friend who had helped him get his first job gave him the rationale for his actions. "The main thing you have to remember," he was told, "is that everything in the world is a hustle."

Malcolm returned to Boston, where he was later arrested for burglary and sentenced to ten years in prison. The year was 1946 and he was not quite twenty-one years old. Prison was another school for Malcolm. He now had time to think and plan. Out of this thinking he underwent a conversion that literally transformed his whole life. By letters and visits from his family he was introduced to the Black Muslim movement (which calls itself officially The Lost-Found Nation of Islam). He tested himself in the discipline of his newly chosen religion by refusing to eat pork. The event startled his fellow inmates, who had nicknamed him Satan. He describes the occasion in this manner:

It was the funniest thing—the reaction, and the way that it spread. In prison where so little breaks the monotonous routine, the smallest thing causes a commotion of talk. It was being mentioned all over the cell block by night that Satan didn't eat pork. It made me very proud, in some odd way. One of the universal images of the Negro—in prison and out— was that he couldn't do without pork. It made me feel good to see that my not eating it had especially startled the white convicts. Later I would learn, when I had read and studied Islam a good deal, that unconsciously my first pre-Islamic submission had been manifested. I had experienced, for the first time, the Muslim teaching, "If you take one step toward Allah—Allah will take two steps toward you." My brothers and sisters in Detroit and Chicago had all become converted to what they were being taught was the "natural religion for the black man."

His description of his process of self-education in prison is an indictment of the American educational system and a tribute to his own perseverance in obtaining an education after being poorly prepared in the public schools. While in prison he devised his own method of self-education and learned how to speak and debate effectively so that he could participate and defend the movement after his release from prison. He started by copying words from the dictionary that might be helpful to him, beginning with "A." He went through to "Z" and then, he writes, "for the first time, I could pick up a book and actually understand what the book was saying."

This aspect of his story calls attention to the tremendous reservoirs of talent, and even genius, locked up among the masses in the black ghettos. It also indicates what can be accomplished when the talent of this oppressed group is respected and given hope and a purpose.

Within a few years he was to become a debater with a national reputation. He took on politicians, college professors, journalists, and anyone black or white who had the nerve to meet him. He was respected by some and feared by others.

Malcolm was released from prison in 1952, when he was twenty-seven years old. For a few weeks he took a job with his oldest brother, Wilfred, as a furniture salesman in Detroit. He went to Chicago before the end of that year to hear and meet the leader of the Nation of Islam— Elijah Muhammad. He was accepted into the movement and given the name Malcolm X. He went back to Detroit and was made assistant minister of the Detroit Mosque. From this point on, his rise in the movement and in the eyes of the public was rapid.

At the end of 1953, he went to Chicago to live with the leader of the Nation of Islam and was trained by him personally. After organizing a mosque in Philadelphia, he was sent to head the movement in Harlem in 1954 before he was thirty years old.

In a few years he was able to transform the Black Muslim movement into a national organization and himself into one of the country's best-known personalities. As the public spokesman and defender of the movement, he literally put it on the map. This was the beginning of his trouble with his leader, Elijah Muhammad. When the public thought of the Black Muslim movement they thought first of Malcolm X.

Malcolm X had appeal far beyond the movement. He was one of the most frequent speakers on the nation's campuses and the object of admiration by thousands of militant youth.

In his pamphlet "Malcolm X—The Man and His Ideas," George Breitman gives the following description of Malcolm's appeal as a speaker:

His speaking style was unique—plain, direct like an arrow, devoid of flowery trimming. He used metaphors and figures of speech that were lean and simple, rooted in the ordinary, daily experience of his audiences. He knew what the masses thought and how they felt, their strengths and their weaknesses. He reached right into their minds and hearts without wasting a word; and he never tried to flatter them. Despite an extraordinary ability to move and arouse his listeners, his main appeal was to reason, not emotion. . . . I want only to convey the idea that rarely has there been a man in America better able to communicate ideas to the most oppressed people; and that was not just a matter of technique, which can be learned and applied in any situation by almost anybody, but that it was a rare case of a man in closest communion with the oppressed, able to speak to them, because he identified himself with them, an authentic expression of their yearning for freedom, a true product of their growth in the same way that Lenin was a product of the Russian people.

From 1954, when he was made responsible for the Black Muslim movement in Harlem, the history of that movement is essentially the history of the rise of Malcolm X.

In public speeches, where he nearly always prefaced his remarks with the statement "The Honorable Elijah Muhammad teaches us," Malcolm X was teaching lessons about the black American's fight for basic dignity that were more meaningfully logical than anything that Elijah Muhammad had ever conceived. He was the public figure most identified with the movement and most sought after as its spokesman. Louis E. Lomax referred to him as the St. Paul of the Black Muslim movement and added, "Not only was he knocked to the ground by the bright light of truth while on an evil journey, but he also rose from the dust stunned, with a new name and a burning zeal to travel in the opposite direction and carry America's 20 million Negroes with him."

In these years, Malcolm X was preaching separation and frightening more white people than the social protest organizations that were demanding integration. The bold act of refusing integration was a challenge to a society that never intended to integrate the black Americans in the first place. With this act, Malcolm X put American society on the defensive by questioning its intentions toward his peo-

ple and proving that those intentions were false. Also he
made black America question itself and face reality. He
identified the enemy of their promise, indicted that enemy,
and still did not relieve the victim, his own people, of
the responsibility for being the instrument of their own
liberation.

To place Malcolm X and his roughhewn grandeur in
proper perspective, one must first understand the nature
of the society that produced him and ultimately destroyed
him. To a large extent, the shadow of slavery still hangs
over this land, and affects the daily life of every American.
Slavery was the black gold that produced America's first
wealth and power. Slavery was the breeding ground for the
most contagious and contaminating monster of all time—
racism.

It was this racism and oppression by white America that
convinced Malcolm X of the necessity of black nationalism
as the vehicle for black liberation, as opposed to "integration," while he was in the Black Muslim movement. Although his black nationalism, while he was in the Muslim
organization, was narrow and sectarian, this did not prevent him from playing a tremendously important role in
the evolution of the black freedom struggle.

Prior to the arrival of Malcolm X on the scene, most of
white America looked upon the established civil rights
organizations as "extremist," although most of them were
creatures and creations of the white controllers of power.
But Malcolm came along and said, "Not only do I refuse to
integrate with you, white man, but I demand that I be completely separated from you in some states of our own or
back home in Africa; not only is your Christianity a fraud
but your 'democracy' a brittle lie." Neither the white man
nor his black apologists could answer the latter argument.

Because they could not answer Malcolm in this area,
they attacked him where he was most vulnerable—the
concept of separatism and that all white folks were "blue-
eyed devils"—labeling him a "hatemonger," "racist,"
"dangerous fanatic," "black supremacist," etc. In reality,
he was none of these things. Certainly he didn't preach
"black supremacy." Malcolm X preached black pride,
black redemption, black reaffirmation, and he gave the

black woman the image of a black man that she could respect.

The fact that Malcolm X, while in the Black Muslim movement, could reject a white person on any terms caused most of white America psychological turmoil. And instilled admiration and pride in most black Americans. For the egos of most white Americans are so bloated that they cannot conceive of a black man rejecting them.

It can be stated categorically that Malcolm X, while in the Black Muslim movement and out of it, created the present stage of the civil rights struggle—to the effect that he was a catalytic agent—offstage, sarcastically criticizing the "civil rights leaders," popping a whip which activated them into more radical action and programs. He was the alternative which the power holders of America had to deal with, if they didn't deal with the established "civil rights leaders."

On December 1, 1963, shortly after President Kennedy's assassination, Malcolm X addressed a public rally at Manhattan Center in New York City. He was speaking as a replacement for Elijah Muhammad as he had done many times before. After the speech, during a question and answer period, Malcolm X made the remark that led to his suspension as a Muslim minister. In answer to a question, "What do you think about President Kennedy's assassination?" Malcolm X answered that he saw the case as "The chickens coming home to roost." Soon after the remark, Malcolm X was suspended by Elijah Muhammad and directed to stop speaking for ninety days. After some weeks, when Malcolm X realized that there were a number of highly placed persons in the Black Muslim movement conspiring against him, seemingly with Elijah Muhammad's consent, he left the movement.

He devotes a chapter in his book (*The Autobiography of Malcolm X*) to the growth of his disenchantment and his eventual suspension from the Black Muslim movement. He says:

I had helped Mr. Muhammad and his ministers to revolutionize the American black man's thinking, opening his eyes until he would never again look in the same fearful way at the white man. . . . If I harbored any personal disappointment whatsoever, it was that privately I was convinced that our Nation of Islam could be an even greater force in the American black man's overall struggle—if we engaged in more action. By that I mean I thought privately that we should have amended, or relaxed, our general non-engagement policy. I felt that, wherever black people committed themselves, in the Little Rocks and the Birminghams and other places, militantly disciplined Muslims should also be there—for all the world to see, and respect and discuss.

On March 8, 1964, he publicly announced that he was starting a new organization. In fact two new organizations were started, the Muslim Mosque, Inc., and the Organization of Afro-American Unity.

Malcolm X was still somewhat beholden to Elijah Muhammad in the weeks immediately following his break with the movement. At his press conference on March 12, he said, in part:

"I am and always will be a Muslim. My religion is Islam. I still believe that Mr. Muhammad's analysis of the problem is the most realistic, and that his solution is the best one. This means that I too believe the best solution is complete separation, with our people going back home, to our own African homeland. But separation back to Africa is still a long-range program, and while it is yet to materialize, 22 million of our people who are still here in America need better food, clothing, housing, education, and jobs right now. Mr. Muhammad's program does point us back homeward, but it also contains within it what we could and should be doing to help solve many of our problems while we are still here.

"Internal differences within the Nation of Islam forced me out of it. I did not leave of my own free will. But now that it has happened I intend to make the most of it. Now that I have more independence of action, I intend to use a more flexible approach toward working with others to get a solution to this problem. I do not pretend to be a divine man, but I do believe in divine guidance, divine power, and in the fulfillment of divine prophecy. I am not educated, nor am I an expert in any particular field . . . but I am sincere and my sincerity is my credential.

"The problem facing our people here in America is bigger than other personal or organizational differences.

Therefore, as leaders, we must stop worrying about the threat that we seem to think we pose to each other's personal prestige, and concentrate our united efforts toward solving the unending hurt that is being done daily to our people here in America.

"I am going to organize and head a new Mosque in New York City, known as the Muslim Mosque, Inc. This gives us a religious base, and the spiritual force necessary to rid our people of the vices that destroy the moral fiber of our community.

"Our political philosophy will be black nationalism. Our economic and social philosophy will be black nationalism. Our cultural emphasis will be black nationalism.

"Many of our people aren't religiously inclined, so the Muslim Mosque, Inc., will be organized in such a manner as to provide for the active participation of all Negroes in our political, economic, and social programs, despite their religious or non-religious beliefs.

"The political philosophy of black nationalism means: We must control the politics and the politicians of our community. They must no longer take orders from outside forces. We will organize and sweep out of office all Negro politicians who are puppets for the outside forces."

Malcolm X had now thrust himself into a new area of conflict that would take him, briefly, to a high point of international attention and partial acceptance.

During the last phase of his life Malcolm X established this Muslim Mosque, Inc., and the non-religious Organization of Afro-American Unity, patterned after the Organization of African Unity. He attempted to internationalize the civil rights struggle by taking it to the United Nations.

In several trips to Africa and one to Mecca, he sought the counsel and support of African and Asian heads of state. His trip to Mecca and Africa had a revolutionary effect upon his thinking. His perennial call had always been for *black unity and self-defense* in opposition to the "integrationist's" program of nonviolence, passive resistance, and "Negro-white unity." When he returned home from his trip he was no longer opposed to progressive whites uniting with revolutionary blacks, as his enemies would suggest.

But to Malcolm, and correctly so, the role of the white progressive was not in black organizations but in white organizations in white communities, convincing and converting the unconverted to the black cause. Further, and perhaps more important, Malcolm had observed the perfidy of the white liberal and the American Left whenever Afro-Americans sought to be instruments of their own liberation. He was convinced that there could be no black-white unity until there was black unity; that there could be no workers' solidarity until there was racial solidarity.

The overwhelming majority of white America demonstrates daily that they cannot and will not accept the black man as an equal in all the ramifications of this acceptance—after having three hundred and forty-five years of racism preached to them from the pulpit, taught in the primer and textbook, practiced by the government, apotheosized on editorial pages, lauded on the airways and television screens. It would be tantamount to self-castration, a gutting of the ego. It would be asking white America completely to purge itself of everything it has been taught, fed, and has believed for three hundred and forty-five years.

It was this recognition of what racism had done to the white man and to the mind of the black man that the following paragraph was and is a keystone of the Organization of Afro-American Unity's program: *"We must revamp our entire thinking and redirect our learning trends so that we can put forth a confident identity and wipe out the false image built up by an oppressive society. We can build a foundation for liberating our minds by studying the different philosophies and psychologies of others. Provisions are being made for the study of languages of Eastern origin such as Swahili, Hausa, and Arabic. Such studies will give us, as Afro-Americans, a direct access to ideas and history of our ancestors, as well as histories of mankind at large."* More so than any other Afro-American leader, Malcolm X realized that there must be a concomitant cultural and educational revolution if the physical revolution is to be successful. No revolution has ever sustained itself on emotion.

When Malcolm X returned from his trip to Mecca and

Africa, he completely repudiated the Black Muslims' program of separation, their acquisitive thirst for money and property and machine idolatry. He felt that they were merely imitating the racist enemy. He still believed in separation from his racist enemy, but his was an ideological separation.

To Malcolm X, the Afro-American must transcend his enemy, not imitate him. For he foresaw that both the Black Muslims and the "integrationists" were aping the oppressor; that neither recognized that the struggle for black freedom was neither social nor moral. It was and is a power struggle; a struggle between the white haves and the black have-nots. A struggle of the oppressor and the oppressed. And if the oppressed is to breach the power of the oppressor, he must either acquire power or align himself with power.

Therefore, it is not accidental that Malcolm's political arm, the Organization of Afro-American Unity, was patterned to the letter and spirit after the Organization of African Unity. Nor should it be surprising that he officially linked up the problems of Afro-Americans with the problems of his black brothers and sisters on the mother continent. Malcolm X's vision was broad enough to see that the Afro-Americans were not a "minority" as the enemy and his lackeys would have us believe. Afro-Americans are not an isolated 25 million. There are over 100 million black people in the Western Hemisphere—Cuba, Brazil, Latin America, the West Indies, North America, etc. Malcolm knew that when we unite these millions with the 300 million on the African continent the black man becomes a mighty force. The second largest people on earth. And so Malcolm's perennial theme was unity, unity, unity.

The formation of the Organization of Afro-American Unity and the establishment of an official connection with Africa was one of the most important acts of the twentieth century. For this act gave the Afro-Americans an official link with the new emerging power emanating from both Africa and Asia. Thus, Malcolm X succeeded where Marcus Garvey and others had failed. Thus, doing this, Malcolm projected the cause of Afro-American freedom into the international arena of power.

When he internationalized the problem, by raising it from the level of civil rights to that of *human rights* and by linking up with Africa, Malcolm X threw himself into the cross fire of that invisible, international cartel of power and finance which deposes presidents and prime ministers, dissolves parliaments, if they refuse to do their bidding. It was this force, I believe, that killed Malcolm X, that killed Lumumba, that killed Hammarskjold.

There is another and more potent reason why the American oppressors feared Malcolm X and desired him dead. And that is the publicized fact that he was going to bring the oppression of Afro-Americans before the United Nations, charging the United States Government with genocide. Many of the oppressors had conniptions when confronted with the prospect of a world body discussing the problems of Afro-Americans.

In the introduction to Malcolm X's autobiography, M. S. Handler has said: "No man in our time aroused fear and hatred in the white man as did Malcolm, because in him the white man sensed an implacable foe who could not be had for any price—a man unreservedly committed to the cause of liberating the black man in American society rather than integrating the black man into that society."

He was, more precisely, a man in search of a definition of himself and his relationship to his people, his country, and the world. That a man who had inhabited the "lower depths" of life could rise in triumph as a reproach to its ills, and become an uncompromising champion of his people, is in itself a remarkable feat. Malcolm X went beyond this feat. Though he came from the American ghetto and directed his message to the people in the American ghetto first of all, he also became, in his brief lifetime, a figure of world importance. He was assassinated on February 21, 1965, while on the threshold of his potential.

About the men of his breed, the writer John Oliver Killens has said: "He was a dedicated patriot: DIGNITY was his country, MANHOOD was his government and FREEDOM was his land."

John Henrik Clarke
New York City—November 1968

PART I

MALCOLM X,
THE MAN
IN RETROSPECT

PREFACE TO PART I

Soon after his assassination on February 21, 1965, Malcolm X became the subject of a number of articles appraising his career and his effect on the black freedom movement. Most of these articles were too hastily written and showed no understanding of what Malcolm X and his mission meant to his people. The evaluation of Malcolm X is related to the evolution of black America in the years since the Montgomery bus boycott set in motion the great human drama now being called "the Black Revolution in the United States."

After the death of Malcolm X, a number of writers discussed how well they "knew" him. Some of these new "authorities" on Malcolm X would not come near him when he was alive. Black writers, however, with few exceptions, did not rush to print with hurriedly written articles on Malcolm X. They seem to have been recovering from the shock of his death. When their articles did begin to appear, they were generally better than the large number of articles by white writers that were published on Malcolm X soon after his death.

Malcolm X was forced out of the Black Muslim movement and into a dangerous wind current of history. Figuratively speaking, he did have the time to balance himself in this wind current before he was swept off his feet and into his death. His challenge to mid-twentieth-century America is both simple and complicated. He

3

merely asked America to keep its promise of democracy to his people.

After leaving the Black Muslim movement he immediately put himself in danger by attempting to organize the black community for self-defense. He called upon all sections of the black community to formulate a solution to the problems facing black Americans. Out of this coalition of various elements in the black community came the Organization of Afro-American Unity. His trips to Africa are significant because they took the black Americans' struggle out of the confines of the continental United States and linked it with the non-white world. The civil rights problem, to him at least, became a human rights problem and he attempted to internationalize it.

C. Eric Lincoln's article for this book, "The Meaning of Malcolm X," represents an extension of his interest in this subject. His book, The Black Muslim Movement in America, *is the first extensive examination of that movement and its effect on black America.*

Reverend Albert Cleage takes up some of the myths about Malcolm X that seemed to have grown faster than they could be printed. His article puts some of these myths to rest. When Malcolm X broke with Elijah Muhammad, he changed his direction, his focus, and his emphasis. He did not discard all of the things that he had learned while he was a follower of the Elijah Muhammad teachings. The Black Muslim movement was the political and spiritual incubator for Malcolm X; it was the area of his basic training and his proving ground. He modified what he had learned in this university of the ghetto, but he never repudiated it. This is, in part, what Reverend Cleage is saying in his article.

In other articles in this section by Charles E. Wilson, W. Keorapetse Kgositsile, James Boggs, Patricia Robinson, Wyatt Tee Walker, and Abdelwahab M. Elmessiri assessments are made of other dimensions in the life of Malcolm X.

No matter how much is said about what Malcolm X was, the speculations about what he could have been will go on for a good number of years. The triumph and tragedy of his short-lived leadership have their own mystique, which is, on reflection, both intriguing and sad, like the memory of lost love.

The influence of Malcolm X on the political consciousness of black Americans has had its greatest growth since his death. His statement, "Freedom by any means necessary," has been both used and abused by young black militants.

His dream of a world where his people will walk in freedom and dignity was temporarily deferred by his assassination. The assassin killed the dreamer but not the dream. This dream is the legacy he left us.

J. H. C.

THE MEANING OF
MALCOLM X *

———————————— BY *C. Eric Lincoln*

THE assassination of Malcolm X upset a good part of the American public. We were upset, and we tend to remain a bit on edge, *not* because Malcolm was a martyr to the cause of civil rights or because of any inherent contributions he may have made to the solution of our race problems, but because he was the uncompromising symbol of resistance and the spokesman for the non-nonviolent "black man" in America. We were uneasy because the murder of Malcolm X could have set off a Chinese-type "tong war" within the black nationalist factions striving for leadership of the masses in the Harlems of America.

We were aghast and dismayed by the 1964 summer riots, by the looting and the wanton destruction of property, but the riots were not organized and led by any recognized leader, and they were riots against property rather than against people. They expressed the resentment and the hatred of the frustrated, penned-up Harlem lower class, but there were few instances of attacks against the human objects of this fury, which included the Negro middle class no less than the hated Jew and the "blue-eyed devils" whose commercial presence in Harlem is exasperatingly ubiquitous and so bitterly resented.

Return to Wary Expectancy

For several months there had been an uneasy calm hanging over the dirty tenements and gaudy storefronts of

* Published in *The Christian Century*, April 7, 1965. Revised for this publication.

Harlem. The return of Malcolm X from his Afro-Asian junket was eyed with genuine apprehension by popular Negro leadership and with jubilant expectation by the black nationalist fringe. Malcolm was as cagey as always. Some Negro leaders thought they saw signs of a "constructive change" in his attitude toward racial goals and the proper techniques for attaining them. The more impatient activists were equally certain that Malcolm had brought them a kind of black-lettered message from García, and they were waiting for the word to be given.

Malcolm X himself was having other problems. He had left the country after severance from the one black nationalist organization with a significant following, and on returning to Harlem he found himself in direct competition with the Black Muslims for leadership of the black dissidents for whom integration and assimilation are not viable solutions.. His first order of interest was to stay alive, an interest neither he nor his followers nor the New York police proved adequate to protect.

The leadership of the Harlem masses is, at least in potential, an office of extraordinary power. It is also a hazardous undertaking. Thus far, with the possible exception of Marcus Garvey, no one has successfully mobilized the masses of America's most populous (and most shameful) black ghetto. Various self-styled leaders, usually oriented toward black nationalism or some other aspect of negritude, have had varying degrees of success in isolating a following, invariably small when measured against the numbers of potential converts who live in that steaming ghetto.

For the past decade or so the Black Muslims have had the largest and best-organized following among the black nationalist groups in Harlem. For most of that period Malcolm himself had been their *de facto* leader, although policy was set by Elijah Muhammad in Chicago. So it was that Malcolm's defection from the Muslims and his subsequent return to Harlem as head of his Organization for Afro-American Unity brought him into direct conflict with the Black Muslim organization.

Negro leaders kept a wary eye on Malcolm precisely

because they anticipated what did in fact occur, a black nationalist "tong war" which threatened the peace of the whole Harlem community and, indirectly, the leadership control responsible Negro leadership claimed to have. The exposure of the pro-Sino-Cuban Revolutionary Action movement caught most Americans of both races off guard because we are not accustomed to thinking in terms of black subversion. The myth of the satisfied Negro has spawned the myth of absolute loyalty. Both are fictions. While the overwhelming majority of the black population is loyal to the American flag and the American way of life, so is the overwhelming white majority. There are exceptions in both cases and the exceptions are multiplied by the increased alienation of non-white Americans.

Until just yesterday there were no non-white world powers of significance. And, more important, black Americans and their cause stood to gain nothing whatever by playing footsie with another *white* power. Times have changed; while we are shedding our negative stereotypes about the black people we may as well be disabused of some other stereotypes as well.

The death of Malcolm X left Elijah Muhammad in unchallenged control of the largest black nationalist organization in the country. Nobody knows how many Black Muslims there are. Some defected to Malcolm X when he left the movement. Others defected because Malcolm's ouster seemed to provide a good opportunity to get out and return to what ex-Muslim Aubrey Barnette calls "the outside world of reality."

Integration or Revolution?

It is a much-debated question as to whether Malcolm made any contributions to the black's struggle for freedom, whether he was a "catalyst to the cause" or just a loud and strident voice crying in some personal wilderness foreign to the real needs and aspirations of black Americans. It is even a silly question, for it presupposes a consensus among black people as to where they want to go and by what means they want to get there. Such a consensus of course does not exist—any more than does an American consensus of our role in (or out of) Vietnam.

Consensus obtains on the proper goals but not on the proper methodology among America's "responsible" *middle-class* leaders who claim to represent the organized thrust of the black American's determination to be free. But we may not safely ignore the dissident masses merely because they are less articulate, or more violent in their articulation, or because they are fragmented into many small groups of undetermined membership. There is a consensus among these groups, too, and it is not the consensus of the black middle class. To the various black nationalist fronts in Harlem and elsewhere Malcolm X was a potential "liberator," a man on a black horse who would someday lead them in a revolutionary struggle against the hated whites.

It does not promote the cause of responsible leadership to deny the importance of Malcolm X to the particular segment of people whose political and/or ideological leader he was, or sought to be, and this despite the threat he represented to the acceptance of the more acceptable procedures advanced by more traditional leaders. Eldridge Cleaver, for example, exists *and* has a following, however annoying that fact may be to more orthodox leadership; the Revolutionary Action movement is a fact, despite its embarrassing and treasonable implications. Similarly, Malcolm X made an impact on the minds of the black masses irrespective of his criminal past or his strong pro-black ideology. Had his turbulent life not been cut short, the chances are that his impact would have widened.

There are many black Americans who are not impressed by Christian philosophies of nonviolence because Christianity itself has so frequently been violent and because the yoke of oppression in the United States was for so long sanctioned by the church. Tens of thousands of others simply have not reached the level of sophistication which would enable them to understand the value and the dignity of nonviolent resistance. Indeed, relatively few Americans, whatever their race, are ideologically or psychologically prepared to suffer with the Ralph Abernathys and the Martin Luther Kings of today's black revolution. Certainly the men with the crash helmets and the cattle prods did not know or did not care what non-violence is all about. So long as men like these are the accepted guardians of the status quo, Malcolm X and the Malcolm X's waiting to be discovered will have meaning for the black masses who live in the black ghettos of America.

Demagogue or Martyr?

As soon as Malcolm was dead his critics turned on him with the fervor of self-righteousness and his defenders sought to elevate him to sainthood and martyrdom. On the one hand, it was pointedly suggested that as a demagogue and a spokesman for violence Malcolm somehow deserved what he got at the Audubon ballroom that Sunday, the day before Washington's Birthday. He had been a thug, an addict, and a thief, it was argued; he was an ex-convict; he had made no contributions whatever to society.

There is a *non sequitur* here which honesty compels us to examine. It is contrary to the "American ideal" and Christian morality to hold a man's past against him if it can be shown that he has overcome that past. Man *is* redeemable; if he is not, surely preaching is in vain. Malcolm X rose above the errors of his youth. Whether or not one agrees with his solution to the race problem, it must be admitted that during the years he presumed himself a race leader he was, under the constant scrutiny of a hostile public, far more circumspect than many of our more "respectable" leaders and politicians. If anything, his past seemed to give him a unique insight into the nature of the problems with which he sought to deal. We owe it to him and to ourselves to acknowledge the facts.

On the other hand, those who saw in the returned pilgrim to Mecca a "new" Malcolm X were at best probably premature in their judgments. The underlying cause of the breach between Malcolm X and Elijah Muhammad was not so much a contest of power within the movement as a conflict of ideology. Malcolm X was a true revolutionary. It is not inconceivable that, given the time, the means, and the opportunity, Malcolm X would have committed himself to the leadership of the "freedom and power—by any means necessary" ideology which is now the cutting edge of black dissidence.

He was indoctrinated to believe that racial strife is the inevitable means of bringing about a reversal of the black man's status, and he passionately believed in and longed for that reversal. True, his conversion to Islam and his desire to be acceptable to orthodoxy may have ameliorated his aggressive tendencies; but the evidence at the time of his death that he was prepared to join the non-violent crusade is scanty, if indeed it exists at all.

Malcolm X must be taken for what he was. He was a remarkably gifted and charismatic leader whose hostility and resentment symbolized the dreadful stamp of the black ghetto, but a man whose philosophies of racial determination and whose pragmatic comments made him unacceptable as a participant in peaceful social change. He had ideological followers—far more than the handful of men and women who belonged to the Organization of Afro-American Unity. His spirit will rise again, phoenix-like, because he is worthy to be remembered, and because the perpetuation of the ghetto which spawned him will not let us forget.

MYTHS ABOUT
MALCOLM X

—————————————— BY *Reverend Albert Cleage*

SPEECH DELIVERED IN DETROIT
FEBRUARY 24, 1967

I AM not a Marxist—I don't pretend to be, I don't even pretend to know anything about it. I am a black man in a world dominated by white oppression, and that is my total philosophy. I would like to get rid of that oppression, and that is my total objective. So I bring to this occasion rather a simple approach—personal reflections on the significance of Malcolm X.

I can remember a number of occasions when I talked to him, when I was with him, when I spoke on platforms with him; and so I am not indebted to printed material for my impressions of Malcolm X. I remember the last time he was in the city—not so much the speech, which was not one of his best by any means; it reflected, I think, much of the tension that he was under, much of the confusion, the constant living on the brink of violence. But I can remember him backstage, in the Gold Room I think they call it, of Ford Auditorium. Recently he had suffered smoke inhalation, the doctor had given him an injection, he was trying to sleep, he was irritable. But he was here because he had promised to be here, because he thought some people were concerned about what he had to say.

I remember him at the King Solomon Baptist Church on one of the occasions he spoke there—sort of in concealment backstage, constantly harassed with the danger of assassination. And I can remember the occasion at the King Solomon Baptist Church when he gave the "Mes-

13

sage to the Grass Roots," which I think is his best speech, his most typical statement, and which I personally think is his last will and testament. I remember him, I talked to him, I agreed with him. He was a Muslim, I am a Christian, and yet I can think of no basic matter upon which we disagreed.

Two years after his death Brother Malcolm was more important to more people than he was at any time during his lifetime. I think this is true. Young people who never saw him, who never heard him, speak of him with reverence and say, "I love Malcolm." This is a tremendous thing. Older people who heard and saw him select from the things they heard and saw the things they want to remember, or even the things it suits their purpose to remember. This too is quite a thing—that an individual should be important enough to be remembered even with distortions or for reasons not quite only of love.

Brother Malcolm has become a symbol, a dream, a hope, a nostalgia for the past, a mystique, a shadow sometimes without substance, "our shining black Prince," to whom we do obeisance, about whom we write heroic poems. But I think Brother Malcolm the man is in danger of being lost in a vast tissue of distortions which now constitute the Malcolm myth. The Malcolm myth or the Malcolm myths, the complex of myths which more and more tend to cluster about Brother Malcolm, remind us of what happened to Jesus Christ. I think I understand much more now the things that are written and said about Jesus, because I can understand how the life of a man dedicated to people can so easily become a focal point for the things people want to make that life mean.

The Malcolm myth or myths depend for substance upon the last chaotic and confusing year or two of his life—fragmentary statements growing out of his trip to Mecca and his efforts to bring the problems of black people in America to the attention of African leaders. Out of this period of his life comes the confusing complex of myths. According to the myth, his pilgrimage to Mecca turned Brother Malcolm into an integrationist. I've heard that seriously stated by people who claim to be scholars and students of the life of Brother Malcolm.

In Mecca, they say, he saw blue-eyed whites and blacks worshiping and living together, in love, for the first time in his thirty-nine years—and his whole concept of white people changed. This is the myth. And he rejected his former position that the white man is the enemy and that separation is inescapable. This is the myth.

The implication here is that this new insight changed his orientation; that with this new insight he was now free to join the NAACP, or to sing "We Shall Overcome" with Martin Luther King, Jr., or to become a Marxist and join the Socialist Workers' Party. And certainly, if we accept this basic myth as being true, as being fact, if this experience in Mecca changed his conception of white people, then all the implications certainly follow logically. If in terms of his experience in Mecca he came to believe that there is no enmity between black and white, that blacks and whites can march together in unity and brotherhood, then why shouldn't he join the NAACP, or sing "We Shall Overcome," or become a Marxist in the Socialist Workers' Party?

I say that is the myth, and from my personal point of view, realizing that we are in the position of the blind man who inspected the elephant and tried to describe what an elephant is, I say I do not believe this myth. I reject it completely, totally, and absolutely. I say if Malcolm X, Brother Malcolm, had undergone this kind of transformation, if in Mecca he had decided that blacks and whites can unite, then his life at that moment would have become meaningless in terms of the world struggle of black people. So I say I do not believe it.

Brother Malcolm knew history and he was guided by his interpretation of history. He interpreted the things that happened to him in terms of his knowledge and his understanding of the past. He would not have been taken in by what happened in Mecca. Brother Malcolm knew that the Arab Muslims had been the backbone of the slave trade. Those of you who have a sentimental attachment to the "Black Muslims" in America, or the Muslims that happen to be black, might not like to remember the slave trade with black Africans in Africa was fostered, encouraged, and carried on by the Arab Muslims in Africa. Brother Malcolm knew this. He would not have been taken in by the window dressing in Mecca. He would not have forgotten this important fact—that blacks and whites do not unite above the basic fact of race, or color. He would not have forgotten this in Mecca any more than in New York or Chicago or San Francisco. He knew that in Saudi Arabia they are still selling black Africans into slavery, they still make forays into black Africa and bring back black slaves for sale in Arab Muslim countries. Brother Malcolm knew this. And to me it is preposterous to say that in Mecca he became an integrationist.

Also, according to the myth, Brother Malcolm tried to internationalize the black man's struggle in America. Certainly he brought the black man's struggle to the attention of African leaders. The implication is that Brother Malcolm felt that the black man in Africa could help us through the United Nations and that we would be better off before the white's man's World Court than before the white man's Supreme Court. I do not believe it. Malcolm knew that one cracker court is just like another cracker court. He knew it, I know it, and you know it. And to say now that he came to the conclusion that if he could get the black man's problem in America before the World Court it would somehow mysteriously be changed and transformed is ridiculous. To take it before the World Court would have been interesting—but certainly no solution. We are no more apt to get justice before the World Court than before the Recorder's Court in the city of Detroit. Crackers run both of them.

Don't be afraid, brothers, don't be afraid—I am not hurting the image of Malcolm. I am just trying to save it, because you are about to lose it, you are about to forget what Malcolm said. By taking the last moments of confusion, when he was getting ready to be assassinated, and saying that the confused little statements he made in those last moments were his life—that's a lie, that wasn't his life. I heard him, I talked to him, I know what his life was, and he understood the relationship between blacks and whites.

Certainly Brother Malcolm wanted to relate our struggle, the struggle of black people in America, to the struggle of black people everywhere. I say to the struggle of *black* people everywhere, because that is a struggle that he understood, that I understand, and that you understand. I am not talking about relating it to the struggle of oppressed people everywhere, but relating it to the struggle of *black* people everywhere. But he expected little help from the Africans and the African nations. Malcolm wasn't running around Africa thinking that the African nations were going to free us. Malcolm wasn't that kind of an idiotic idealist. He went to our black brothers because they were our brothers. He talked to them about our problems because their problems are our problems, and we are as concerned about their problems as we want them to be about our problems. But he didn't go to Africa expecting them to free us.

Sometimes we forget that, and we sit around waiting for somebody in Africa to send somebody over here to free us—"like Malcolm said they were going to." He never said it and they are never going to do it. If you are going to be free, you are going to free yourself, and that is what Malcolm told us. The African nations can't free us, they can't save us. They couldn't save Lumumba in Africa, they couldn't wreak vengeance upon those who perpetrated his death in Africa. They couldn't save the Congo; they couldn't save the black people of Rhodesia; they couldn't free the black people of South Africa. Then why should we sit here in our own oppression, our own suffering, our own brutality, waiting for some mysterious transformation when black armies from Africa are coming over here and free us? They could use some black armies from over here to free them.

Malcolm never said it, and don't be mislead by the statement that Malcolm tried to internationalize the black man's struggle. He tried to tell us quite simply that the white man has given you hell here in the United States and he is giving black men hell all over the world. It is one struggle—black men fighting for freedom everywhere, in every country, in the United States, in Africa, in Vietnam, everywhere. Black men fighting against white men for freedom. He tried to tell you that the white man is not going to free you. I don't care what persuasion or philosophy he has, he is not going to free you, because if he frees you, he must take something away from himself to give it to you.

Funny how we can so easily forget what Malcolm said. I don't believe it. Certainly he wanted to relate it to the black man's struggle throughout the world. He knew we were struggling against the same enemy. He knew that we could expect no more justice from the World Court than from a Supreme Court. So much for the Malcolm myth.

Brother Malcolm's contribution is tremendous. What Brother Malcolm contributed to the black man's struggle in America and throughout the world cannot be equaled or surpassed by the life of any man. Oh, we can think of individuals like Marcus Garvey. When he looked at the world and said, "Where is the black man's government?" it was tremendous. Because he understood that the black man was engaged in a struggle against an enemy, and that if he was engaged in a struggle there were certain things that were necessary—he had to have power, he had to have a government, he had to have economies, he had to have certain things. Marcus Garvey understood it. But no man surpasses Malcolm in his understanding of the meaning of the struggle in which black people are engaged everywhere in the world. And there was no subterfuge or confusion or weak-kneed pussy-footing in Malcolm as long as he lived.

I want to tell you this: We get all confused because we don't know who assassinated him. I don't believe that the Honorable Elijah Muhammad assassinated him. You believe whatever you want to, I do not believe it. And because we get confused about who assassinated him, we say there was never any good in Elijah Muhammad or the "Black Muslims." I don't believe that either. I believe that the basic truths that Malcolm X taught came from the basic philosophy and teachings of Elijah Muhammad. I believe that the basic contribution which he made, the basic philosophy which he taught, stems di-

rectly from the teachings of Elijah Muhammad and the
"Black Muslims." I do not accept all the teachings of
Elijah Muhammad or the "Black Muslims," but I understand what Malcolm X did to those teachings. He
took the teachings of a cult, with all the mythology of
the "Black Muslims," and universalized them so that
black people everywhere, no matter what their religion,
could understand them and could accept them.

I can accept the teachings which he abstracted from
the cult philosophy and mythology of the Honorable
Elijah Muhammad. I do not believe in the story about
Yacub and creating the white man as the devil in six
thousand years, but that has nothing to do with the essential truth. I do not believe that the white man is the devil.
He does devilish things, but I don't believe that he is a
devil. Because to say that he is a devil is to say that he is
more than human, and I don't believe that. You know
that in Christian religion the devil was flung out of
heaven; he was an angel, he was more than a man, and
to believe that the white man is a devil is to attribute to
him supernatural powers. That is a cult mystique. There
is nothing about the white man that is supernatural. He
is just exactly like we are—that's why we can understand
him so well. There is nothing mysterious about what he
does. He wasn't condemned to be a devil for six thousand
years—he just acts like a devil because it suits his purpose, and he mistreats us, he oppresses us, he's brutal to
us, because it's in his interest—not because he is a devil.

It is closer to the truth to say that he is a beast, and
that is what Malcolm said. You would like to forget that
now, but every time I talked to him, he referred to the
white man as a beast. And those of you who are white
here will agree with him that most white people are
beasts—you can't deny it. On the basis of the way the
white man has treated black men in America and
throughout the world for four hundred years, you cannot deny that he certainly had a truth there when he
said that the white man is a beast. But not a devil. A
beast is lower than a man, a devil is higher than a man.
Certainly the white man is not a devil, but he is in many
instances a beast.

Malcolm was different when he was in the "Black Muslims." You have got to remember that, too—he had a power base then. You know, as quiet as it is kept, it is one thing to operate out of something, to talk out of something, to have something behind you when you go into a town or a city—to go knowing that there are people there who are preparing things for you. It is another thing to step out by yourself and try to go around the country without a power base, without any protection, without any organization in front. And that was the difference when Malcolm X stepped out of the Muslim movement and became an individual. Then he faced the harassment, the danger, the confusion, and everything in these last years that those who want to distort Malcolm X want to make so much out of. At the beginning, when he was with the Muslims, there was a power base from which he operated, a philosophical foundation upon which he could build. And he built well and he operated well in terms of a power base. He abstracted the general truths that we still remember. And these things we have got to preserve—*we* have got to preserve, brothers, I'm telling you, *we* have got to preserve.

We have a great tendency to turn our leaders over to somebody else. Who is the custodian of Malcolm's tradition? Who is the custodian? But we aren't acting like it. You know who the custodian is, don't you?—there he sits, right there. If Mr. Breitman stopped writing, nobody would write anything. And he's doing it in terms of what he believes is a proper interpretation. If we want to preserve our heroes, we have to become the custodians of that tradition. Who is the custodian of DuBois? Black people? No, we don't have one thing that he wrote. The Communist Party has it, and they will let us read what they want us to read. I'm talking to you black brothers, I don't care what the rest of these people think. We have got to become the custodians of our own heroes and save them and interpret them the way we want them interpreted. And if you don't do it, then you have to accept what somebody else says they said. Who is the custodian of Paul Robeson? (Voice from audience: "The Communists.") All right, we don't have it. The great things he said, all of the things—where are they? The CIA has has taken over perhaps all of the African Encyclopedia that DuBois was working on in Ghana. Nobody knows where it is. We don't protect these things. We are careless and we get caught up in the myths that other people spin for us. In another five years our children won't know what Malcolm X was really like. Because we won't write it down, and everything that is written that they can put their hands on will be saying that Malcolm X said something he never said, that Malcolm X meant something he never meant.

I say Malcolm X was tremendously important, beyond even our comprehension today, because Malcolm changed the whole course of the black man's freedom struggle—the whole course of that freedom struggle not only in America but throughout the world. Black people everywhere in Africa, in the United States, everywhere, black people are fighting today a different battle than they fought before Malcolm began to talk. A different battle because Malcolm laid down certain basic principles that we can never forget. He changed the whole course. The first basic principle that Malcolm laid down that we can't forget is this: *The white man is your enemy.* That is a basic principle, we can't forget it. I don't care what else they drag in from wherever they drag it—remember one thing, Malcolm taught one truth: The white man is our enemy. We can't get away from it, and if we accept and understand that one basic truth, his life was not lived in vain. Because upon that one basic truth we can build a total philosophy, a total course of action for struggle. Because that was the basic confusion which distorted the lives of black people, which corrupted the movements of black people. That was the basic area of our confusion, and Malcolm X straightened that out.

The white man is an enemy—he said it. We must break our identification with him, and that was his basic contribution. He didn't just say it, he didn't sit off someplace and just write it—he went out and he lived it. He asked for moments of confrontation. He said we have got to break our identification, we can't go through life identifying with the white man or his government. You remember what he said down there at King Solomon Baptist Church: You talk about "your" navy and "your" astronauts. He said forget it, we don't identify with these people, they are the enemy. And that is the basic truth. We must break our identification with the enemy, we must confront him, and we must realize that conflict and violence are necessary parts of a struggle against an enemy—that is what he taught. Conflict, struggle, and violence are not to be avoided. Don't be afraid of them —you heard what he said. There has got to be some bloodshed, he said, if black men want to be free—that is what he taught. Now you can't take that and say that he believed in blacks and whites marching together. He said black men have got to be willing to shed their blood because they believe that they can be free. The white man is an enemy.

We must take pride in ourselves—you know that is what he said. But he didn't make a mystique out of Africa. He didn't sit down in a corner and contemplate his navel and think about the wonders of Africa. He said we have a history that we can be proud of. Africa is our history, African blood is our blood, African soil is our soil. We can take pride in our past—not by sitting down and contemplating it, but by using it as the basis for a course of action in today's world, as a basis for confrontation with the enemy, as a basis for struggle, for conflict, and even for violence, if necessary. We fight because we are proud; and because we are proud, we are not going to lie down and crawl like snakes on our bellies. We are not going to take second-class citizenship sitting down, saying, "Well, in a few years maybe things will change." We want to change it *now*. That is what Malcolm told us, that is what we believe, and that is the basis of our struggle today.

A corollary of that, which you must understand and which is essentially Malcolm's contribution, is that integration is impossible and undesirable. Integration is impossible—he said it time and time and time again, under all kinds of circumstances—integration is impossible and undesirable. Now this was harder for black people to take than for white people. Because white people never wanted it in the first place, and were determined that it would never come to pass in the second place. But black people had been led to believe that it was a possibility, always just around the corner. So black people had pegged all of their organizational efforts toward integration. We sang "We Shall Overcome Someday," believing that overcoming meant integrating. The NAACP pegged its whole program on the possibilities of integration. We are going to build an integrated world, we are going to build a world in which black people and white people live together, we are going to build an integrated world—that is what Dr. Martin Luther King said. "I've got a dream for America tonight, a dream when the children of slaves shall walk hand-in-hand with the children of slavemasters." And we believed it until Malcolm X told us it is a lie. And that is a genuine contribution—it is a lie.

You will never walk hand in hand with anybody but black people, let me tell you. If you do, it is just a moment of mutual hypocrisy in which you are both engaged, for some purpose best known to yourselves. You may build a position of strength, a position of power from which you can negotiate with strength instead of weakness, and if you are willing to negotiate, then you can talk to the white man as an equal. That is as close to brotherhood as there is—there is no other brotherhood. If you talk to a man as an equal, he is your brother. But there is no other kind of equal. You cannot get down on your knees and talk up to a man and talk about brotherhood. Because you stopped being a brother when you got down on your knees. And if you are afraid to get up and look him in the eye and take a chance of getting killed if necessary, then there is no hope of brotherhood for you. Integration is impossible and undesirable—Malcolm taught it.

We have our own communities. The white man "gave" them to us. He forced us into them. He separated himself from us. And white people went all around the country all the time Malcolm was alive, saying, "He wants separation." They had separated themselves from us in every area of life, and yet they said, "He is bad, he is wicked, he wants separation." And if he had asked for integration seriously, they would have killed him more quickly.

He said we are going to control these separate communities. We have them, the white man "gave" them to us, and we are going to stop being ashamed of them. We are going to live in them and we are going to make them the best communities in the world. We are going to make the schools in them black schools and good schools. We are going to make our housing black housing and good housing. We are no longer going to believe that a block is no good till a white man comes and buys a house on it. We are no longer going to believe that if we can move into a community where half of the people on the street are white, that is a better community. We are going to take our separate communities, we are going to work with them, we are going to control them, we are going to control their politics, we are going to control their economy—we are going to control our community.

Malcolm X laid the entire foundation for everything Stokely Carmichael says. Stokely hasn't said one word that was not completely implicit in everything that Malcolm X taught. He is just a voice carrying on upon the basic foundation that Malcolm X put down. Integration is impossible and undesirable. We are going to control our own communities. We are going to stop worrying about being separate. We are not worried about bussing black children into white neighborhoods. We are not worried about open occupancy, except that we want the right to live anyplace, and unless we are given that right, we will take it. And when we take it, we will still live together, because we do not want to live with you. That is a philosophy, that is Malcolm X's philosophy. We have learned it, we still remember it, and there is nothing you can do today to take it away from us. But I'm telling you, brothers, we have got to write it down because they are about to mess it up so we won't recognize it next year.

The whole civil rights movement has changed. The

NAACP is washed up, through, finished. The Urban League is nothing but the social service agency it started out to be. The civil rights movement now is nothing but Stokely Carmichael and Floyd McKissick—that's it. Because they got the message. They are building today on what Malcolm said yesterday. The civil rights movement, the freedom struggle, the revolution—call it what you will—black men fighting for freedom today are fighting in terms laid down by Brother Malcolm. No other terms. You can't go out into the community—the brother here said "let's go out into the community"—you can't go out into the community with anything other than what Malcolm X taught. Because they won't listen to you, they won't hear you.

The whole movement has changed. The last great picnic, as Floyd McKissick said, on the White House lawn, that "great freedom march"—that was the end, that was it. From here on in, black people are trying to build, to organize. Malcolm in his last days was trying to make the transition to organization, to structure; to fight not only in terms of words, of ideas, but to build the organizational structure. He didn't do it. But he was making the transition because he realized that the next stage is an organizational stage—that if you want to be free, if you want power, you have got to organize to take it. When you were just begging the white man to give you something, you didn't need organization. All you needed was a kneeling pad so that you could kneel down and look humble. But if you want power, you have got to organize to get it—you have got to have political power, you have got to have economic power, you have got to organize. Malcolm realized that, and the feeble beginnings he made in the area of organization were pointing the way. Today we have got to carry on that organizational struggle that Malcolm pointed out.

I was in New York, I went to his headquarters while he was over in Africa, I talked with his lieutenants. They didn't have the slightest idea of what was going on. They loved Malcolm, and they were sitting in the Hotel Theresa in a suite of rooms, but they didn't have the slightest conception of how to organize. They were waiting for Brother Malcolm to come home so he could tell them what to do. I said, "My God, one man never carried such a load all by himself! He has men here who are supposed to be doing something and they are sitting there waiting for him to come back." And they were carrying around his letters—he would write back a letter and they were carrying it around like it was the Bible: "Look, we've got a few words from Brother Malcolm."

He did not want reverence—he wanted people who could do something, who could organize, who believed in action, who were willing to go out and sacrifice; and he didn't have them. And all of us today—black people, brothers from coast to coast—when we get together and do reverence to Malcolm, let us remember that the last message was organize. We didn't do it and that is why he died. We didn't have organization enough to protect him. We didn't have organization enough to give him funds to do what he had to do. We let him die. The message is the same today, and still we are not organizing, we are not doing the work that has to be done. If you love Brother Malcolm, write your poems at night and organize and work in the daytime for power. Because until you get power, Malcolm X is just a memory. When we get power, we will put his statue in every city, because the cities will belong to us. Then we can do him reverence.

But until we get power, let's not play with images and myths. Let's remember that he gave us certain principles, certain ideas, and we have got to do something with them. All of us have the task—to organize, to build, to fight, to get power. And as we get it, as we struggle for it, we will remember that we are struggling because we believe the things that he taught. That is the message of Malcolm, and don't let anybody get you all mixed up. He never turned into an integrationist, never. He wasn't fooled in Mecca, he wasn't fooled in Africa. He told it like it was and he knew it like it was. That is our Malcolm. Some other folks may have another Malcolm—they are welcome to him. But brothers, don't lose *our* Malcolm.

LEADERSHIP:
TRIUMPH IN LEADERSHIP
TRAGEDY

BY *Charles E. Wilson*

When the life of a leader is snuffed out by assassination or by sudden death, his followers are thrown into a state of near shock. And when these followers, like American Negroes, have little faith in ideologies or institutions, but have instead put their trust in the strength of unselfish, fearless, dedicated leaders, then their loss is exceedingly grave. With no available person to replace the fallen leader, the very life of the group is threatened. If, as a leader, the fallen one had too little time to realize his promise, then his passing is tragic. When all these conditions obtain, the situation is complete tragedy. Such a complete tragedy befell the Negro masses at the death of Malcolm X.

While he was known as Malcolm X for most of his public life, he led really three existences—Malcolm Little (Big Red), Malcolm X, and Malik El-Shabazz. Only his own strength of personality and capacity for human growth could weld these dissimilar elements into a single human strand. His was a stormy career—as stormy and tumultuous as the days in which he lived. Yet those days were filled with that electric quality which is the atmosphere that surrounds the world of greatness. His quips were priceless, his homilies devastating, his idiom sure and sharp, his witticisms crisp with insight. A product of the advanced communications era, he sought to tame the media to his will and to his ways.

During his life as a leader, Malcolm was forced to

expend as much energy struggling with the fears and timidities of his own people, and with the constraints, contradictions, and jealousies of the civil rights movement, as he expended in the struggle with his real foe —the exploitive, racist power order. The practical restraints and ideological shackles of Negro leadership sapped his energy and limited his effectiveness. The straightforwardness of his speech titillated his white listeners and frightened his Negro bourgeois audience. But that same kind of speech lifted the spirits of the tired black masses who had no one else "to tell it like it was."

At his death, white America's newspapers could hardly restrain themselves from gloating. The now defunct New York *Herald Tribune* wrote: "The slaying of Malcolm X has shown again that hatred, whatever its apparent justification, however it may be rationalized, turns on itself in the end. . . . Now the hatred and violence he preached has overwhelmed him and he has fallen at the hands of Negroes." His death was used as a none too deftly disguised message to would-be militants. The non-violent as well as the violent joined in maligning his name.

Since his death, however, his stature and image have grown. His unfinished work has slowly begun to attract others to carry the burden. His vision has begun to capture the young and the dispossessed who struggle against oppression both here and abroad. Paradoxically then, the life of Malcolm, which at his death seemed to be so vast a tragedy of leadership, is now several years later transformed into a triumph of black manhood.

The Basis of His Leadership Appeal

As an important historical figure of our time, the details of Malcolm's life are well known. Less well appreciated is the way in which those early experiences contributed to making him what he was as a leader, and as a man. His life was scarred quite early by tragedy, and he and his family were victims of racism's wrath. Those selfsame early scars were to be the basis for his close identification with the dispossessed and downtrodden as well as his uncanny ability to sense their moods when articulating their sentiments.

A gifted student, yet a school dropout and dance hall dandy at fifteen, then in rapid succession a hipster, a liquor head, a junkie, a procurer, a pimp, and finally the head of a burglary ring. By his twenty-first birthday he had already been convicted and sentenced to ten years for armed robbery. Within the gray walls of Massachusetts State Prison at Charlestown, Malcolm Little gave way under the pressure of his own restless, inquisitive spirit and the prompting of the Muslim teachings to become Malcolm X. With the abandonment of his former identity Malcolm adopted one of the few routes out of degradation available to lower-class Negroes.

Malcolm received formal tutelage for his leadership role as a spokesman-administrator from the Honorable Elijah Muhammad. His native intelligence, keen wit, and capacity for leadership won him the position of minister of Harlem's Muslim Mosque No. 7, where he drew scores of new members and captured the ear of countless others.

The dynamics of Negro nationalism and Negro radicalism, parts of the Muslim mystique, provided Malcolm with a unique chance to reach out to the masses. Historically, Negro nationalism has articulated the felt needs of the masses rather than the Negro bourgeoisie. It is characterized by four elements:

1. sought to withdraw psychologically and/or physically from the society;
2. tended to attract an unstable membership composed primarily of persons on their way up to middle-class respectability;
3. tended to be an urban phenomenon;
4. bound by a religious doctrine seeking either to reinterpret the Old Testament tradition into the current political and social context, or to lead toward the establishment of a separate theocratic state.

These movements have generally lacked the sustained support of Negroes, for Negro radicalism flourishes for a time only to retreat to limbo. Malcolm emerged at just such a period in history, when Negro nationalism was on the rise.

Being a skilled debater with a piercing ghetto-eyed point of view and a flair for words made Malcolm as popular on college campuses as he was on the street corners of Harlem. Articles about him or interviews with him seldom failed to catch the depth of thinking and the clever persuasiveness of his arguments. On one occasion he was asked to characterize the participation of white liberals in the civil rights movement. Malcolm X said:

A man who tosses worms in the river isn't necessarily a friend to the fish. All the fish who take him for a friend, who think the worm's got no hooks in it, usually end up in the frying pan. All those things dangled before us by the white man posing as a friend and benefactor have turned out to be nothing but bait to make us think we are making progress.

Unbound by the cultural constraints that shackle the civil rights movement, Malcolm X could loose his own brand of caustic criticism on whatever target he thought merited censure. The cultural restraints on the civil rights movement have forced the adoption of strategies, by and large, which lack the capacity to affect meaningfully the long-standing oppression and exploitation to restraints prompt the compartmentalization of the racial issue, removing it from consideration in relation to economics or politics. As a psychological consequence of this compartmentalization, Americans are taught to see the issue of racism as a national problem rather than an international one and to see the present conflict as a crisis of conscience rather than the consequence of capitalism's inhuman use of human beings. For Malcolm X to be overtly free of some of these restraints was to free him to speak his piece clearly and forcefully.

The message of Malcolm X as filtered through the white non-listening system titillated the masochistic, plagued the frightened and guilt-ridden, and appalled the naïve. He never tired telling these whites that their stereotype of Negro servility, as reflected within their more modern view of Negro non-violence, was false. He seldom lost an opportunity to remind them that their society's anointed Negro leaders were little more than vassals. The last few summers have provided a fiery testament to Malcolm's viewpoint.

To some Negroes, as well as most whites, the strident rhetoric of Malcolm was simply un-Negro, though fascinating, foreboding, conjuring all the dreaded consequences of centuries of slavery and exploitation. He never tired of pointing to white verbal inconsistency and behavioral purposefulness.

Malcolm's experience with Muslims was not limited to speechmaking. As an administrator of Harlem's Mosque No. 7, he learned to develop and utilize some of his capacities in the direct service of the religious cause he espoused. The disciplined, oligarchal organizational fabric of the followers of the Honorable Elijah Muhammad provided Malcolm X with a kind of support for his administrative training. The training he secured was not generally available to the rank and file of lower-class Negroes.

In addition, as part of his training and experience, he derived an opportunity to enter the arena of international relations. As the personal envoy of the Honorable Elijah Muhammad, in 1959 Malcolm X journeyed to the United Arab Republic, Sudan, and Nigeria. The trip undoubtedly helped Malcolm X to widen his vistas and place the racial issues in a broader international framework.

During his period of service to the Muslims Malcolm X benefited from a number of experiences and opportunities, all of which broadened his view, sharpened his skills, and provided increased access to the Negro masses. His opportunities for public speaking, his administrative responsibility, as well as world travel, combined to place him in the forefront of leaders. But his rise to prominence within the movement caused jealousy among other members of the sect. His own personal disillusionment grew as he discovered information about the alleged misconduct of those in whom he placed great trust. These factors tended to reinforce the feeling of estrangement he felt toward the parent group and weakened the bonds that had fastened him to the movement headed by the Honorable Elijah Muhammad. The statement about "the chickens coming home to roost"—a reference to the assassination of President Kennedy—precipitated a long-anticipated suspension of Malcolm as minister of the Harlem Mosque. As a further rebuke, Malcolm X was prohibited from making public statements or appearances. The announcement of his final break with the Muslims, in March of 1964, was a mere formality. Malcolm had completed his active apprenticeship and was about to set out as his own master.

After the Break with the Muslims

When Malcolm X broke away from the Muslims he attempted to carry many of the concepts he had learned into his new venture. Initially he called his organization Muslim Mosque, Inc., and declared his continued allegiance to the Honorable Elijah Muhammad.

"I believe in the Honorable Elijah Muhammad," he said then, as Malcolm claimed his new organization was designed to propagate the kind of moral reformation needed to rid the Negro community of the evils which sapped its vitality. His "Go-It-Alone Plan" for Negro areas demanded complete black control of black communities, excluding the outsider who would be frequently pulling the strings behind the scenes. Whites were therefore to be excluded from membership.

One month later, a trip to the Holy City of Mecca set the stage for a further development of his understanding. Treated to the spectacle of Muslim pilgrims practicing true brotherhood, Malcolm X underwent a major metamorphosis. This change is best expressed in his own words in a letter to his aides at the Muslim Mosque: "Each hour here in the Holy Land enables me to have greater insights into what is happening in America between black and white." Even his attitude toward whites was affected by his experiences in that holy place. Malcolm became convinced that only a sharp turn by white Americans toward the spiritual path of truth would stave off the impending racial holocaust.

Lifted by his experiences in Mecca, gifted with fresh insights on world problems, Malcolm, now truly Malik El-Shabazz, grasped a new vision, a new direction, a new sense of political relevancy and a new awareness of the possibility of an alternative to the sterile pursuit of middle-class standards which had become so much a part of the life of the Muslim movement. On his way back to the United States in May of 1964, Malcolm detoured through several of the new African states, where he was warmly received.

On his return to the United States, Malcolm announced the formation of a new organization, a broader, more secularly oriented group, the Organization of Afro-American Unity, OAAU. This group proposed to try to attract the widest possible spectrum of Negroes, religious and non-religious, passive resisters and direct actionists, to struggle for full human rights here in America. In addition to his domestic goal, Malcolm was relentlessly seeking to internationalize the Negroes' struggle by bringing the American racial situation before the United Nations. While this idea was by no means a new proposal, Malcolm raised the idea from the level of vague possibility to a level of distinct probability.

To these ends Malcolm lent his considerable talents, softening his uncompromising rhetoric, becoming more humane and infinitely more sophisticated. He became less and less doctrinairely antagonistic toward whites. In addition he even went so far as to apologize to other civil rights leaders for earlier slashing attacks on them. In October of 1964, he suggested that he was sorry that he had led so many well-meaning Negroes into the Muslim fold.

His efforts within the United States sought to forge a meaningful link between Mother Africa and Africa's displaced American children. Repeatedly he called on Negroes to look culturally and spiritually to Africa. He exhorted his brothers and sisters to accept their African cultural component and suggested active use of the word "Afro-American" in place of the word "Negro." The very name of his OAAU—Organization of Afro-American Unity—reflected his continued efforts in this direction. Malcolm X strongly urged Negroes to adopt self-defense techniques and be on their guard against the duplicity of the power structure.

United States Government authorities came to view Malcolm as a threat because of his popularity, not in the present but perhaps in a not too distant future. Despite official Washington's assessment of his popularity on the grass-roots level, every poll of Negroes and of whites placed Malcolm far down the list of "Negro leaders." Malcolm's swing to the political left did little to endear him to an America which flirts with fascism and is obsessed by the notion of international communist conspiratorial plots.

Outside the American Straitjacket

If on the domestic scene Malcolm's efforts were hampered by recruitment problems, organizational shortcomings, and problems of style, in the international arena his activity made surer progress. In the eleven months between his departure from the Muslim fold to the time of his death, Malcolm X tried to gain the support of sovereign African states for his plan to bring the U.S. racial problem before the United Nations under the Human Rights Provisions of the UN Charter. Tirelessly he lobbied in eighteen different countries. As an "observer" at the Summit Conference of African prime ministers, Malcolm X delivered an eight-page memorandum condemning U.S. racism and sought to enlist aid from these African leaders in his campaign.

The memorandum drew tremendous applause, but no formal stand on the issue of bringing the question before the UN was taken by the delegates at that session. When that memorandum is combined with scathing denunciations of America's imperialism abroad and this nation's inactivity in enforcing the existing civil rights codes at home, Malcolm X was indeed fanning the flames of anti-Americanism on the African continent. Touchy, even supersensitive about its image, the American Government in the person of various agencies—the State Department, the Justice Department, and the Central Intelligence Agency—placed him under round-the-clock surveillance. Efforts were made to poison him in Cairo prior to delivery of the famous eight-page memorandum.

Malcolm openly acknowledged that his phones were tapped. In the *Saturday Evening Post* he quipped: "If I said on my home telephone right today I'm going to bomb the Empire State Building, I guarantee you in five minutes it would be surrounded."

Long before Martin Luther King, Jr., was to announce his objection to the war in Vietnam, Malcolm was on record as opposing the employment of America's superior tools of destruction—the jets, the napalm, the jellied gasoline, and the white phosphorous—on the people of Vietnam.

The American intervention in the Congolese Civil War (November 1964) galvanized Malcolm into even greater activity. He whipped up opposition to the United States, calling the U.S. Government's continued support of Moise Tshombe a vital force in the seemingly unending Congo turmoil. Several writers hailed Malcolm as the driving force behind the shower of abuse that rained on the United States during the December 1964 Congo debate at the United Nations General Assembly.

In January 1965, Malcolm claimed that his international efforts had been crowned with success, that links had been forged between U.S. Negroes and African Governments and Orthodox Muslims. That same month *The New York Times* reported Malcolm was urging African states to exploit the racial situation in the United States as a lever in their discussion of international problems with the American Government. Malcolm hoped that not only would the Africans benefit in their dealings with the United States from the increased leverage produced by this strategy, but that Negroes would also derive greater leverage within the society.

This type of national internationalism was just too much for the American Government and the leadership of this "moderate" society. In this society the race problem is considered purely a local argument and the current "Negro revolution" is expected to remain essentially a religious reform movement—moralistic, legalistic, and "removed" from the power realities. For Negro bourgeois and moderate civil rights leaders the approach called for by earlier figures like DuBois and pursued by

Malcolm was far too daring. They would prefer to struggle to bring about racial change by Robert's Rules of Order.

Malcolm boldly sought to break the bonds which have constricted Negro thinking and Negro leadership. Malcolm was in fact preaching a non-Negro doctrine— power, success, mobilization, international awareness, and leverage. In pursuit of the black man's place in the world, Malcolm was correctly adjudged guilty of un-Negro activities.

An Assessment of Malcolm's Leadership

Malcolm's untimely death on that bleak wintry day in February 1965, in a tired old ballroom one writer called "a dirty place to die," stripped the Negro masses of their champion, their own "black shining Prince." He was a symbol, as Ossie Davis eulogized him, of "our manhood, our living, black manhood!" A rare breed of man who was truly irreplaceable. His work was largely unfinished, had hardly just begun. His legacy to his people amid obvious tragedy—the brilliance of triumph.

Like all aspirants to leadership among Negroes, Malcolm was bound by the conflicts and contradictions of Negro life. He was saddled by a truncated view of the society current among Afro-Americans and victimized by status needs and the lack of a relevant strategy needed to bring about a change. The single issue protest activity that Afro-Americans employ is predicated on the illusion of a concerned public opinion and a power order that is responsive, when in reality there is essentially an apathetic mass manipulated by an unsympathetic power circle.

Malcolm's failures were a failure of leadership style and a failure to evolve a sound organizational base for his activities. Thus Malcolm is a domestic victim of the protest style. Malcolm tried to employ the protest style with all the dramatizing rhetoric and verbal pyrotechnics at his command in order to mobilize an effective organization. The protest style is just not suited to the task of mobilization. Although the protest style is

extremely popular with the most deprived, the style un-
knowingly plays right into the hands of the present
power order. For the style creates the impression that a
single issue reform of the power order is possible or that
an all-encompassing racial loyalty is essential. The power
structure, by design or inadvertently, acts in matters of
race relations in such a manner as to keep the Negro
community hopelessly divided and therefore relatively
powerless. The protest style, because it deals in a rhetoric of the extremes, actually heightens the differences
between the various subgroups within the Negro community. Instead of forging permanent links between the
various segments of the community, the protest style can
at best only organize single issue efforts, mass demonstrations—noisy demonstrations to be sure—but cannot
alone evolve that strategy and the disciplined activity
required to forge long-term operational unity.

Although in their hearts some of the Negro masses
understood Malcolm and the nature of his message, their
minds could not fully grasp the nature of his concepts.
Malcolm was at one and the same time talking to some
of them, talking over the heads of most of them, and
scaring the pants off the rest. It may be that the protest
style speaks to the Negroes' cultural emphasis on ex-
pressivity which exists in place of an emphasis on in-
strumentality (practical, goal-directed action). Malcolm
was a truly charismatic figure—a person who could legit-
imately identify with his audience of the dispossessed,
who had suffered the same demoralization that they had
suffered. But unlike many of them he had somehow
worked his way out of the dilemma. While Malcolm might
well have given them what he knew they needed from the
standpoint of domestic political style, Malcolm was also
a victim of his own charisma.

As a direct consequence of Malcolm's style as well as
the result of the demands of the task of international
negotiation, his energy, effort, and time were diverted
from the tedious job of building a reliable organization
at home. The task of building a viable radical organization is already fraught with obstacles without adding any
self-imposed ones.

From the outset an organization of a movement comprised primarily of Negroes can expect limited financial support; a radical movement will find an even smaller trickle of funds available. The kind of organization that Malcolm would have had to build required, in addition, time to recruit and to develop individuals with appropriate organizational and administrative skills. Little sympathy or constructive help can be expected from other Negro organizations because of their own limitations of staff, and concept. The middle-class Negro can be expected, by and large, to pursue his own private goals through naïve self-seeking, individualistic opportunism. The upper middle-class Negro, like other essentially upper middle groups, is essentially conformist and frequently apolitical. Upper-class Negroes have only a passing concern for reform and hardly any concern for serious societal revision. In this Malcolm's media image as a so-called racist may well have blocked his effort to reach the upper-class and middle-class Negro.

Malcolm's organizational failure, however, may have been as much a failure of the Negro community's followership as it was due to his own stylistic approach. Negro followership could not keep pace with this vital, growing, maturing leader; nor was Malcolm always willing to wait till the people caught up with him. He was therefore alone, isolated, and vulnerable.

Assessment of Malcolm's failures must be tempered by the fact that his actual life-span in the big arena was actually far too short. He just did not have the time to wrestle with the simple issues, let alone to solve the more complex problems! Yet in his life he made such a profound impact on these problems that many of the most restless Negro youth now try to add to their own sense of bravado by mimicking his words and placing his likeness on all kinds of sweaters and on every describable type of poster. The young have taken to copying and repeating the failures of Malcolm. That is, these young people have maintained their self-purging rhetoric of violence but have developed few instrumentalities or institutions through which they can realize their political or cultural objectives.

Malcolm's triumphs are so fundamental that they are often overlooked or seldom appreciated, and, therefore, not repeated. Malcolm was a triumph of concept—that is, Malcolm broke with the "no view" position of the American civil rights movement, as well as with the parochial "no involvement in politics" view of the Black Muslims. Each of these positions, because of its own peculiar narrowness, leads nowhere. Civil righters go nowhere because they refuse to accept the radical nature of the race problem (that is, the race problem is at the very root of this society and there is a vital relationship between capitalism and racism). At this juncture, Negro civil rights leadership is effectively tied either to the Democratic Party coalition or the "progressive Republicans." All the civil righters can do in such a position is to seek imaginary reforms, or a kind of progress which does not deal with the social, cultural realities of our times, or does not affect the present power order.

But Malcolm likewise rejected the Muslim program. For despite the Muslim talk of violence and retaliation, they do nothing unless their own immediate interests are attacked. Their definition of brotherhood does not seem to deal with the rest of the sons and daughters of Africa, but only with their own narrow group. As such, Muslims are no immediate threat to the power structure.

Malcolm became Public Enemy No. 1 when he chose the road of national and international involvement, the road of struggle, the road of anti-colonialism and anti-capitalism. He helped those about him—in the words of a well-known educator and social worker—

to distinguish between democracy and hypocrisy, to see the relationship between their past conditions of servitude and their current plights and begin to recognize their own responsibility and capacity for self-development.

Malcolm transformed the so-called Freedom struggle (passive) into a Liberation struggle.

Malcolm's adoption of the old Leftist strategy of the post-World War II era—viz., hauling the United States before the World Assembly for its crimes—also represents a triumph of conception. That he attempted to achieve through his own personal efforts reflects the shortcomings of his operational approach, but, nonetheless, that conception is still a goal of radical groups and a sore spot with the American Government.

Whether the dominant Negro bourgeoisie—which is truncated in its political thought—or the Negro working class—now lacking any class conception—accept it or not, Malcolm's life as a leader was a triumph in conception. As long as these groups cling to their hopes and dreams that this society will keep its promises to all its citizens, men like Malcolm will remain outcasts and marginal characters.

Malcolm was and still is a triumph of relevancy. Even his style, which had limited effect, was at least relevant to the group Malcolm wished to lead. His call for extreme measures for extremely serious situations was not unreasonable. His call to Negroes to join the world struggle against colonialism was hardly inappropriate. Now in retrospect one can appreciate his assessment of President Johnson, and Goldwater, the former Republican candidate; in hindsight that assessment stands as a high-water mark of relevancy.

Johnson and Goldwater, I feel that as far as the American black man is concerned, both are just about the same. It's just a question of Johnson the fox, or Goldwater the wolf. Conservatism's only meaning is 'let's keep the niggers in their place.' Liberalism's meaning—'let's keep the kneegrows in their place, but tell them we'll treat them a little better. Let's fool them with more promises!' Since these are the only choices for the black man in America, I think he only needs to pick which one he chooses to be eaten by, because both will eat him.

Similarly there are hundreds of illustrations of Malcolm's unique gift of verbal relevancy and cogency (relevant in style, relevant in word and deed). Yet each of the phrases, each of the maneuvers, leads to his most supreme triumph. Malcolm, by his own efforts and struggles, by his gifted intellectual resources, by his introspection, became black. Not a non-white Anglo-Saxon, not a colored man, not a Negro, but a black man. A man who still realized a degree of his greatness in spite of the oppressive pressures of the racist society. A man who perceived error in a society that makes a habit of being always right. As a man he acknowledged his own errors. A man who devised a way to learn in a society which makes capital of the know-it-all. A man who learned to recognize the humanness trapped in men, even within the arrogance of white men. A man who was impatiently patient with the fumblings of his brothers, both black and white. A man of courage in a nation of impersonal cowards, cowards who kill so efficiently if they do not have to look at the victim face to face.

"Asalaam Alaikum" (Peace be unto you) and "Now, now, Brothers, break it up," he was heard to say before he was foully murdered. These words capture Malcolm's supreme triumph. His triumph as a man, as a black man, a beautiful black man, truly a black Prince!

Triumph in Tragedy

It is said, a people get the leaders they deserve. Conversely, they lose those leaders they cannot protect or do not deserve. Ahead of his time, ahead of his people, at the forefront of their struggle was Malcolm. His death and failures were tragic. But as one of current history's great figures, Malcolm's mistakes, shortcomings and all, triumphed over his personal tragedy.

Malcolm, known to the fighters for freedom throughout the world now as Malik, joins the rolls of the great leaders of the children of Africa who have tried to throw off the yoke of European oppression so that their fellows might be able to give this tired old globe Africa's great gift—humanness. To most of his fellowmen, in America he was known as a racist. But what can they know? For in this land, things and people are rarely called by the right name.

Malcolm was a triumph in tragedy for he was a black man, a black leader to all people. For simply he was one of them, he was the best of them, he reflected their needs, their desires, their aspirations. Would that the people would honor him— not by repeating his failures, but rather by reflecting his triumphs. . . .

MALCOLM X AND THE BLACK REVOLUTION: THE TRAGEDY OF A DREAM DEFERRED

———————————— BY *W. Keorapetse Kgositsile*

What happens to a dream deferred?
Does it dry up
like a raisin in the sun?
Or fester like a sore—
And then run?
Does it stink like rotten meat?
Or crust and sugar over—
like a syrupy sweet?

Maybe it just sags
like a heavy load.

Or does it explode?

Langston Hughes

I WRITE this with something bordering on fear. Among many other things Malcolm, like nationalism, is too many different things to too many people. Perhaps there would be nothing especially unfortunate and regrettable about that, but because of the different levels of our consciousness shaped by the varying degrees of filth and cowardice in us, our general understanding of Malcolm is, therefore, necessarily a distortion. Also running through my mind are the following words of Setswana wisdom: A Motswana doctor throws his bones and when they tell him of an irretrievable loss he will say:

"Se ileng se ile
Se ile mosimeng, motlhaela-thupa
Lesilo ke moselatedi."

Loosely translated, this says, "What is gone is gone/ It has gone down the hole, the-unreachable-by-a-rod/ The irrational (i.e., the unwise and ill tempered) is he-who-follows-it." But then again I realize that Malik, our monumental spiritual thrust, is not gone down any hole. If we had been stronger and more intelligent in 1965, Malcolm, the brother we thought we knew and admired, would still be with us today. And today, black man, where is Rap Brown? Max Stanford? Mandela? Sobukwe?—among many other free black men and women? You see, until *we* actually stop these racist maniacs who are opposed to any world order that challenges their decadence and racist perversions, they will continue to kill our leaders and any voices which, by articulating what is or should be in every black heart, become a direct threat to the warped white sensibility and its hideous creations. But to stop the madness of these perverts, we have to move to positions of power. Before we can move to positions of power we have to know ourselves so that we can, among many other necessary things, identify the enemy with a very precise clarity. This necessarily involves formulating a revolutionary ideology which will facilitate the building of our self-reliant communities and our veritable social institutions. Which is where Malcolm was at. Which is why Malcolm was murdered. But let us look beneath the sore.

To talk of a revolutionary ideology is to talk about the spirit of a people. And Malcolm, as I have said, was our spiritual thrust. Many people who have written about Malcolm have overlooked, deliberately or unwittingly, the importance of his inner landscape, his spirit. But LeRoi Jones, not surprisingly (he has been talking about the supremacy of the spirit for the past few years), could not overlook such an important aspect of Malcolm's energy:

Malik was the surge at one point, and his relationship to the Nation of Islam is as graphic a picture of world spirit as exists. And his break, into a secular (political) intelligence, understanding. His murder rendered most of the things directly associated with him into ruin. His, finally, was an abstract energy, a symbolizing of certain times of certain spirit. He was

murdered because he summed up the whole black-white struggle in America, and the world, too easily. He has risen, in a
wide arc-circle to embrace a whole public consciousness. He
was pimp-prisoner, student-monk, firebrand-wiseman and martyr. In each place his spirit settled, something was turned on,
and over. A beginning, an ending.

Jones is talking about what did not die, what cannot
die, which is what we must understand. Blood to blood,
we are talking about things deeper than the eye; Malcolm, the mover and the moved, Malik, the pledge of
fire, of song, the authentic lover. Fire and love, the most
powerful forces on Malcolm's inner landscape, informed
his movement, the practical manifestations of his abstract energy which Jones talked about. Fire and love,
those two forces in the inner landscape, are a spiritual
measure—a way of enabling us to know that we *can* if
we are willing and determined. But for us to know if we
can, actually, we must see the promise, the hope, in us
or around us, that what we are striving for is actually
possible, and know that after that point there can be no
turning back. Malcolm knew he could, that we can. Malcolm was willing and determined. Malcolm underwent
the internal revolution and internalized the Black Revolution, the world revolution.

Brother Malcolm was our dream, our promise, our
hope, a concrete vector of our desire and possibility, the
actual embodiment of what we strive to be, intrepid,
righteous, dedicated to the destruction of evil, dedicated
to the rebuilding of man and our possibilities as only the
sincere lover can be, constantly moving. To know you
love, to know you are loved; this is supreme. This was,
and will always be, the godly power in Malcolm, his
energy, spiritual. Malcolm was our sun, our son. When
we know we love, words of love become acts of love
recreating the powerful gods in us, making us *our* moment, the supreme rhythm—that is, the pulse of the most
desirable forces in our sensibility, which is spiritual. We
belong to our time, we belong to each other through our
journey to, and in, the breath we seek, a spiritual clean-
liness informing our vision to keep on pushing relentlessly to reshape the world in the image of this vision.

Fire and love, greater than our weakness or shortcomings, past reason or reasonableness, create a force relentlessly demanding a complete union with the soul, "an abstract energy, a symbolizing of certain times of certain spirit." Gwendolyn Midlo Hall says in "St. Malcolm and the Black Revolution" *(Negro Digest,* November 1967), "Spirituality is a powerful, highly contagious emotion, and in my view, mankind's most profound emotion. A revolution in the psyche of one man can become an all-powerful force for social change. St. Malcolm was such a man."

We can now look at the festering sore, the tragedy of our dream deferred. Malcolm, our dream, died unprotected. I have said before (see "Is the Black Revolutionist a Phony?" in *Negro Digest,* July 1967):

Brother Malcolm was assassinated at the beginning of his revolutionary maturity because of our collective weakness. Countless other perverted atrocities are continually perpetrated on us because of our collective weakness. Brothers, what I am driving at is, for instance, that if our historical enemy—now practically our natural enemy—knew that should anything have happened to Brother Malcolm there would be chaos in Harlem that night; that the following day there wouldn't be a single white store on 125th Street; that the very foundations of this system would have to cope with a Black uncontrollable power, the chances are that Brother Malcolm would still have been with us.

I have since realized that one of the major reasons Malcolm died *unprotected* is that many of us who were supposed to, did not actually know precisely who we were. There is nothing unusual in this filthy world when a very concrete, revolutionary man like Malcolm is killed by the enemies and oppressors of black people. In fact, these sinister neo-European devils, be they in Africa, Asia, South or North America, have shown us in very exact terms what they are prepared to do to any people who are determined to determine their own destiny. If they cannot buy you off or scare you or turn you into some freak apologist of their hideous schemes, then they organize to isolate and immobilize you or they kill you. We are familiar with what they have done to Nkrumah,

Sukarno, Robert Williams, Mandela, Sobukwe, Agostinho Neto. They even killed Luthuli and King, who preached a peaceful alternative, an appeal based on a level of morality the Western white man is too beastly to deal with for his own salvation. LeRoi Jones has pointed out that the Western white man cannot even feel because if he could he would feel the pain he is to the majority of the peoples on this planet. At the time I am writing this piece these sinister maniacs are carrying out plans to either kill or immobilize every black man they consider a threat to American domestic colonialism and dollarism around the world. What they are trying to do to Huey Newton, Rap Brown, Eldridge Cleaver, LeRoi Jones, Stokely Carmichael, to name a few, is exactly what the French tried to do to the leadership of the Algerian liberation front. It has happened in all colonial countries. I was in Detroit recently and there were these devils on TV discussing how they were going to improve their methods of controlling us. Finally one of them gave the police commissioner orders to arrest Brother Glanton Dowdell and General Baker as soon as any "racial incidents" broke out. I suspect that not knowing precisely who we are, we have not always been able to understand what we are up against very clearly, the black-white relationships and struggle in this country, as well as in Africa.

The position of Afro-Americans in America is that of a colonized people. There are three types of colonial situations: In the first kind the colonizers come into the country, say, as the English did in Kenya; then they oppress and exploit the people on African soil in the name of some country they owe allegiance to. In the second kind the settlers take over the country, as in South Africa or Zimbabwe, break off ties with whatever European country they owed allegiance to, and consider themselves "African." The Amerindians also suffer this kind of colonialism in North America. In the third kind European refugee bandits who have usurped a country like North America oppress and exploit Africans they brought over as slaves. The conditions of Africans under these three kinds of colonialism are the same, though the tactics that the colonizer uses on the colonized might vary from place to place. Which is what Malcolm kept hammering at over and over again so that we could better understand who we are in relation to the oppressor. Pointing out some significant things about the Bandung conference, Malcolm said:

The same man that was colonizing our people in Kenya was colonizing our people in the Congo. The same one in the Congo was colonizing our people in South Africa, and in Southern Rhodesia, and in Burma, and in India, and in Afghanistan, and in Pakistan. They realized all over the world where the dark man was being oppressed, he was being oppressed by the white man; where the dark man was being exploited, he was being exploited by the white man.

If we understand this clearly, then all the talk about injustice, discrimination, segregation, lack of equality before the law or before any other white institution, is just so much sterile bullshit, a trap very carefully worked out by the oppressor to make sure that our minds and feelings remain imprecise as to who we are and what we can actually do. But "America is doomed," as Malcolm pointed out with poetic precision. So is the rest of the colonial world because we are beginning to be clearer about our roots and identity, the gateway to our powerful thrusts into the future, with self-respect. Malcolm preached a cultural return to Africa, a strong spiritual bond to guide our goals, to guide the formulation of our ideology and the necessary revolutionary tactics and strategies. We are beginning to understand who we are historically. We are beginning to understand who we are socially—our best possible usefulnesses to our communities. We are beginning to understand who we are in our time—the direct relevance of our lives to our strong collective thrusts into the future. We are beginning to clearly understand who we are politically—our direct allegiances and alliances.

Malcolm's legacy, Malcolm's purpose and direction, Malcolm's impact on the Black Revolution the world over, nationalism, and Pan-African unity—these and many more of the practical manifestations of Malcolm's spirit—"the outer trimmings," Jones aptly described them—have been talked about in this book and many others, so I consider it unnecessarily repetitious to talk about them. One thing, though, I will point out: Malcolm, like Nkrumah, Touré, Felix Moumié (the Cameroonian brother whom the French poisoned with thallium), Nyerere, Fanon, Ho Chi Minh, to name just a few among our many heroes who have earned our respect, taught us to get rid of our fear and cowardice and wage an uncompromising, total struggle like our Vietnamese brothers. No concessions, Malcolm warned us, because to look forward to and expect concessions from the oppressor is to put yourself in a trick the enemy has, until recently, succeeded in placing us into. The nature of this paradox is ridiculous: I desire what I do not desire. Concessions lead you away from revolutionary struggle, lessening your chances of liberation. "Revolution is based on land. Land is the basis of all independence. Land is the basis of freedom, justice and equality," Brother Malcolm taught us. Because it is on land that a people builds a nation. The Setswana word for "peace" is *kagisano,* which literally means "building together." Brother Malcolm continued, "Revolution is bloody, revolution is hostile, revolution knows no compromise, revolution overturns and destroys everything that gets in its way." Look around you today, look around the world if you need any evidence to verify the truth and validity of Malcolm's statements above. And always remember this perceptive observation Malcolm makes upon looking back at the intelligence of something he did at the age of twelve: "All I had done was to improve on their strategy, and it was the beginning of a very important lesson in my life—that anytime you find someone more successful than you are, especially when you're both engaged in the same business—you know they're doing something that you aren't."

Fanon, demystified, said, "To put Africa in motion, to cooperate in its organization, in its regrouping, behind revolutionary principles. To participate in the ordered movement of a continent—this was really the work I had chosen." If we understand "Africa" here to include African societies wherever they may be, that too was

Malcolm's spirit. It is recurring in many of us today
because:

> There are memories between us
> Deeper than grief. There are
> Feelings between us much stronger
> Than the cold enemy machine that breaks
> The back . . . there are places between us
> Deeper than the ocean.

The recurrence of Malcolm's spirit is the source of
our power, the power of the best possible productive uses
of our lives. "The ingredients are simple," I have written
elsewhere ("More Steps Towards Our Freedom"),

and have always been there, within reach. *Self-respect*—you
cannot do anything of real human value unless you respect
yourself and your family, all the brothers and sisters around
the world. *Dedication* and *commitment* to reshaping our lives
—even our literature and the rest of the arts have to be, must
be, committed and committing. The undesirable and the meaningless we will destroy. *Belief* with clarity—unless you believe
in possibility—possibility is what always moves us—unless
you believe that you can actually do something, you cannot
do it.

And with our memory pried open to the bone of feeling:

> In the stillnesses of the night
> We see the gaping wounds where
> Those murderers butchered your flesh
> As they butchered the flesh of our land.
> Spirit to spirit we hear you
> Then blood on blood comes the pledge
> Swift as image, in spirit and blood
> The sons and daughters of our beginnings
> Boldly move to post-white fearlessness
> Their sharpnesses at the murderer's throat.

ASALAAM ALAIKUM.

THE INFLUENCE OF MALCOLM X ON THE POLITICAL CONSCIOUSNESS OF BLACK AMERICANS

BY *James Boggs*

"MALCOLM said . . ." For the last few years the inclusion of these two words in any discussion has been sufficient to establish an almost mystical bond between members of the black movement in the United States. Like a secret handshake or password, the reverent quotation of Malcolm has identified the speaker as (1) repudiating the "Negro revolution" or integration into American society and advocating instead the Black Revolution and struggle for Black Power; and (2) repudiating nonviolence and advocating instead the fight for freedom by all means necessary.

Hundreds of thousands of black men and women who at the time of Malcolm's death three and one half years ago had not even reached the stage of reformist activity today consider themselves black revolutionists and regard every word uttered by Brother Malcolm following his break from the Muslims as the gospel truth. Young people from thirteen to thirty play and replay the records of his speeches, study his autobiography, and refuse to attend school or go to work on the anniversaries of his birth and assassination. Such has been the tempo of revolutionary development in the United States since 1965.

Chiefly responsible for this fantastic growth in political consciousness have been the spontaneous rebellions which have hit America's cities summer after summer, most dramatically in Watts, Newark, and Detroit. These rebellions in turn have reflected the growing alienation of black people, and particularly black youth, from American society. Having witnessed over TV nearly every day for the past fifteen years the bestiality and savagery of rank and file American whites against black men, women, and children seeking to exercise the elementary civil rights of sitting at a lunch counter or buying a home or going to school, black people have concluded that it is not only futile but, even more important, demeaning to themselves to seek acceptance by a morally inferior white society. At the same time the war in Vietnam, in which a disproportionate percentage of black youth are drafted to kill and be killed by people of color, has brought home to them the fact that automation and cybernation have now made black people expendable and that a nation which has built itself on the extermination of one race and the enslavement of another can hardly be expected to stop short of Hitler's "final solution." Out of the rebellions has come a growing black revolutionary consciousness and out of growing black revolutionary consciousness has come growing identification with Brother Malcolm.

Malcolm split from the Muslims at the end of 1963 and was killed in February of 1965. His chief energies during his all-too-short year of independent activity were devoted to clarifying the fundamental link between the Black Revolution in the United States and the Black Revolution all over the world—in Africa, Asia, and Latin America. Among black revolutionaries today there is no doubt whatsoever that the CIA engineered his murder because they recognized the grave threat to American Masternationship which this linkup involved. Malcolm was only the first to be killed for this reason. As long as Dr. Martin Luther King, Jr., steered clear of international issues, he was safe from the CIA. When he began to lead a challenge to the foreign policy of the United States in Asia, even his philosophy of non-violence could not protect him from a violent death.

Malcolm did not have the time to build an organization to implement the revolutionary concepts which he was the first to articulate in the language with which black masses could identify. A brilliant organizer who had been chiefly responsible for building the Muslims into the most

highly disciplined mass organization that the black community has ever known, he was killed in the very act of
unfolding his plans for building a black political organization.

Today the task of building a disciplined revolutionary
organization to carry on the struggle for Black Power has
not advanced much beyond where it was at the time of
Malcolm's murder. Instead of applying themselves to this
essential task, black leaders have tended to rely upon the
spontaneous eruptions of the masses to wrest concessions
from the white power structure. Thus the black movement has not yet done the necessary scientific analysis of
the system which has exploited black people and now
threatens them with extermination. Nor has it clearly
defined the enemy and evolved a concrete strategy and
tactics to defeat this enemy and gain power for itself,
based upon a careful evaluation of the strength and weaknesses on both sides.

Lacking this kind of scientific analysis, Black Power
has become a slogan rather than a historic perspective
around which to organize a revolutionary struggle for
the political, social, and economic power necessary to
destroy the existing system and build a new one. "By all
means necessary" has been interpreted to mean acts of
violence rather than a strategy for liberation which will
employ whatever tactics are most useful at a particular
time—sometimes violent, sometimes non-violent, sometimes offensive, sometimes defensive—but always with
the clear objective of defeating the enemy and establishing one's own power. The struggle over "land," which
Malcolm defined as essential to the "Black Revolution"
as distinguished from the "Negro Revolution," has been
interpreted to mean an idealized territory rather than the
terrain or land of the major cities where blacks are fast
becoming a majority surrounding the centers of political
and economic power. Identification with Africa has come
to mean identification with anybody or anything African
rather than identification with those revolutionary forces
in Africa which are carrying on a war to unite and
liberate the entire continent from colonialism and neo-
colonialism.

Without such a comprehensive perspective and program, black revolutionaries constantly find themselves on the defensive against white radicals who lend a grudging support to Black Power but who in actual fact patronize and paternalize black revolutionaries as "unfinished products" who will one day see the light and recognize the superiority of Marxist theory and the necessity of an alliance with the white working class.

Actually it is these old radicals who are the unfinished products, i.e., politically undeveloped. None of them, either in the United States or in Europe, has seriously confronted the fact that all the successful revolutions since the time of Marx have been in undeveloped countries and that not a single one has taken place in an advanced industrial country with a large working class. Far from struggling for political power, the working class in the advanced countries has tended more and more to concentrate on economic demands which could be realized within the system. Instead of attacking the system, it has sought membership or integration into it.

Meanwhile, capitalism in each of these advanced countries has been revolutionizing technology and with it reducing the working class. Meanwhile, also, out of capitalism have come colonialism and neo-colonialism with their systematic exploitation and degradation of more people than simple capitalism has ever exploited.

Nor has any Marxist seriously examined the fact that the workers in the advanced countries have not put up any opposition to colonialism or neo-colonialism but have instead supported their ruling classes as colonial powers. This phenomenon is particularly flagrant in the United States where black people constitute a colony *inside* rather than *outside* the oppressing nation's borders and where therefore white workers could not pretend ignorance of the evils of colonialism. White workers in the United States have historically enjoyed all the benefits of racist exploitation of blacks and today are the most militant supporters of racism. After the Civil War it was the re-enslavement of blacks by the laws of the Southern states which provided the opportunity for European immigrants to come into the northern United States and become the industrial working class. Today, as automation and cybernation steadily reduce the number of industrial jobs, white workers regard every struggle by blacks as a threat to their own well-being.

Thus, far from being revolutionary, white workers today in the United States are counterrevolutionary. Far from being allies of the Black Revolution, they are its most intransigeant enemies.

Black people in the United States, on the other hand, have the combined antagonisms to the systems of a colonially oppressed and an urbanized, modernized people. Growing in numbers and concentration inside the nation's biggest cities, ceaselessly educated in the potentialities of modern technology by the mass media and the world about them, they have both the social force and the compelling necessity to fight for total political control as the only means to ensure their survival and development. Every issue of the world in which we live is for black people in the United States a matter of life and death. The rapid development of automation and cybernation to reduce the need for human toil and to create the opportunities for human development; the distribution of goods according to need; the overthrow of the existing educational system with its built-in racism and Western biases; a new revolutionary constitution which will establish a new law and order between nations and within this nation on the basis of the right to self-determination by those who have been systematically damned to underdevelopment—these are only some of the issues to which Black Power naturally and urgently addresses itself. Thus the perspective of Black Power is a new society much closer to the classless society projected by Marx than anything that the old Marxists have even dared to envision.

The Black Revolution is not anti-socialist or anticommunist, but it is very much anti the Socialist and Communist Parties which persist in urging the black movement to seek solidarity with a working class which is as much an enemy to the black movement as is the bourgeoisie and which, as an integral part of the American way of life, i.e., social mobility for whites on the backs of blacks, has an organic kinship with fascism and an organic hostility to the egalitarian concepts of social-ism or communism.

The chief reason why the old Marxists cannot see this potential in the Black Revolution is that they cannot see beyond its color. (The argument that blacks are a mi-nority is a specious one since they know very well that all revolutions have been started by a minority.) But the critical problem of the black movement is not these left-wing racists who can envisage Workers' (i.e., white) Power liberating blacks but cannot envisage Black Power liberating all humanity. The real problem is the idea of racial inferiority still lurking in the minds of black revolu-tionaries and inhibiting them from setting about the task of developing the scientific theory and the revolutionary organization necessary to achieve Black Power. Not until they do this will black revolutionaries take the giant step necessary to cross the great dividing line which Malcolm drew between the "Negro Revolution" and the "Black Revolution."

MALCOLM X,
OUR REVOLUTIONARY SON
AND BROTHER

———————————————— BY *Patricia Robinson*

I for one believe that if you give people a thorough understanding of what confronts them and the basic causes that
produce it, they'll create their own program, and when the
people create a program, you get action.

Malcolm X

MALCOLM was a destroyer of myths and the webs of
mystification. He was a humanist with a world view. Yet,
he was not a man. He was a black son and brother who
had audaciously returned to us from a very long trip
through lands ruled by god-kings and magician-tricksters.
He brought back the truth about the racket of racism,
oppression, and imperialism; how it had been run down
on us for so long, who runs it, and for what "sacred"
purpose—power over other men.

I might point out here that colonialism or imperialism, as
the slave system of the West is called, is not something that
is just confined to England or France or the United States.
The interests in this country are in cahoots with the interests
in France and the interests in Britain. It's one huge complex
or combine, and it creates what's known not as the American
power structure or the French power structure, but an international power structure. This international power structure is
used to suppress the masses of dark-skinned people all over the
world and exploit them of their natural resources.

February 14, 1965

Malcolm had been allowed his first birth by a woman.
For most of written history, the boy has turned to his

father as the great guide to and through the outer world. Malcolm's father died too early, raging and resisting and pointing the way through the kingdom of the white man backward to the kingdom of the black man.

Fathers are guides beyond the borders of the home, after the motherly realm where the small child plays and begins to experience the body. It is a historical fact; fathers have ruled the world a very long time and it is their accepted domain. Women and children are their subjects, their property.

The sons, however, are to be bred and trained to continue the hierarchic male rule. Through history ruling fathers have fought mostly with each other—so sure and arrogant have they been of their power to rule over others. They await only their sons (not their daughters) to join them in this historical quest for continued power over other men. In the long progression of male rule, men have believed themselves, and have seduced others to believe, that they are in the images of sacred gods, existing high above women and children and "lesser" men whose feet are embedded solidly in the earth or who lightly traverse the land in unplanned and exultant play.

It is only the sons who are encouraged to go out with the father to discover the world and its workings. They alone can really make the outer trip. It is the sons who can fall victim to staying there and trying foolishly to imitate and rule in the patriarch's place. And it is the son who can return to us, the women, the girl children, the poor, and the have-nots, who are still ruled in dumb suffering, to tell how we have come to be subjugated, used, and exploited. It is the son who can return, awaken the people to their own human worth, their inherent dignity, their true beginnings. It is the son who has the real chance to turn spy on the father-rulers, who have for far too long deceived the people and enchanted and enslaved the world population.

I feel like a man who has been asleep somewhat and under someone else's control. I feel that what I'm thinking and saying is now for myself. Before it was for and by the guidance of Elijah Muhammad. Now I think with my own mind, sir!

New York *Times*, February 22, 1965

Elijah Muhammad had been for Malcolm the father-guide who took up where Malcolm's father was forced to stop. He took a hustling, hung-up Malcolm into the other world where black men ruled, where black men were taught by this "messenger from God" the divine black word and the divine black way—into a fantasy world, for black men no longer ruled anywhere. It was a dream trip and it dreamed thousands of young, black city-males. It was that longed-for central black kingdom within a hostile white kingdom because we had been unable to go back to Africa to dream up a kingdom there. The Garveyites had been prevented from leaving the United States by the white slave master. Malcolm's father had been murdered by white males threatened by his rebellious black masculinity.

Black fathers have never ruled anyone in the United States. Not even the usual victims of male rule, the women and children. They have resisted and rebelled against the ruling white father, threatening to wrest from him more of the profits and surplus from his exploitations of the rest of the world; or to go off in a separate nation to make their own means to obtain a surplus or profit. Then the black man could be in high position and privilege and exert control over the surplus as he had done in Africa before the white European ever appeared off the African shores.

An idyllic African classless society (in which there were no rich and no poor) enjoying a drugged serenity is certainly a facile simplification; there is no historical or even anthropological evidence for any such a society. I am afraid the realities of African society were somewhat more sordid.

All available evidence from the history of Africa, up to the eve of the European colonization, shows that African society was neither classless nor devoid of a social hierarchy. Feudalism existed in some parts of Africa before colonization, and feudalism involves a deep and exploitive social stratification, founded on ownership of land. It must also be noted that slavery existed in Africa before European colonization, although the earlier European contact gave slavery in Africa some of its most vicious characteristics. The truth remains, however, that before colonization, which became widespread in Africa only in the 19th century, Africans were prepared to sell, often for no more than thirty pieces of silver, fellow tribesmen and even members of the same "extended" family and clan. Colonialism deserves to be blamed for many evils in Africa, but surely it was not preceded by an African golden age or paradise.

> Kwame Nkrumah, "African
> Socialism Revisited,"
> *African Forum,* 1968

Other black men in the United States, like many colonized people, joined in pitiful imitation of the real ruler, the white entrepreneur, draped in condensed wealth and imitating the old, historical god-kings. Power in the United States has been in the image of maleness and whiteness. Elijah Muhammad, black and male, was a caricature of the usurper king who only appeared to offer his black subjects a nation of their own if they followed him. Inexplicably, this black nation would arise here (not yet in Africa). The mythical, ancient God would, as before, destroy the oppressor nation and set the oppressed nation free.

Mystification and enchantment are old tricks that African medicine men and "sacred" kings practiced to keep themselves in power. Elijah Muhammad was a black father figure using out-of-date stratagems to put himself in power over a black people in the United States when the power in poor dark countries was beginning to be seized violently by all the damned—all the people who have for centuries been the beast of burden, the slave and property of kings and an elite, the women and the children who were the cheap labor force of factories and the plantation-farms. The black oppressed in the United States were stirring in embryonic consciousness already stimulated by African, Asian, and Latin American revolutionaries. They only awaited a teacher, a demystifier of their very own.

Malcolm saw the need for a real black nation—beyond the static fantasies of the Nation of Islam. Through his readings in prison and his travels for the Honorable Elijah Muhammad, Malcolm began to see the process by which other black and brown people had secured their nationhood, by violent revolution.

Ruling fathers understand that violent revolution brings on their own overthrow, loss of high social status and the privilege to exploit others. Unless sons agree to continue the hierarchic system whereby there are rulers and ruled, they are banished from the kingdom, imprisoned, or killed. This has been the general pattern of East and West since the rise of cities.

In November 1963 Malcolm addressed a Northern Negro Grass Roots Leadership Conference and explained that we were a nation within the United States, a black colony ruled by white outsiders. We were like all the world colonies exploited and controlled by white men. Black people all over the world were waking up to their common enemy. If black people wanted to own their own nations that was black nationalism and all nations that wanted to own themselves had had revolutions. "A revolutionary is a black nationalist. He wants a nation." Real white nationalist revolutions were violent ones, as we could remember from our white-controlled education.

The white man knows what a revolution is. He knows that the Black Revolution is worldwide in scope and in nature. The Black Revolution is sweeping Asia, is sweeping Africa, is rearing its head in Latin America. The Cuban Revolution—that's a revolution. They overturned the system. Revolution is in Asia, revolution is in Africa, and the white man is screaming because he sees revolution in Latin America. How do you think he'll react to you when you learn what a real revolution is?

November 9, 1963

On December 3, 1963, Malcolm was suspended by Elijah Muhammad for unauthorized remarks after the assassination of President John F. Kennedy. On March 8, 1964, Malcolm gave the press "a declaration of independence." He felt then that Elijah Muhammad, like Garvey, was correct. "I too believe the best solution is complete separation with our people going back home to our own African homeland." But until then this black son, banished now by the father, wanted a unity in the black colony that would repair the worst of our exploitation and suffering. The son did not seek to rule over others, the usual historical pattern. He wanted to join with and teach all who had been oppressed, why and by whom they were oppressed.

The thing that you have to understand about those of us in the Black Muslim movement was that all of us believed 100 per cent in the divinity of Elijah Muhammad. We believed in him. We actually believed that God, in Detroit by the way, that God had taught him and all of that. I always believed that he believed it himself. And I was shocked when I found out that he himself didn't believe it. And when that shock reached me, then I began to look everywhere else and try to get a better understanding of the things that confront all of us so that we can get together in some kind of way to offset them.

February 14, 1965

Malcolm experienced that essential rebirth in the world. It had been stimulated by the betrayal of the black father, Malcolm's trusted guide. But the black father who could not rule here in white America had revealed to the son the black world from which we'd come.

One of the things that made the Black Muslim movement grow was its emphasis upon things African. This was the secret to the growth of the Black Muslim movement. African blood, African origin, African culture, African ties. And you'd be surprised—we discovered that deep within the subconscious of the black man in this country, he is still more African than he is American.

February 14, 1965

Elijah Muhammad had given Malcolm the root lesson but, like all rulers, not the basic knowledge that revolutionary violence was a just response to reactionary violence —that very violence that has kept the great and lesser father figures in power over others through most of history. The son had discovered the truth for himself.

On November 24, 1964, Malcolm returned for the last time to us from abroad. He had been away since December 4, 1963. At the Audubon almost every week thereafter Malcolm lectured to those of us who had waited for centuries—the return of the truly revolutionary black son and brother who could and would help us to find the concrete way to the overthrow of the great white tricksters and their capitalist economic system. With the wisdom born from the betrayal of the black father and his own individual revolution against tyranny, Malcolm turned to the poor masses, the women and the young people.

For how many countless centuries has the black woman of Africa and the Western world repressed the knowledge that she and the children had been betrayed by the black men who lusted for high position and its gold and money symbols—and used them to exploit black people? For how long had she kept silent in the times when her black man was oppressed by foreigners—or earlier, when she herself, turned traitor to her children and her people, had consented to rule with the black fathers in Africa for the few crumbs and the secondary position they gave her? For that matter, how many white vestal virgins in the symbolic temples of white power have turned whore down through history for a few trinkets?

How long had the poor black women of the world been the planter, the builder of homes, the burden carrier, sunk in their slave acceptance of male and god rule? Black women in the twentieth century had, like their sons, heard the revolutionary exaltation of the Russian, the Spanish, the Algerian, the Chinese and Vietnamese, and the Cuban women who have gallantly helped their revolutionary husbands, brothers, and sons to resist and overthrow the tyrants who have exploited them. And she had looked in her white Western prison for those sons whom she could help to overthrow the oppressor father and his aggressive exploitive system.

The girl children who were not preferred as the sons awaited their brother's return with the truth to counter their own miseducation, their own feelings of inferiority and powerlessness.

Look at yourselves. Some of you teen-agers, students. How do you think I feel and I belong to a generation ahead of you —how do you think I feel to have to tell you, "We, my generation, sat around like a knot on a wall while the whole world was fighting for its human rights—and you've got to be born into a society where you still have that same fight." What did we do, who preceded you? I'll tell you what we did. Nothing. And don't you make the same mistake we made. . . .

December 31, 1964

Malcolm had said to the black women earlier in December 1964 that we were the real educators. We were the setter of fires that would burn until our people set themselves free. It was up to us to educate the coming generation to their historical responsibility to the oppressed and have-nots of the world.

I think that an objective analysis of events that are taking place on this earth today points toward some type of ultimate showdown.

You can call it a political showdown, or even a showdown between the economic systems that exist on this earth which almost boil down along racial lines. I do believe that there will be a clash between East and West.

I believe that there will ultimately be a clash between the oppressed and those that do the oppressing. I believe that there will be a clash between those who want freedom, justice and equality for everyone and those who want to continue the systems of exploitation.

January 19, 1965

On Sunday afternoon, February 21, 1965, all of us, who had waited for centuries for that revolutionary son and brother to be reborn, gratefully and humbly accepted the revolutionary responsibility as it passed out of Malcolm's slowly descending body.

> The Valley Spirit never dies,
> It is named the Mysterious Female.
> And the doorway of the Mysterious Female
> Is the base from which Heaven and Earth sprang.

> It is there within us all the while;
> Draw upon it as you will, it never runs dry.

TAO TE CHING 6
Translation, Waley,
The Way and the Power

NOTHING BUT A MAN

BY *Wyatt Tee Walker*

I HAVE not yet read or heard anyone speak of the historical significance of Malcolm X. More tragic than his death (for all men die sooner or later) was that it was precipitated in the early days of a basic change in his philosophy. Perhaps it would be more precise to say "jelling" of his philosophy, for his break with the "old man," Elijah Muhammad, was *the change* and all that followed until his murder was really a quest for what this sensitive and dramatic "angry man" knew could be found somewhere *in spite of America*. For me, his search was consciously or unconsciously the reclamation of the black man's masculinity.

Sociologically, what focus the Negro family has had, parentally, has been for the most part matriarchal—that is, centered in the mother figure. The racist critics who disparage the instability of Negro family life fail to note that there was no concept of family life in the Negro community in the South until just a hundred years ago. Then, following "Emancipation," the leftover evils of slavery, some of which are much in evidence today, contributed largely to the suppression of the father figure in the already weakened and sometimes broken family circle. Reconstruction, followed by "separate but equal" and the coupling with antebellum "tradition," prevented the Negro male from becoming a man. The only course left was *survival by accommodation*—being an Uncle Tom.

The male head of the Negro family could defend neither

his woman nor his children; he was impotent politically and economically; he absolved violence and death without cause or purpose. Having had to stand by and see his children starved and his women raped, the Negro man either resigned his manhood or physically fled his responsibility as the only alternatives to sure death. The end result of this circumstance was for the Negro child to be almost totally dependent upon the female head of the family for strength, direction, hope—whatever! Children for the last three or four generations have grown to manhood and womanhood under this matriarchal influence necessitated by loss of the Negro male's masculinity.

This is why Brother Malcolm has historical importance. As he was symptomatic of the terrible ills that beset our nation domestically, he was also symptomatic of the solution to those ills. Black and white people who regretted and resented the presence of a Malcolm X would have done better to have regretted and resented the society that *produced* him. It must be noted that as Malcolm made an impact on society, in reciprocal fashion he felt its impact on him. How was it that a Malcolm X never appeared on the scene until the non-violent movement led by Martin Luther King, Jr., had reached thunderous proportions? All of the problems have been just about the same for the last one hundred years.

One who is a thoughtful student of sharp social change can recognize the telltale dynamics of revolution. Given a Martin Luther King, Jr., there had to be a Malcolm X. In earlier days, Dr. King was considered by most in the national community (circa 1960) a dangerous, wild-eyed perverter of religion with demagogic power and obvious Communist sympathies. Whites were not alone in swallowing hard at his "extremist tactics." Enter Malcolm X, and Dr. King, in contrast to the fiery outpourings of Malcolm X *al la Muhammad*, necessarily became more palatable to the American scene. King, the pioneer of a new militancy, provokes a response that purports to "out-King" King.

Thus, Malcolm represented a newly found assertiveness that had lain dormant too long in the minds of men of color. Casual observers of the present American scene in race relations mistakenly assess Malcolm as "more militant" and Dr. King as "less militant," when in reality each practiced distinctly different methodologies. Dr. King, by the nature and practice of non-violence, could not be more militant; Malcolm's practice was far less militant than his theory. Militancy is more accurately measured by how determinedly one pursues and *achieves* his goals. Dr. King chose non-violence as his methodology and has steadily escalated and broadened his attack against the evils of bigotry and prejudice so much so that his work now tangentially is of significance to international affairs.

Malcolm's methodology was verbalized as "an eye for an eye" in earlier days and softened to self-defense in later days. The goals of both, though not always described as such, were basically securing a fair shake for the black man in America. Dr. King's techniques have proved to be not only religious and morally rooted but also practically and realistically productive. However charitably one may view the work of Malcolm X, the same caliber of results is not evident.

Not everyone can buy the non-violent stratagems of Dr. King and company (though I am proud to be counted in his number). Few, precious few, can academically and functionally accept non-violence as a way of life. All those who are left are not necessarily spineless or violent. There are certainly those like Malcolm, whose manhood was challenged? strengthened? by the repeated heroism of men, women, and children of the Deep South in the face of awesome hardships, physical and emotional. The non-violent movement in the South broke the shackles from many chained minds in the North through its raw courage alone.

A Malcolm X, a Jesse Gray, a Milton Galamison had to do *something*, though they would not *or* could not abide by the discipline of the King-led forces who "turn the other cheek." To some degree, this may explain some character of disconnectedness in the thrust of the Negro community in our large urban centers of the North. The new-found assertiveness of the Negro in the North went off in as many different directions as the personalities through whom it was filtered. At some points, as in the case of last summer's [1964] looting and so-called "riots," its misdirection and lack of discipline degenerated into senseless violence. In almost every instance, it expressed itself most vehemently at that point in society where the Negro male has been emasculated most—confrontation with law enforcement officials.

Malcolm "brought whitey down front" and men who had cowered inwardly and outwardly in the presence of the nameless white face in whose world he moved admired his spunk and grit. Vicariously through him, some Negro men got up off their knees for the first time in their lives and touched their manhood as if it were a new Christmas toy.

What am I saying? We should make the late Mr. Little "St. Malcolm"? Not at all. Malcolm was guilty at times of useless illogical and intemperate remarks that helped neither him nor his cause. I personally could never buy black nationalism, nor could I recommend it even if conditions for black men were infinitely worse than they are. But all the world must agree that Malcolm had the "book" on white America and he read it loud and clear for all to hear.

The press generally, more from naïveté than from malice, wrote Malcolm off rather quickly at death, almost summarily, as "living and dying by the sword." This was neither a fair nor accurate assessment of the late Malcolm X. Careful study of Malcolm's preachments, particularly after his break with Elijah Muhammad, reveal primary focus on being pro-black as versus being anti-white, as was erroneously described in epitaph. A secondary focus was his insistence on the right of an individual to protect the sanctity of his home, life, and property with arms as over against his newspaper-produced reputation of encouraging black to take up arms against white. These are fine shades of differences but absolutely crucial to understanding the historical importance of Brother Malcolm.

The current low-budget movie, *Nothing But a Man,* is the story of another Malcolm, fictitious yet very real, who can be found all over this land. Dove Anderson, the main character, wasn't looking for trouble or running away from it either. His unverbalized goal in this magnificent picture was to be "nothing but a man." That's what Malcolm X was all about. He was the symbol of Negro males who, though groping, have not yet found the answer to how they can be "nothing but a man," which is, really, more than enough.

ISLAM AS A PASTORAL
IN THE LIFE OF
MALCOLM X

BY *Abdelwahab M. Elmessiri*

THE *Autobiography of Malcolm X* is a hymn of praise to the soul of man, which can survive in the face of the most corrupting circumstances. This heroic achievement is possible because man is always capable of dreaming of a world of pastoral innocence and of maintaining a measure of spiritual purity even after becoming the most cynical of all cynics.

The pastoral, whether in the *Thousand and One Nights* or in ancient Rome, is an ideal characterized by simplicity and purity, and is considered superior to the norm or statistical average predominant in a sophisticated culture. The pastoral ideal is used by the revolutionary or visionary writer to undercut and expose a complex yet stagnant *status quo*. He may not believe that such an ideal actually exists, yet he believes in the possibility of vision and its superiority over fact and reality. In this sense the pastoral mode is as inevitable as history and revolution.

Islam, for Malcolm, was such a pastoral. It provided him with an idealistic or visionary frame of reference that liberated him from the racist assumptions of his society of which he was the victim, and to which he must subscribe. But why did I choose the term "pastoral" to describe the Islamic-Arab world Malcolm personally saw, and the Islamic beliefs he eventually embraced? Arabia and Cairo, after all, do exist, and Islamic culture is indeed devoid of racial tensions. This is admittedly true, but the Arab world is not exactly the paradise Malcolm saw. Malcolm did not see the seamy side of the Islamic-Arab world because he was dealing with totalities. He discovered that as far as he, the Afro-American, was concerned, the Arab-Islamic world as a totality did not stunt human potentialities. That is why he could abstract his pastoral ideal from this Muslim world. White Protestant America for him was devoid of such human idealistic possibilities. He found it totally destructive.

Morever, the traditional pastoral is supposed to be devoid of any tensions because it is totally ahistorical and mythical. The pastoral writer deems it a theoretical rather than a real possibility. The modern revolutionary pastoral, on the other hand, has its roots in reality and it derives its potency from the fact that it is realizable. Soviet Russia is such a pastoral for many Marxists. It is not exactly the land of milk and honey, a secular Promised Land; it is rather a community in which possibilities for controlled and directed human development exist. Mao Tse-tung has his own pastoral vision of a new socialist man who is not motivated by the profit incentive. The Red Guards and the great Cultural Proletarian Revolution are the means of implementing the vision. The Islamic-Arab world, in spite of all its historical tensions, provided Malcolm with a pastoral vision of a world morally superior to America, at least insofar as human and racial relationships are concerned. By returning to America to realize his new vision through social action, Malcolm showed that he belonged to the tradition of historical revolutionaries who want to alter reality, not by transcending or breaking away from it, but by reshaping it according to their vision of the "good life."

The structure of the *Autobiography* as a whole could be seen as the development of Malcolm from being a practical, soulless hustler to becoming a visionary who discovers, through the help of an Islamic, pastoral norm, "idealistic tendencies" in himself. The *Autobiography* begins with a reference to the pregnancy of Malcolm's mother: a clear symbol of fertility and new life. The father, a preacher of a form of black nationalism, is also an emblem of a new national birth. Yet the very second line of the *Autobiography* tells of the hooded Ku Klux Klan riders who surrounded Malcolm's house in the night and taunted his father. The very fact that Malcolm survived and that he wrote his *Autobiography* is a testimony that man, by refusing to sell his soul to the devil of race and materialism, and by maintaining a belief in the superiority of the possible over the actual, can achieve salvation.

Al Jahilyya: The Pre-Islamic Phase

Everything in Malcolm's society conspired against him and his humanity. Once the father died, the welfare people moved in to convert Malcolm's little community into fragmented economic units. They looked at the members of the family "as numbers and as a case in their book, not at human beings" (p. 22).* Later in life, Malcolm was once more literally converted to a number when he was sent to jail. His number became a part of him, "stenciled on his brain" (p. 152). Malcolm discovered that the conversion of men into numbers is a cultural necessity for America, because while this country can solve the problem of sending man into outer space, it cannot deal with human beings (p. 268).

If the relationship is between object and other objects, rather than between a man and other human beings, manipulation replaces social responsibility and love. Everyone preys on everyone else. The early part of the *Autobiography* tells of lust replacing love (p. 121), of white and black men exploiting white and black prostitutes, and vice versa. It also tells of the legion of gamblers who preferred doing nothing to real human struggle. In their heart of hearts, they discovered that human labor, "slave" they called it, did not really pay in exploitative, manipulative, capitalist America. In the capitalist gospel it says, do unto others, before they do unto you.

The most manipulative of all the characters was the hustler. Malcolm noticed that the ghetto hustler, a product of white racism, had no inner restraints whatsoever

* All references are to *The Autobiography of Malcolm X* with the assistance of Alex Haley (New York: Grove Press, 1966). In order to reduce the number of footnotes I have referred to the page numbers in the essay itself.

because, in order to survive, he was "out there constantly preying upon others, probing for any human weakness like a ferret" (p. 311). The hustler, in competitive white America, could never trust anyone (p. 87), and had to keep on the go, shoving and pushing.

Reduced to the status of a hustler, a gambler, or even an object, man loses what distinguishes him as a human being. In the *Autobiography,* the many references to man as an animal serve to dramatize the reductive brutality of white society. Malcolm found that white people considered him, at first, a pet canary (p. 26). Later he became, for them, a fine colt, a pedigreed pet (p. 27), and a pink poodle (p. 31). This useless pet became a mere parasite (p. 75), only to become a vulture in Chapter Six.

But not for a moment did Malcolm surrender his innocence, for he knew all along that he became a vulture through living in "this competitive, materialistic, dog-eat-dog white man's world" (p. 267). Malcolm, with his sharp analytical mind, discovered that this awareness made the ghetto hustler a potential revolutionary. Seeing himself as a victim rather than a victimizer, the hustler had "less respect for the white power structure than any other Negro in North America" (p. 311). As a matter of fact, Malcolm implicitly suggests that the moral standards of the community of hustlers are in a sense superior to those of white Protestant America. The relationship between Shorty and Malcolm is characterized by a certain warmth totally absent in the rest of the world of dollarism. For one thing, the hustlers form a community. For another, their code of ethics is consistent because it applies to both blacks and whites—an ethical height yet to be reached by these United States.

Basha'ar Al-Baath or the Emergence of the Pastoral

If even the hustlers of the *Autobiography* kept their souls, the mass of people showed a remarkable cultural stamina. They did not only survive, but they also had visions in a world of crass materialism. It is ultimately the capacity to have visions of a world of pastoral beauty that saved Malcolm.

The first reference in the *Autobiography* to any visions of salvation is made in the first few pages of the first chapter. Malcolm remembered very well his father's favorite sermon: "That little *black* train is a-comin' . . . an' you better get all your business right!" (p. 4). The images used show the stubbornness of the black man in America. He converts the most mundane of activities, business, and the least poetical of objects, a train, into spiritual symbols. Malcolm also remembered his father invoking the myth of an African Adam "driven out of the Garden into the caves of Europe" and using the cleansing metaphor of the coming storm to describe Africa's redemption (p. 6). No wonder, with this capacity to resist entrapment in mere matter, that the Negroes, when in church, "threw their souls and bodies wholly into worship" (p. 35). White America did not obliterate their souls the way it did to their white brethren, who, as Malcolm observed, "Just sat and worshiped with words" (p. 35)—a sad sight indeed!

But it was through music and dance that the Afro-American could transcend his agony and achieve specific selfhood and identity. In the *Autobiography*, Malcolm joyfully asserts that his long-suppressed African instincts broke through when he was dancing (p. 57). References to Afro-American music and songs are just too many to enumerate. But they stand as some kind of emblem of the triumph of the Afro-American soul and its desire to reach the skies. (The music and the dance are in sharp contrast to the animal imagery which points to the voraciousness of the white man's culture and its desire to reduce and fetter the Afro-American.) Nowhere is this emblematic significance of music made clearer than in Chapter Five, when a reefer-smoking Negro, hearing Lionel Hampton's "Flyin' Home," believed he could fly and actually jumped from the second balcony, breaking his leg. Both the incident of the temporary "spiritual liberation" and its tragic aftermath were immortalized in another Afro-American song: Earl Hines' hit tune "Second Balcony Jump" (p. 74). Malcolm was detached enough to see the futility and moral inadequacy of this kind of flying, but he was also compassionate enough to see its beauty. Later in life, Malcolm himself would fly like the "boy Icarus," but with wings given to him by Allah and the religion of Islam (p. 287).

The music and the other redeeming elements in the world of the Afro-American preserved his soul and saved him from being crushed by the racist ethics of white America. Though they all implied a degree of rejection of the stagnant *status quo,* they never liberated the Afro-American completely because they did not provide him with a new total vision which could serve as a total critique of American culture. Islam, a total ethical system, was for Malcolm both the total critique and the pastoral ideal.

Islam

The process of conversion to Islam began with small ritualistic steps such as the refusal to eat pork in prison (p. 156) and the ablution (p. 193). Yet it ended with the revolutionary adoption of a new system of values.

While still in jail, Malcolm was introduced to the version of Islam advocated by Elijah Muhammad's group. He embraced it and felt its moral superiority. But Malcolm went beyond the group's moral assumptions because of their failure to reject America's ethical values completely. Although the Black Muslim's creed did undoubtedly contribute to Malcolm's liberation and redemption, it was, like the other pastoral elements in his pre-Islamic life, morally and psychologically inadequate. For this reason let us move on directly to discuss Malcolm's conversion to "orthodox" Islam, demonstrating in the course of the discussion the ways in which he transcended the beliefs of the Elijah Muhammad group.

Malcolm showed an intuitive understanding of Islam and its God. Many Americans have studied Islam before, but they were satisfied with their culture and its underlying assumptions, while Malcolm was undergoing a moral crisis and dreaming of a better world. That is why after hundred of years of theological studies and European missionaries, no Westerner as yet has captured the essence of the Islamic God the way Malcolm did. Malcolm, for instance, discovered the egalitarianism and universalism of Allah. The Christian God is universal, yet Malcolm knew that He was appropriated by a Western culture that gave Him specific colors and definite cultural attributes. A Harvard seminary student, lecturing on the Christian re· ligion, grew very evasive and embarrassed when Malcolm told him about the real color of Jesus and St. Paul (p. 190). Allah, on the other hand, remains free from human prejudices and false distinctions. He is the God of *all* people, in *all* places, and of *all* colors. Malcolm reached this conclusion not through theological ratiocination, but through personal experience. In the Islamic-Arab world, people insisted on seeing him as an American. Isn't that his nationality, after all? The Egyption pilot, whose complexion was darker than Malcolm's, invited him to the cockpit as an "American Muslim" (p. 324), not as a black Muslim. A Persian Muslim in Malcolm's compartment greeted him saying, "Amer . . . American" (p. 329). The astonishment was complete and the realization of the nature of the Islamic God became final when Dr. Azzam, who "would have been called a white man," did not act white in the least (p. 331). To his utter dismay, Malcolm discovered that he was the only one who was color-conscious. This new outlook signaled the beginning of his total liberation from American values. Malcolm, in a very significant passage, which begins with a reference to the morning, tells us about his reappraisal of the term "white," and his heroic leap from racist judgments to ethical evaluations (p. 333). The term "white man" loses its racial content because he saw people with white complexions who were genuinely brotherly. He so thoroughly exorcised the devil of racism that when he noticed that people who looked alike stayed together, he could see it not as racial segregation but as a voluntary action of people who simply have something in common with each other (p. 344).

This personal interaction with Muslims enabled him to grasp the revolutionary implications of the Islamic concept of the Oneness of God. Whites standing in front of the One God ceased to be mere whites and became full human beings (p. 360). He, an Afro-American, also stood before the "Creator of All" and also felt like a complete human being (p. 365). He could achieve this completeness because to accept the Oneness of God means to accept the

Oneness of Man (p. 341). Consistent and generous as ever, Malcolm embraced the logical conclusion of his new Islamic position; later in life he rejected the pseudo-Islamic myth of the white man being the devil.

In the Christian world, people have to have images and icons to be able to see their gods. In the Islamic tradition, God can never be represented nor is He ever incarnated in any human or superhuman form. The Muslim prophet is also the Iconoclast, the breaker of statues and images. The reasons are not hard to discover. To paint an image of God is to impose a human limitation or prejudice on Him. The Islamic God is universalistic and prefers to remain this way. Malcolm showed his remarkable acumen in his rejection of the elaborate mythical scheme, Protestant in origin, devised by the Black Muslims (p. 168). They believe that God was incarnated in the person of a half-white, half-black man named Mr. W. Fard. The whole idea of incarnation, which has many anti-humanistic and anti-democratic implications, is totally alien to the spirit of Islam. Malcolm grasped this fact, and pointed out the dangers of deifying the human. He believed in Elijah Muhammad as a leader not in the ordinary human sense but also "as a divine leader." In Mecca, on the hilltop, and in the presence of the One and the Unique he realized how very dangerous it is to believe in the "divinely guided" and "protected" person (p. 365). Nowhere in his *Autobigraphy* does he talk about the form of Allah or His personal attributes.

One and Unique He is, but He is never alien to the human self. The Islamic God refused to endow his prophet with supernatural powers which could contravene natural processes. Muhammad stubbornly refused to yield to the temptations of becoming an ordinary, supernatural prophet, and remained a man living among men. If the messenger of Allah, a casual speaker with Him, is an ordinary human being, then anyone can speak to Allah. Allah tells Muhammad in the Koran that if people asked the prophet about Him, they should know that Allah is near, and that He will answer all their prayers. Malcolm was almost echoing the Koran when he said, "Allah always gives you signs, when you are with Him, that He is with you" (p. 319). It is this humane God whom Malcolm had in mind whenever he reiterated the sentence "I knew Allah was near" which runs like a refrain throughout the *Autobiography*, especially in Chapter Seventeen.

The Muslim prophet was not only a messenger of God, but also a political leader of Arabia. He did not only offer a new vision of life, but he also fought for the liberation of slaves. That is why Balal, one of his first converts, was at once a religious follower and fighter for freedom. In short, the separation between a religious and ethical ideal, on the one hand, and social and political practice, on the other, is not a Muslim phenomenon. The imam in Islamic culture still plays the role of the minister and the leader of the community, and his Friday sermon is still both religious and political. The Islamic view of social action as being inseparable from ethical and religious beliefs was not lost upon Malcolm. It seems to me that this is the single most important point that caused Malcolm to break away from the Black Muslims. Moving among the Afro-American masses, he discovered that the Nation of Islam could be a significant force only when it is "engaged in more action" in the overall struggle of the masses (p. 289). When his efforts at reorienting the Nation of Islam to social action failed, he decided to build his own organization which would carry into practice what the Nation of Islam preached (p. 315). He was too much of a Muslim to be a mere priest; he could not help being a social activist, like the messenger of Allah.

One final characteristic of the Islamic ideal which Malcolm perceived and fully appreciated is its communitarianism. The Islamic sabbath is on Friday, *Yawm Al-Juma'a,* or the day of the community. Allah in the Koran says that His hand is always with the community rather than with the individual. In his first encounter with Muslims, Malcolm immediately felt "the atmosphere of warmth and friendliness" (p. 321). Coming from a racist, competitive society it was almost like stepping "out of a prison" (p. 321). People loved him, and accepted him "as a brother" (p. 322); and they offered him their food and even their beds. An Egyptian wife, incapable of seeing competitiveness as the sole motivation of man's behavior, innocently asks, "Why are people in the world starving when America has so much surplus food?" (p. 322). He who comes from a capitalist, sophisticated society knows better: In America they let the surplus rot, according to the most advanced technological methods, of course! Islamic communitarianism makes social action an inevitable outgrowth of moral consciousness. Malcolm embraced the communitarian ideal and the ideal of social action. His life after his actual conversion to Islam testifies to this fact.

Though he left a part of himself in the Holy City of Mecca, and though he took away with him a part of Mecca (p. 349), he refused to degenerate into any form of escapism or desire to "return." He went back to his people to fight with them for their rights. The separatism of the early nationalist groups was rejected in favor of a more sophisticated concept of return to Africa. The "return," from that point on, came to mean a philosophical and cultural "return," rather than a purely physical one. The physical going back to America, however, was as important as the psychological return to Africa. This dual "return" reveals Malcolm's commitment to his community and his desire to bring salvation to it. It also reveals his insistence on his dual, complex identity as an African and as an American. He was no mad prophet who wanted to break all historical and human limits.

Having accepted the Islamic ethical ideal, and having exorcised the ghost of white Protestant America, the new man Malcolm could now discover himself and his real and beautiful soul. The *Autobiography* reaches its climax when liberated Malcolm, in his new pastoral world, in the Holy City of Mecca, discovers "idealistic tendencies" (p. 333) in himself. This is a far cry from the pink poodle, the vulture, and the hustler white America wanted him to be. The *Autobiography* is indeed a hymn of praise for the soul of man, which can endure and even triumph.

PART II

MALCOLM X
AT CLOSE RANGE—
PERSONAL VIEWS

PREFACE TO PART II

Malcolm X was easy to meet and difficult to know. He listened to all and learned from many, while being careful not to mistake the trivial for the profound. The article "The Last Days of Malcolm X" by Earl Grant was extracted from a much longer work that is a book in preparation. Grant is one of the few people who can say that he was a personal friend and associate of Malcolm X. All of the contributors to this part of the book knew Malcolm X personally.

The other contributors to this section—including Betty Shabazz (Mrs. Malcolm X)—present a picture of a Malcolm X not generally known to the public. What comes through in these articles is the profound humanness of the man himself.

Malcolm X and his activities got some of the best and worst press coverage of any personality of our time. Fortunately, Malcolm X was the master of press conferences and he always got the best out of them. Many writers arrived at sweeping conclusions about Malcolm X without ever confronting him or seriously trying to understand the nature of the movement that his personality, almost solely, brought into being. Those who viewed him at close range got a different picture than others who attempted to view him from a distance with detachment and what some people call objectivity.

The many dimensions in the personality of Malcolm X made him a difficult person to understand and interpret.

He was a person always in the process of growth and change. He had outgrown the Black Muslim movement led by Elijah Muhammad long before he was forced out of it. It was inevitable that Malcolm X would eventually see the major weakness of this movement and try to grapple with it. The major weakness is the escapist method it uses to offer identity and dignity to black Americans.

In an attempt to bolster its appeal by identification with Islam, the Black Muslim movement advocates complete withdrawal from American society—either by the concentration of all blacks (apparently to the exclusion of whites) in a part of the territory of the United States, or by a mass return to Africa. This approach is not feasible under prevailing circumstances. The main consideration is this: Withdrawal from American society is most decidedly not what most black Americans want. First and foremost they want justice in a country that promises justice and dignity to all of its citizens.

The personal evolution of Malcolm X brought him to an understanding of this fact. The United States, the country that made him, was his special vantage point—his window on the world. From this vantage and from this window he attempted to see how the struggle of the black man in the United States related to Africa, Asia, and the other parts of the Third World. This was the essence of his evolution and growth.

J. H. C.

THE LAST DAYS OF
MALCOLM X

——————————————————— BY *Earl Grant*

I

On December 5, 1963, the national press reported that
Malcolm X had been suspended from the Black Muslim organization and silenced for ninety days. I knew something
was seriously wrong. I had resigned from the Black Muslims two years before; as a former Muslim I knew that
they never advertised their internal affairs. Since leaving
the Muslims I had not had any contact with Brother Malcolm. Now, out of curiosity and anxiety, I telephoned
Malcolm at his home. He was surprised and pleased to
hear from me.

He now wanted to speak with me privately, so we
arranged a meeting at my home later on that evening. Remembering Malcolm's penchant for promptness, I went
downstairs to meet him at the exact time agreed upon. As
he drove up my heart contracted with excitement and sadness: Coming to my home was the one black man in the
United States who was best able to understand, define, and
identify with the problems of black Americans in the
twentieth century.

During this first meeting, Brother Malcolm didn't discuss the formation of any new organization because he was
still hoping to continue his work as a Muslim involved in
some way with the Nation of Islam. When Malcolm's
hopes were replaced by the certainty that he would never
be allowed to function with the Black Muslims, he moved
away from them and began to formulate goals of his own.

Three or four of us began to meet together with Brother

83

Malcolm. As the weeks passed, we were encouraged as a larger number of men and women, many of them former Muslims, started joining our ranks. Soon there was a core of about twelve of us brothers, the men you read about in the press as "Malcolm's lieutenants."

Throughout 1964, during the last year of Malcolm's life, we were with him constantly—on the streets, at our headquarters. We struggled to form new organizations that would speak to black men, unify us, and give us direction, truth, and power. Brother Malcolm set up the Muslim Mosque, Inc., as a religious, spiritual organ, and the Organization of Afro-American Unity for political and social action.

The story of that year and of our struggles is a long story about confrontation with the truth of the workings of power in this city [New York] and in this country. Let me now tell you about the end, about the last, terrible thirteen days.

By February 1965 we brothers were sleeping and eating with our guns at our side. (These are men I shall not forget.) I moved into my living room and slept on a small folding bed. My rifle was always nearby.

Every morning, at about 3:00 A.M., I would get up and telephone certain of the brothers, strategically located ones. Our conversations were terse, just long enough to find out if everything was quiet.

After making these calls I'd get dressed, pick up my rifle, and go up on the roof of my building to look around. Then, down the stairs, stopping to check out each floor landing. When I got down to the basement I'd look around there, then go up to the street floor and survey the lobby. If that was clear, I would go outside and see what was happening on the streets.

Like all the other brothers, I closely examined all the parked cars and kept a lookout for any strangers in the neighborhood. Finally, I would walk completely around the block before returning to the house and my cot. Many times, before dawn, out in the hard, bitter cold, I would think of Brother Malcolm's sardonic words. He often told us that by putting so much pressure on us, the power structure was actually doing us a favor. Being hunted day and night, he told us, served to keep one's mind sharp and one's body toned.

It was around 3 A.M., on the morning of February 14, 1965, that my sleep was pierced by the ringing of the telephone. Trouble somewhere. It was one of the brothers from Long Island. Come right away, he told me, because the minister's house was on fire. Malcolm and his family had escaped unharmed, but his home was badly damaged. I told the brother I'd be there in less than hour. I called some of the other brothers who lived in Harlem. We and our rifles headed for Queens.

We found Brother Malcolm safe, and very happy to see us. He had sent Betty and the children to shelter at a neighbor's house.

It was now around 4 A.M. The fire was out by now, and the fire engines were pulling away. From the outside one could see that the house had been burned out inside. Policemen, firemen, and some bystanders mingled in the early morning chill. Malcolm took me inside to show me the damage. As always I had my camera with me, and at his request I got pictures of everything.

Brother Malcolm began to describe the evening. He said he had been more tired than usual and had taken a sleeping pill so as to get some rest. Without being disrespectful, I completely lost my temper. I asked him if he knew what he had done. That if he had wanted to sleep that deeply he could have called me first and some of us brothers would have come out and stood guard around his house all night. He looked down at me with that big fatherly smile of his and I just gave up and walked off mumbling to myself.

Brother Malcolm indicated that the first bottle bomb had been thrown through the living room window. The crash had awakened him. By the time of the explosion he was up, moving. Then there was another crash and explosion near his bedroom on the side of the house. He awakened his wife and the two of them began to get the children out of the burning house. He said that at this time he could see that the entire front of the house was ablaze.

There were at least two more bombs used in this cowardly attack on the sleeping family. One of these bombs had been thrown into the children's room, but, thanks to Allah, it had not exploded. Brother Malcolm was infuriated: He could accept being attacked himself, but he wanted his family left alone.

Out in the back yard we found a burned spot on the ground about five feet from his rear bedroom window. This area smelled of gasoline and we found chunks of broken glass and a burned-out wick. Evidently there were several degenerate persons involved in this cowardly attack. The one in the rear had lost control of his flaming bottle and dropped it. Had this bottle been thrown into the house, Malcolm and his family would have been trapped.

Malcolm told me that after he had gotten his family out of the house he was surprised to hear running footsteps inside. He figured that, since their coordinated attack had failed, the attackers had entered the burning building to try to finish off the sleeping family.

He kept two guns in the house: a rifle we had given him and a pistol given by a friend. In his haste to save his family he had picked up the pistol instead of the rifle. Upon hearing the continuing commotion in the house, he had tried to shoot, but the pistol would not fire. Later, investigation proved that this was a gun bought from a phony gun salesman in Harlem before the so-called riot. I told Malcolm that I had found out that all of those guns had broken firing pins.

We walked to the front of the house to talk to the Deputy Fire Inspector and the Deputy Police Inspector. Since it was cold this February morning and since Malcolm had begun to cough, I insisted that we get out of the bitter, damp air.

The four of us went to sit in the police squad car— Brother Malcolm, myself, and the two deputy officers. They began to question Malcolm. They asked Malcolm how could anyone else but him have burned his house. These two characters were trying to blame Malcolm for trying to kill his entire family! I could hardly believe my ears. First they claimed they had not seen any bottles in the house. (Then later, one was supposed to have been found on the dresser in the oldest girl's room.)

Malcolm proceeded, calmly, to tell the story. He told

how he had heard the explosion, awakened his family, and led them out to safety in the back yard. Then, Malcolm looked the Deputy Inspector of Police right in the eye and told him that he had tried to fire a pistol into his house. I waited for some reaction. Here was Malcolm X, the man whom the entire power structure was against, telling a police officer that he had tried to shoot a pistol a few minutes earlier. The very possession of a pistol in New York requires a police permit, which the whole world knew Malcolm did not possess.

Here was a golden opportunity for the power structure to move legally against Malcolm. I'm certain this Deputy Police Inspector had been thoroughly instructed in the provisions of the Sullivan Law on pistols. Yet he acted as though he was not hearing Malcolm. Brother Malcolm repeated, about three or four times, that he had tried to fire shots into his burning house. And the police officer's hearing did not seem to improve any at all; I was later to remind Malcolm of this.

The police department's refusal to understand English and to question or arrest Malcolm about the pistol is understandable when one examines their strange actions on the day of the assassination. More about this later.

We sat in the police car for about forty-five minutes. Still careful of Malcolm's health, we took him into a neighbor's house to keep him from becoming chilled and sick.

By now a large number of the brothers had arrived on the scene. I took them through the burned-out house and we began to board up the windows and doors. Then Malcolm sent for me. He told me that he still had to make his speaking engagement in Detroit. He intended to travel wearing his charred overcoat so that when our people saw him, they might better understand the high cost of freedom. We regretfully escorted him to the airport. We would have wanted to assign a bodyguard to travel with him; but we brothers had no extra funds. So Brother Malcolm flew off to Detroit, alone.

II

It was all disturbing and puzzling. We brothers got together and began talking about what was going on. I told them about the police officer who could not hear. The way I looked at it, it seemed that those who had prevented the brother from landing in Paris had apparently drawn some members of the New York City Police Department in on their plans. How else could you explain a Deputy Police Inspector who preferred to act as though he had never heard of the Sullivan Law?

I told the brothers that from this moment we could expect the worst to happen. Furthermore, we could not look for any protection from the police. As a matter of fact, we had better keep our eyes on the police. This was not to say that all policemen were hired killers. But the Deputy Police Inspector's actions clearly indicated that someone big did not want Brother Malcolm in jail where the police could be blamed for anything that might happen to him.

The next day the press reported that "In the absence of firm clues, it was assumed that the fire bombs were thrown from a passing automobile." Assumed by whom? The fire was completely inspected by both the Police Department and the Fire Department. A bottle was thrown through the front window and one dropped in the back yard. Yet the public was being told to believe, in effect, that bottles were thrown from a passing car through the front window, some of them curving around the house and falling in the back yard, and one actually entering a side window and sitting itself upright on a dresser. This is the same class of lie that the press has told in the Kennedy and King assassinations.

There was so much that had to be done for Malcolm as soon as he came back from his speaking engagement in Detroit. For one thing, we had to find a home for him and his family. Then there was also the task of preparing for our next meeting at the Audubon Ballroom. Again, at this time, I asked him if we could search the people as they entered the hall. He asked, "For what purpose?" He knew that the same people who had ordered the bombing of his house were easily capable of attacking him on the street if they found it expedient.

On February 17, Brother Malcolm gave a press conference in our offices at the Theresa Hotel. On that occasion, he made a statement saying, "We are demanding an immediate investigation by the FBI of the bombing. We feel a conspiracy has been entered into at the local level, with some local police, firemen and press. Neither I, nor my wife and children, have insurance and we stand in no way to gain from the bombing. My attorney has instructed me and my wife to submit to a lie detector test and ask that the same test be given to the police and firemen at the scene."

The next day, the eighteenth of February, Malcolm appeared on the Contact radio show in New York. Just before the program went on the air another one of those curious incidents occurred that hinted at the Police Department's role in setting the stage for Malcolm's assassination. Some of our brothers were outside the building, watching Malcolm's car. Some were in the waiting room with him and some were in the hallway outside the waiting room. The police were also inside and outside the building.

As I left the waiting room and entered the hallway, I saw a plainclothes policeman standing about halfway down the hallway. Directly across from him was one of our brothers, standing with his coat opened in front. The two were looking each other over. I received quite a shock as I passed between them. Here was this brother standing about ten feet from a New York City policeman with his coat open and with a big pistol showing. This police officer was acting as though he had never heard of the Sullivan Law.

I proceeded down to the end of the hallway. Then I turned around and came back for a second look. Yes, the police officer was still looking at the brother and his gun. As I passed this time I quietly told the brother to button his coat.

I went on into the waiting room to find Malcolm and

tell him about the incident. He nodded and said, "Now, you should know what to expect from them. They are also in on it, brother."

He continued, saying that he had asked for a police permit during one of the times he was questioned about the bombing of his house. But he did not think the police would give a pistol permit to a man whom they themselves were trying to help to kill. I think it should be said that at no time, up until now, did Malcolm ever carry a weapon of any sort. Also he did not want the brothers to carry a gun. I told him that the strange actions of the police left the brothers no choice. Then he said, very simply, "Anyway, it will be all over soon." I never told him how much it hurt me to hear him speak that way. I knew he was tired; if only there was some way for him to rest.

After the radio program was over, we all left by a side exit and headed to the place where his family was staying. He was very happy about the number of brothers who were with him that night. We saw him safely home, then prepared for our next move.

III

Brother Malcolm called a business meeting for Saturday night, February 20, 1965, at a sister's house. There were about a dozen of us present. Malcolm was very tired and restless but he said it was important that the meeting be held. He said that he wanted a complete reorganization of the OAAU to be made. It had not been operating to his satisfaction. The OAAU had not been able to take advantage of the attention drawn to it by his activities. And, also, he wanted women to be given a more clearly defined role in the OAAU.

We reviewed the many events that had recently occurred; we started with the refusal of the French Government to allow him to enter Paris. And we wondered who had instructed the police officer at the radio station that he was not to arrest a man carrying an unauthorized pistol.

On his way to his house, after the meeting, I asked him to spend the night with me. He said, "But, brother, you have a family." I told him I also had a loaded rifle and eight years in the military service and that I intended to shoot first and ask questions later. He thanked me and said he would go on out to the place where his family was staying. He said he was going to try to keep away from the brothers in the OAAU because he alone was responsible for his present position. I said the brothers would never agree with him. He said "No, Brother Earl, I don't want anyone hurt on my account. I always knew it would end like this. The brothers and sisters have been so good to me and my family. I will always love all of them. They are the best black men and women that I have ever known. I knew that as poor as they are, they made every sacrifice for me and my family. No, brother, I have to face this alone. I want to keep away from them for the next few days. Right now it is not safe for any of them to be near me. As you have seen, it is not safe even for my family. The power structure is frightened by the existence of the MMI/OAAU. They realize its importance even better than some of the OAAU members themselves. And you can see they are out to kill me. Brother, I'm sorry I never had a chance to tell you about my father. He, too, tried to help our people and was hunted and finally killed by the powers of that day. Now I know how he must have felt, with a family and all. I don't care about myself. I only want to protect my family and the OAAU. No matter what happens to me personally, it is important that the OAAU continues to exist, do you understand that?

"Don't look so sad. I'm no stranger to danger. I have lived with danger all of my life. I never expected to die of old age. I know the power structure will not let me. I know that I have done the very best that I could to help our people. You and I have talked of these things before and I have tried to prepare you for them. They come in the lives of every struggling people. As I told you when we first began, after I was expelled from the Black Muslims, I did not want an organization that depended on the life of one man. The organization must be able to survive on its own."

I asked him again to come live with me, but he refused. After being sure that he was safely on his way home, our group dispersed, everyone returning home to prepare for the next day's meeting.

IV

About 9:00 A.M., on the morning of February 21, 1965, my telephone rang. It was Brother Malcolm calling from the New York Hilton. I sprang out of bed. Calling from the Hilton Hotel? What was he doing *there*? He told me that he had felt restless out at the house and had decided to go spend the night in the hotel. There was no point in asking why he had not come up to my apartment; we had already gone through all that.

Malcolm told me that three people already had tried to find out what room he was in. He thought the police must have let them know that he was staying in the hotel. He said a white man had called him that morning and spoken briefly with him. I told him to remain in the hotel room until I arrived. He said, no, he would be all right now that it was daylight.

Then, just like that, Malcolm stated that he needed four thousand dollars and did not know where he could get it. I was shocked. This was the first time Malcolm had ever discussed business on the telephone. His policy was always to assume that our telephones were tapped and never to reveal any personal information.

Worried, I told him that I was on my way down to the hotel. But again he insisted that he would be all right now. He told me to make some telephone calls for him and to meet him at the Audubon Ballroom at 2:00 P.M., our usual time.

After finishing my assignment for Malcolm, I got ready to go over to the meeting. I packed my tape recorder and camera, checked my rifle, and made some last-minute phone calls.

I left my house at about 1:45 P.M., a little late for me. I got to the Audubon a few minutes after 2:00 P.M. When I got to the building I noticed that there were no policemen in sight; there were usually several stationed out front and along the sides of the building.

Upstairs in the auditorium there were already about

fifty people seated around. I saw only a few of our members present and they were all busy preparing for the day's meeting. At this time there was no one posted at the front door.

It was about 2:30 P.M. before I had completed setting up all of our equipment. Brother Malcolm still had not arrived. As more of our members came in I sent them to usher people to their seats. Some members were stationed at the front door and others along the side of the auditorium.

Soon a brother reported that Brother Malcolm was entering the building. With two other brothers I walked to the front of the main meeting room to meet him. As Malcolm came up the stairs he smiled and greeted us, but to me he seemed extremely worried. I asked him where his car was and he replied that he had parked it nearby.

Later I found out that Brother Malcolm had parked his car quite a few blocks from the Audubon and that he had walked up Broadway alone, toward the building. I believe that he was attempting to offer himself as a target, alone and away from his followers. This was his way of protecting us from what he knew was certain to happen soon. I guess we all knew it but tried not to believe it.

When he entered the main meeting room we paused for about three minutes in the rear of the room. He asked, "How do things look?" I told him they were about as well as could be expected.

Brother Malcolm began to tell us about the strange phone call with the white voice and about the three Negro men who had tried to find out his room number. In very worried tones he said, "I don't feel right about this meeting. I feel that I should not be here. Something is wrong, brothers." I asked him to cancel the meeting or to let another brother speak in his place. He said he would think about it and we walked to the front of the hall and into one of the small offstage rooms.

I could not remember ever seeing Brother Malcolm so tense and nervous. He wanted to know if the other speakers had arrived. Some people were to make an appeal for a fund to help replace his burned-out house. He was concerned because they had not shown up yet.

There were about six of us in the small offstage room. After about fifteen minutes, Brother Malcolm asked us how the crowd looked. Someone said that the people were beginning to come in. At this point, I left the room to check our equipment.

A few minutes later I was called backstage again. There was a discussion going on to decide who would speak. Malcolm said that he had not prepared a speech for today. Someone suggested that Brother Benjamin should speak in Malcolm's place.

Malcolm would sit and talk for a few minutes; then he would jump up and go to the door leading to the main room and look into it. Then he would slowly sit back down in his chair. All this was upsetting me very much. I told him that he should leave the building right away, and that I felt that Benjamin could speak for him. He said he was worried about the way things had been going but that he would be all right.

I told him that I had to get back to our equipment, but he said, "No, I want you to go and call my family and ask if they are coming." I said that one of the secretaries could do it because I had other things to do. He said, "No, I want you to do it." So to please him I went out into the small lobby at the entrance to the main room and telephoned his family. The brother who answered the phone told me that the family had already left and would soon be at the Audubon.

I went back and reported this information to Brother Malcolm and again I asked to be excused so that I could get the recording equipment and cameras ready for our meeting, as was my usual practice. I had never been asked to take care of the running of a Sunday meeting; that was the responsibility of the secretarial staff. So I couldn't understand why Brother Malcolm insisted on involving me with these things.

Next Brother Malcolm told me to go out and call the person who was handling the fund appeal for replacing his house. I replied that I had spoken to this man before I had left home and he had told me that everything was set. Malcolm, looking extremely nervous and tired, said, "No, I want you to go and call him now." Again, I told

Brother Malcolm that I already had been assured that everything was set for the fund raising. And, besides, let the secretary call him. His first response was an expression of great sadness and tiredness. He looked much older than usual; for a small moment he looked like an old man. He knew that he had only a short time to live and his only concern was to protect his poor followers. He looked at me and then murmured in a voice so low that it was difficult to hear him, "None of you understand. You just don't understand. Brother Earl, I want you to go out and call the man about the fund raising again." He said, "Do this for me, brother," and he tried to smile. This was the last time I was to see Brother Malcolm alive.

I left the small room and proceeded to the telephone in the front of the main room. I called the man and again he said everything was set. He gave me a message for Malcolm and said that he would hold the phone until I returned with Malcolm's reply. I lay the phone down and as I was turning to leave the phone booth, the first shot rang out.

V

There was a pause, then a long series of shots. It was impossible for me to re-enter the main room because there were so many people stampeding out of it. The two exits were jammed by people trying to get out.

After a few moments I saw a man with a gun in his hand running and stumbling toward the stairs to the street. Some of the brothers and people from the audience were grabbing and kicking at him. Then he fell down and they began kicking him in the face.

I was about ten feet from him. His face was unforgettable; he looked like someone about to explode. His eyes were wide open and almost seemed to bulge from his head. He seemed hypnotized. Also, another strange thing was that despite the kicking he was getting all over his body and face, he never uttered a sound! He seemed to be drugged against pain. This man was later identified as Talmadge Hayer.

As Hayer and the crowd beating on him stumbled down

the stairs, I was able to re-enter the main meeting room. There was pandemonium! Chairs and tables were turned over everywhere, and people were running and screaming. One man, said later to have been shot in the foot, was lying on the floor next to a small child. On my way to the stage, I passed another person lying in the center of the floor; he was crying, "Help me, I'm shot." At this point I had passed two people said to have been shot.

I jumped up on the stage to see if I could help Brother Malcolm. He was lying on his back; his eyes and mouth were slightly open. There was a small trickle of blood on the corner of his mouth. He did not appear to have been struck in the face by any of the bullets.

The brothers and sisters were doing the best they could for Brother Malcolm. When they were able to get his coat and shirt open, I took one look and knew that it was too late. No man could have that many bullet holes in his chest and still survive. Really, there was nothing I could do for Malcolm now. I thought to get my camera and get some photographs. They might be useful later.

It was now about ten minutes after the first shot had been fired. Some brothers had run out to get a doctor. Although we were directly across the street from Columbia Presbyterian Medical Center, it took almost half an hour for a stretcher to arrive.

Then, about five minutes later, a most incredible scene took place. Into the hall sauntered about a dozen policemen. They were strolling at about the pace one would expect of them if they were patrolling a quiet park. They did not seem to be at all excited or concerned about the circumstances.

I could hardly believe my eyes. Here were New York City policemen, entering a room from which at least a dozen shots had been heard, and yet not one of them had his gun out! As a matter of absolute fact, some of them even had their hands in their pockets. This scene told me lots about the role the "Old Ones" in the power structure played in Malcolm's death.

As Malcolm's body was wheeled out of the building, I asked the brothers if anyone else was hurt.

I was especially worried about the secretarial staff that

I had left in the small room with Malcolm, and about his family. The brother said that as far as he knew, no one else had actually been shot.

We all walked to the back of the hall, down the stairs, and into the streets. The policemen filling the streets only seemed interested in shoving around Malcolm's followers. We tried to enter the hospital, but the policemen blocked the way. Seeing them blocking the way reminded me of some of the pictures I had seen from Nazi Germany.

I spoke to as many of our people as I could and told them to go home and remain quiet. Some of the brothers wanted to go and start shooting every Black Muslim that could be found.

Obviously, as one could learn from studying the newspapers at the time, the Black Muslims had been unwise enough to allow themselves to be placed in a position to be blamed for Malcolm's death. However, at this time, we had no evidence that they had actually done the shooting. The brothers reminded me that some Black Muslims had been ejected from the meeting earlier. I said yes, it was true that some of them were present, but to my mind that was just part of the plan of the "Old Ones" in the power structure.

I told them that the situation made me think of the incident in which the Nazis burned down the Reichstag building. The Nazis lured Van der Lubbe into the building and at the same time had their own experts set fire to it. Van der Lubbe was certainly in the building, but he did not do the job alone. The Black Muslims were set up by the power structure to be immediately blamed for the crime.

After about half an hour of this talk, I finally got these brothers calmed down. They began to see the logic of what I was saying. Everyone promised to go home and not to begin shooting at any Black Muslims.

There was not much that we could do now at the scene of the shooting, so we all left for home. I returned my equipment to my apartment, then I went back out into the community.

Our office at the Theresa Hotel was closed. Across the street a small crowd of people had gathered in front of the Black Nationalist Bookstore. They were all shocked by

Malcolm's death. The speakers found it hard to believe that black men could be found who were degenerate enough to pull the trigger on Malcolm. I listened to them for a while and then moved on down Seventh Avenue toward the Black Muslim restaurant. It was closed and surrounded by policemen. I was glad of that because, with the restaurant shut, there would be fewer targets for some distraught brother to find.

VI

From speaking with many of the brothers and sisters, some of whom were in the small room and others of whom were in the main auditorium, I have been able to get a better understanding of the events that took place on that fateful day.

It seems that after I had left to make that second phone call, Brother Malcolm had slowly stood up from his chair, thanked the secretarial staff for their help, and started for the door which led onto the stage. He paused a moment and waited for Brother Benjamin to finish introducing him. As Benjamin walked off the stage, Brother Malcolm approached the microphone, laid his notes on top of the rostrum, and began to speak.

One of the brothers who saw the entire event was seated in the rear of the auditorium. Another brother was returning to the auditorium from an errand he had run for Malcolm; he was about halfway up the left-side passageway when the first shot was fired. He remembered that when the first shot struck, Brother Malcolm had raised his hands up in front of him as if to protect himself. People in the audience began to run for the doors. Then there were more shots fired.

Malcolm fell backward onto the stage. The brother who was in the passageway on the left side of the building decided not to try to get to the stage. He figured that the people doing the shooting would have to pass near him on the way out.

Soon the brother saw three men carrying guns, running toward the back of the auditorium. They were still shooting into the crowd. At this point, someone began firing shots at them. The first one of the murderers to be felled was a man of medium build. Then another of them was shot, a heavyset, light-complexioned person. The brother believes he was hit high up in the body because the bullet knocked him against the wall. These first two were both hit while they were still in the auditorium.

Talmadge Hayer was shot next as he approached the back of the room. The bullet knocked him off his feet and he fell face down. He rolled over on his back and tried to shoot back, but his gun was empty. Before he could be shot again, he was up on his feet and again heading for the exit door. The crowd swarmed around him. One couldn't shoot him again without hitting innocent people.

The crowd was holding onto one of the other killers who had been shot. As they stumbled into the streets, a policeman came to his rescue. The policeman drew his pistol and threatened to shoot into the crowd if they didn't turn the killer loose. The policeman took the bleeding man and put him into a squad car which then drove him away. This man has never been identified.

The next day, the twenty-second, the *Daily News* reported that "Two men were taken by force from a howling mob of Malcolm's followers who were pummeling them on the street after the assassination. . . . Police said that four of Malcolm's guards were standing just below the platform when he was hit. They were among the two dozen persons who chased the *attackers* into the streets and started tearing them apart."

The New York *World-Telegram and Sun* reported that "Stanley Scott, a United Press International reporter, said Malcolm's followers seized two men and were yelling, 'Kill them, kill them' until an eight-man police flying squad wrestled the pair free."

On February 25, the *Morning News* of Paterson, New Jersey, stated that "Police said Wednesday they have photographs of the five-man assassin team. . . . While officials refused to go into details they said they had used the photographs to obtain positive identification of the four members of the murder team still at large."

The New York *Times* on the twenty-second reported that Patrolman Thomas Hoy, twenty-two, said he had been stationed outside the 166 Street entrance to the Audubon Ballroom when, "I heard the shooting and the place exploded." He rushed in, saw Malcolm lying on the stage and "grabbed a suspect" whom, he said, some people were chasing.

"As I brought him to the front of the ballroom, the crowd began beating me and the suspect." He said he put this man—not otherwise identified later for newspapermen—into a police car to be taken to the Wadsworth Avenue station.

In a lengthy article entitled "Muslims Rehearsed Malcolm Killing," the *Journal-American* reported that a high police official said that the Black Muslims rented the ballroom for an apparent "dress rehearsal" of the assassination:

The killers must have had prior knowledge of the ballroom and building itself in order to execute their plan with such a degree of speed and precision.

The Black Muslims had never used the ballroom before. It seems to be more than a mere coincidence that they should suddenly choose to hold a meeting in the very place that Malcolm was to appear the following Sunday.

During the Muslim meeting there would have been ample opportunity to study exits and entrances, to plan step-by-step the timing and determine the escape routes. It is conceivable that a dry run took place during the meeting.

The Paterson *Morning News* of February 25, 1965, described Talmadge Hayer as a well-mannered star athlete turned high school dropout, Black Muslim, and accused thief and murderer.

He was arrested for possessing twenty-five stolen guns, rifles, and pistols in his Marshall Street basement.

The mother of one of the men jailed in the case remembered Hayer as "the kid who used to sell *Muhammad Speaks* on River Street."

In the February 22, 1965, edition of the New York *Journal-American,* Deputy Detective Inspector Thomas Renaghan, in charge of Manhattan's Sixth Division, said, "He's a Black Muslim."

All of the above illustrates another way in which the "Old Ones" in the power structure operate. They had to have someone whom the public would immediately blame, even before the press went to work. They had gotten rid of Malcolm and arranged for the Black Muslims to be the scapegoats.

On the twenty-fourth of February, the New York *Journal-American* reported that Negro FBI agents were working on the Malcolm X case in Harlem.

The New York *Herald Tribune* of the twenty-third reported that "several undercover plainclothes policemen were in the uptown meeting hall at the time Malcolm X was shot dead there on Sunday."

The Police Department's excuse for allowing the shooting to occur is that the cops present were probably thrown off guard by a phony diversionary scuffle before Malcolm was shot.

All right, let's say they *were* thrown off guard before the first shot. What were they doing the rest of the time that there was shooting and scuffling? What were they doing during the time the three killers were shooting and being shot at? Were they in the throngs chasing them out of the building?

An unidentified police official stated that "It is sufficient to say that we had him covered." Yes, Malcolm was covered by the police. He got the same kind of "coverage" from the New York City police that the late President Kennedy got from the Dallas police.

One paper reported that "Africans call Malcolm X the American Lumumba." In Dakarta, Indonesia, demonstrators invaded the grounds of the U.S. Ambassador's residence and plastered anti-American signs on the house. Leaders of the crowd said they were protesting the murder of Malcolm X. They blamed the U.S. Government for the murder.

The *Daily Times* of Lagos, Nigeria, commented, "Like all mortals, Malcolm X was not without his faults . . . but that he was a dedicated and consistent disciple of the movement for the emancipation of his brethren no one can doubt. . . . Malcolm X has fought and died for what he believed to be right. He will have a place in the palace of martyrs."

It was obvious that at least one portion of the operating

plan for the day of the assassination had been defused. The power structure's hoped-for bloodbath between the Black Muslims and the OAAU had not occurred. Now they had to make another try at stirring up trouble.

The morning paper headlines of February 23, 1965, announced the bombing of the Black Muslim Mosque No. 7. The bombing happened about 2:15 A.M., although there were policemen guarding it from the street and inside the building. The press called it "an apparent stroke of quick and violent revenge." The immediate assumption was that we, the followers of Malcolm X, were responsible.

This assumption is not only absolutely false, it is also insulting. Were the authorities really thinking that, after the death of our beloved brother, we had gone out on a bitterly cold February morning, sneaked past police guards, and climbed up on the empty building and bombed it? Imagine that. An empty building with policemen guarding it!

Certainly give us the credit of having the good sense to attack a building filled with the alleged enemy. Naturally we were questioned; they did have the nerve to come to our offices.

Malcolm's body was now in the Unity Funeral Home at 2352 Eighth Avenue, and the funeral was to be held at Bishop Alvin S. Child's Faith Temple Church of God in Christ, located at 1763 Amsterdam Avenue. Both of these places were continually menaced by bomb threats.

I did not go to the funeral home to view Malcolm's body until the last hour of the last day he lay in state. Every time I passed near the place, I was so overwhelmed with feelings of sadness and grief, I would pass on by. And I have never been back in the Audubon Ballroom. I don't think I could stand to see people dancing in that place.

I don't think I have ever been busier in my life than I was those five days after Malcolm's death, before he was buried. I found myself suddenly the president of the Muslim Mosque, Inc.; before, under Malcolm, I had been vice-president. There were legal papers to be signed and all the plans made for his funeral. We had to think out all the details, ushers had to be picked and stationed, other brothers had to be chosen as pallbearers.

Many of the brothers were jumpy about the bomb threats. They wanted to go out and take care of those whom they thought were making the threats. I had my hands full just trying to keep them quieted down.

Our group was at Faith Temple early on the morning of February 28; several thousand people waited outside. The brothers were sent to their stations, as ushers and as guards. We had tried to plan for every eventuality.

The press arrived and we showed them to the left front of the church. Then so many of them came in we had to place them in the choir section, behind the pulpit. A large section in the center front was reserved for African and Muslim dignitaries, most of whom were too cowardly to show up.

It wasn't long before the church was filled up. Many of them were recognized as Black Muslim members. I think Brother Malcolm's death worked a lot of them up. I, myself, saw and spoke to about twenty-five of them. I can say that they were truly saddened.

The funeral began about 10:00 A.M. The services were opened by Ossie Davis and his wife, Ruby Dee. Around the coffin stood an honor guard of brothers.

Ruby Dee read messages of condolence from the African, Pakistan, West Indian Society of the London School of Economics, The Freedom Fighters of Ohio, Inc., The Michigan Committee of the Freedom Now Party, the Los Angeles NAACP Youth, the Government of Ghana, and the Pan-African Congress of South Africa.

Then Omar Osman of the Islam Center of Switzerland and the United States spoke next and said: "We express deepest sorrow in the death of our brother. We knew him as a blood brother especially after his pilgrimage when he learned we are all brothers. He had come to know that all races can live in peace and harmony with each other. And after he returned he never preached any racism. But he did not change his fighting spirit. He preached full freedom. He would not bow down his head to any tyrant."

Osman expressed anger with Carl T. Rowan's attempt to smear Malcolm. "I was most shocked; he says that we in Africa misunderstood Malcolm. No, brothers! We understood him. We heard what he said. I have known Malcom for two years. He preached justice for his brothers and sisters. He toured Africa speaking widely, speaking to the people in the streets, and they loved him. In Islam, which he embraced, we accept all people as brothers and he preached justice for his brothers everywhere. The highest thing a Muslim can aspire to is to die on a battlefield and not die at the bedside. In the struggle for justice, Malcolm reached a height few people in history have achieved. Those who die on the battlefield are not dead. They are alive." There was thunderous applause.

At this time, Ossie Davis stepped forward and delivered the eulogy. When he was finished with the eulogy, Alhajj Heshaam Jaaber of Ansar of Islam, Inc., said the brief prayer said for every Muslim at his death.

Some of the brothers and sisters as well as members of Malcolm's family came forward for their last look at him. He lay wrapped in seven white shrouds. His body had been prepared by Sheik Ahmed Hassoun. The Sheik, a Sudanese, had taught in Mecca for thirty-five years before becoming Malcolm's spiritual adviser.

As I stood by his coffin, I looked down upon a face that I had loved so much. The tears were streaming down my face as I said "As Asalaam Alaikum" to him for the last time. I thanked him for allowing one so unworthy as I to share his life with him. I asked his forgiveness for my being unable to have done more for him.

The coffin was closed for the last time and placed in the hearse for the trip to Ferncliff Cemetery in Hartsdale, New York.

Along the route, newsmen riding in the procession noticed an occasional Afro-American take off his hat in a symbolic gesture of respect for their fallen spokesman.

At Ferncliff Cemetery, the grave was uncovered and the coffin placed over it, facing toward the east, the direction of the Holy City, Mecca. Sheik Alhajj Heshaam Jaaber, wearing a brown cloak and black-banded white turban, delivered Muslim prayers at the graveside. The coffin was slowly lowered into the grave and the people, the little people whom Malcolm had loved and died for, began to push the earth into the grave with their hands. There were also a few white students who helped bury him. I think Malcolm would have wanted it that way.

I returned home and fell into a deep sleep. It was the first real rest I had been able to get in months. There was no longer any reason to jump when the phone rang or to sleep with a loaded gun. The best year of my life was at an end. But I, and all of the brothers and sisters, would live it again, Allah willing.

MALCOLM X
AND THE PRESS

BY *Art Sears, Jr.*

THE SUN beamed pleasantly down on East Cleveland, Ohio, that mid-June 1967 afternoon, when I took the short walk from my weekly newspaper [*The Cleveland Call and Post*] office to the nearby hotel which served as "Mecca" for black visitors.

The weather and the exciting challenge of a new job— I had been in the city for only a month after working three years for a Negro weekly newspaper in the South— helped to put added spring in my steps.

Lifting me above everything, however, was the conspiratorial flavor of a meeting which I was going to have with a man whose very name at the time left most black publishers and editors cold and indifferent. To the white press, he was an unheard-of sleeping giant.

And little did they realize that it wouldn't be many months later before his name would be a feared household word, his message a revolution on the fabric of Western thought.

The word had earlier fanned across the country, through black news channels, that this "mysterious" personage was seeking space in black newspapers for his leader's column.

The column was "Muhammad Speaks," penned by Mr. Elijah Muhammad, spiritual and physical leader of the Black Muslim movement. Mr. Muhammad's "courier" that June day was the late Malcolm X, then as nationally unknown as Mr. Muhammad's movement.

There I was, practically skipping along, instructed to

accept whatever material the mystery man had to offer, to make no commitments, then quickly return to the office.

Management of the paper, like most of the black media across the country, clearly wanted nothing to do with either Mr. Muhammad or his spokesman.

I realize now that the hotel was a most unlikely place to meet Malcolm, reflecting on that day years later, and thinking of the disciplined lives led by the followers of Mr. Muhammad. The hotel was alive with the blaring sounds of the big band rehearsing for its nightly girlie show in the hotel's nightclub.

The bar was loaded with its daily complement of souls apparently too disillusioned about life to care about anything but oblivion seen through the amber liquid in the glasses from which they sipped their favorite cocktails.

Obvious prostitutes strutted through the lobby, eyeing prospective "dates." The numbers operators were making their appointed rounds, slipping dollar bills and pennies into their pockets along with the familiar white slips which bore the numbers the operators' clients hoped would enable them to strike it rich, when the winning figures would be announced late in the day.

I shouted a cheery greeting to them all. For almost anyone who lives in any ghetto knows who's who. It takes but a very short stay to absorb the atmosphere; to learn where one goes to play a number, or to get a girl, or to find an after-hours party where the real happenings are.

I bounced onto the brightly lit old elevator, relaxed as the contraption wheezed and creaked its way up to the third floor. I stepped off into a dimly lit hall, turned left, walked to the corner suite, and then, with a delicious nervousness, rapped on the mahogany door.

The door opened. A brown, round face popped into the doorway. I identified myself, and then was warmly ushered in by the gentleman I assumed was Malcolm X.

But no, there before a dark mantel stood, I knew in an instant, Brother Malcolm.

It's funny how easy that is to say now. Brother. But at that time, pumped full of prejudice against a man I was told our paper didn't care to do business with, I could only see an enemy of whom I must be wary. I must be friendly to him but non-committal.

He stood there, at ease, warm and charming. But a shudder raced through my body as I noted Malcolm's ghostly pale color, as if he had spent all his life in a dimly lit room, such as the one we then stood in.

He was tall, athletically built with wide shoulders. Added to the incongruity of my reaction was the thought that his glasses made him appear ascetic and deeply religious. He looked like a man who had found the truth, whatever that might have meant to him, a man who exuded an aura of unshakable confidence and conviction.

At that time I could think in terms of truth as we're taught it through the King James Version of the Holy Bible. Not of the truth Malcolm was to articulate so devastatingly clearly in the years to come.

He introduced me to Jeremiah X, the gentleman who opened the door. At that time Jeremiah was head of the young Philadelphia Muslim temple which Malcalm had helped to establish. Jeremiah, slightly rounded, also wore glasses. Their smiles and their manner were so warm that I shivered again. I'd never met anyone who was so immediately outgoing. I was still wary, however, remembering the charge I had been given before leaving my office.

"I am Malcolm X, Mr. Sears," the tall, handsome spokesman smiled. "I represent a revolutionary new movement in this country, a movement designed to free black men from the shackles which the white man has placed upon us and which separate us from one another.

"My leader, Mr. Elijah Muhammad," Malcolm continued, with a smile so warm I wasn't sure it was friendliness or some secret only he knew, "praise be to Allah . . ." and then he was off on a terse yet full analysis of the Muslim movement.

Even then, Malcolm's eloquence was evident with all the polish and the finesse he later was to use, rapier-like, to reduce his opponents to ineffective apologists for the *status quo*.

As he continued unfolding his talk to convince me of the worth of the Muslim movement, his words served as a bewitching point, transfixing me. I no longer knew exactly what he was saying. But the tenor of his conversation was overpowering, devastating, truthful.

Magnetically, it seemed, he pulled me into his mind's eye. But I resisted, suddenly, remembering my orders. And much like many other black people during those times, and even later, for whom the message was heady, frightening truisms, I had a feeling that I couldn't permit his thoughts to enter my consciousness.

Then too, I realized, I wasn't there for personal soul-searching, but to turn him off on behalf of my employer.

And although his introductory remarks have long since receded into some wilderness of my brain, the memory, the effectiveness of his presentation, and the worth of it all will never be forgotten.

I was reeling, some forty-five minutes later, when I departed from the hotel suite, armed with a weighty sample of the columns Mr. Muhammad wished to have appear in our newspaper. I felt a newfound but unadmitted glow flashing inside as I walked slowly back to my office. I was proud that I had kept the faith for the boss—made no commitments, took my leave of Malcolm without incurring any obvious wrath.

But personally, he had affected me more than I dared to admit. For the rest of my life.

I immediately reported to the boss that Malcolm was impressive, had what I considered a unique, new message. I didn't elaborate, for I knew that Malcolm's efforts, so far as my newspaper was concerned, were to no avail.

As Malcolm indefatigably crisscrossed the nation, trying to woo the publishers into accepting Mr. Muhammad's column, no doubt similar meetings, from the hearts of the nation's ghettos, were repeated again and again by black reporters who were taking the weight off their publishers, denying Malcolm the support he should have had.

Later, as the white press took up its cries against Mr. Muhammad, Malcolm, and the movement, the black press had no one to blame but itself. (Most still take no blame, however.) For the black press had the first opportunity to set the record straight, to at least have presented the Muslim viewpoint in a framework of creditability and provided its readership, as well as the world, with the story of one of the most important movements designed to free black people in this century.

But the press opted out. Most of it, that is. For there were a handful of black newspapers which eventually carried the Muslims' message. But not nearly a fraction of those which should have as representatives of the ghettos of the nation.

It was nearly five years later when I next saw Malcolm. And then he was, as I was to see him on several occasions during the next several years after that, serving as the opening, pacesetting spark for the Muslims' annual gathering at the Chicago Convention Hall, where he eloquently galvanized thousands upon thousands of the faithful to a state of preparedness for the acceptance of Mr. Muhammad's messages.

Malcolm would step to the podium, as slim and as impressive as he had been when I had first met him. With a broad smile, he'd say, warmly and intimately, "Asalaam Alaikum," and the gathering would roar in return, "Asalaam Alaikum!"

During the intervening years after the initial meeting, I didn't interview Malcolm. But I hung onto his every statement, followed his progress through the media—the newspapers, the radio, and television. Each time I saw him, he seemed to glow more than the previous appearance, seemed more sure than ever, if that were possible, more devastating, as "respectable" black and white leaders fought futilely to defuse the movement, which grew to engulf the world with its messages of the worth of black people and the insistence that black men must learn to do for themselves.

I never ceased, at these times, to reflect on the initial meeting, as I listened to Malcolm and read about his efforts. I had become more vocal about my belief that most of Malcolm's message was good; I became less and less Establishment in my analysis, as did many others, as the system tried harder and harder to discredit the movement and Malcolm.

If not "The Way," Malcolm's approach was certainly becoming one of the most powerful solutions for empowerment of black citizens.

I joined the staff of *Jet* and *Ebony* magazines in Chicago in late 1959. And at least once a year thereafter, I had the opportunity to see and hear Malcolm at the big Muslim meetings in Chicago.

In mid-1962, I was transferred to *Jet*'s New York office. My first thoughts were of the possibility of seeing and talking to Malcolm again.

And it wasn't two months later that I got the opportunity. I went up to Harlem and to the Muslim Restaurant, which had become a place to meet Malcolm. But he wasn't there. I was able to get his home phone number. I called him.

His wife answered the phone and asked me to please wait.

In a moment he came.

"Well, hello there," were his opening words. "I haven't seen you since 1957 in Cleveland, at the ———— Hotel. . . ." I was stunned.

How could he have remembered all those years, considering the thousands of miles he'd traveled, the countless speeches he'd given, and the thousands of persons he'd met personally? I never asked him. But until this day, I reel a bit when I think of that phenomenally brilliant mind which remembered a fledgling journalist who wasn't much more than a cub reporter at the initial meeting.

It was typical of Malcolm. It suggests why he attained such great heights in the spawning and the expansion of the movement. He later said himself that he was quick to learn and never forgot, once he learned a message or met a person.

In the succeeding years, an interview with Malcolm was mine for the asking, no matter how pressed he was. If he was out of town or out of the country, he'd be sure to contact me as soon as he returned. Sometimes it was weeks. But he'd answer his calls. No one was unimportant to him.

Malcolm had assistants. But never do I recall hearing any one of them on the other end of the phone declaring, "Hold the line for Minister Malcolm X, please." Instead, Malcolm was always there himself, as patient as he could be if I were on another call, as if he had nothing better to do than to idle his time away with a reporter digging for angles.

It was this personal attention to people that most impressed me. No matter how mundane my questions, Malcolm gave full attention to me. And he'd do it with all the deliberateness as if, for example, the President of the United States had called him to Washington to discuss what states the Muslims wanted to develop for their idea of an all-black nation.

The last time I had the opportunity to tape-record an interview with Malcolm was in the early evening at my midtown New York office.

He was obviously weary and spent when he arrived. For the first time, a slight stubble appeared on his face, as though there hadn't been time to shave. His eyes were glazed with fatigue.

His smile was pleasant, but wan. His steps weren't as confident as I'd most often seen them. I regretted I'd asked him in that day.

But once we entered the conference room, sat down, and I turned on the tape recorder, the tiredness seemed to drain out of Malcolm. Replacing it was all the confidence and self-control he'd always displayed. He warmed fast as we began discussing his newly formed Organization of Afro-American Unity (OAAU).

On several occasions, during the hour-long interview, I asked for amplification and clarification on specific points. And with affectionate kindness, and with the patience of a dedicated teacher, Malcolm reiterated and restated many of those answers over and over.

I had long enjoyed going to his offices on the mezzanine floor of the Theresa Hotel, where I never could catch him working at a desk. Or even in the office. He was always either on the streets, trying to win more friends and supporters, or on the road, or making an appearance on television or radio.

But his presence was always there in that office. It reflected on the faces of his colleagues and co-workers. I recall with special warmth his secretary, who wore her hair in the natural style; how attractive and personable she was. His colleagues, too, were found there late into the night, fulfilling their assigned tasks, as if they were driven by the sheer enthusiasm of Malcolm alone.

I know that I wasn't as close to Brother Malcolm as many other black reporters. And I know that I wasn't privileged to spend as much time in his presence as many of them.

But those brief occasions I did share with him in discussing the world and the problems besetting black citizens were priceless and irreplaceable. They were also vital moments of learning.

If there's any way to describe Malcolm, it is that he was purely a thoroughbred, a man for all seasons; a man who worked at achieving the impossible dream. A man whose efforts are now daily quoted and extended by thousands who can now truly see the value that was always there in Malcolm.

No one was too small for his time or attention.

Shakespeare had one of his characters say about one of his subjects, "When comes such another?" The answer, obviously, must be, in the case of Malcolm, "Never."

For only once in a lifetime does one have the privilege of touching greatness. Such a man was Malcolm.

MALCOLM X:
THE APOSTLE OF DEFIANCE—
AN AFRICAN VIEW

BY *Mburumba Kerina*

Future written history of our brothers and sisters, the African-Americans, will begin with the brutal assassination of Brother Malcolm. Much of this extraordinary period will continue to be haunted by the phantom of this Black Prince of Hope of all Africans at home and abroad.

The biographies of Malcolm X will no doubt provide fascinating history of the dynamic and hypnotizing leader whose wisdom and deep perspicacity are reflected in his positive leadership and action rather than in mere public pronouncements—one who has created the most enduring impressions upon all black people in America and Africa. Indeed, his life reflected the great potential of a bridge of unity being built between the peoples of Africa and their brothers and sisters in the Western Hemisphere.

In the few years that he held the high office of public spokesman for the Nation of Islam, he gave that enviable position of responsibility a special form adapted to his distinctly African-American heritage, experience, talent, and character. White America and a few of his critics have occasionally, with much bitterness and fear, called him names, but without success, for Brother Malcolm proved to be an indomitable leader and an indefatigable statesman, very well capable of giving the political life in America important impulses and worth.

To the white people in America who feared him and those who have closely associated with him in the Nation of Islam over the past years (including of course the American power structure), he has been known as firm, overpowering, and has been often referred to as a "serious threat to the American Establishment." This is the most unique quality about Malcolm X. As a leader and a spokesman for the Nation of Islam, circumstances beyond his control often made him exert a firm will in order to make the widely divergent interests of all our brothers and sisters in America somewhat compatible.

The political liberation struggle of our people in the United States has been plagued with a variety of community groups with vested interests, antagonizing one another and falling victims of the American octopus power structure which in turn divides and subdivides the entire African-American people accordingly. As a great leader, Brother Malcolm mastered this challenge by always pursuing a policy of finding an objective basis beneficial to the common desires of the entire black population in the United States while remaining aloof, and not taking sides in the struggle between the competing individuals and factions within the Nation of Islam. Until his unfortunate assassination, he was to thousands of American blacks a "Saint of Hope." He remained devoted in upholding the policy of the black liberation struggle, which, among other things, he stated to me in Mosque No. 7, New York City, in 1963 in the following words:

The triumph of the black man's struggle in America and Africa demands absolute unity, organized action, solid leadership based among our people and with defined aims.

With millions of African people joining the mainstream of history as sovereign independent nations, the present era of the African-Americans might well be called "the Era of Defiance." Two decades ago hardly anyone dreamed of such a revolutionary awakening among our African-Americans. A revolution it is, vast in its magnitude and impact, and exhilarating for all who hold the African-American's right to complete freedom, to determine his own destiny in his own community and to choose his own leaders and government representatives according to the dictates of his own conscience.

Malcolm X was the inventor and the embodiment of this

new revolutionary black consciousness. He labored for its creation and propagation among the black people not only in America, but also in Africa, England, and the Caribbean. He continued to the last day of his life to defend the rights and humanity of the black people of the world against the aggression of those white powers which seek to enslave, oppress, and exploit them. It is due to his initiatives that the issue of "civil rights" as against that of the "denial of fundamental human rights" to African-Americans became a controversial problem. This development marked the turning point in the life of Brother Malcolm. He outgrew his false slave "Negro" identity to become an African-American. He further outgrew the so-called civil rights issue, which has blinded many African-Americans to the real problem of their denial of fundamental human rights. Thus, in so doing, Malcolm X was about to elevate the "Negro" into a new black human being which the American Establishment has, since the period of slavery, denied him. As Malcolm X's mind began to reflect on the international problems and particularly those affecting the destiny of all black people in the world —in Africa, Asia, the Caribbean, England, North and South America—so also did Brother Malcolm start to outgrow the spiritual confines of the Nation of Islam, which he enlarged from four hundred to four hundred thousand, plus the many sympathizers.*

It was during that period that I first had the privilege of meeting him. Our meeting place was Mosque No. 7. Much of what we discussed centered around the crucial issue of the black man's emancipation and his destiny in the world, and the role of the black leaders, scholars, and activists. Concerning the black leaders and their respective organizations, Malcolm made the following observations:

The dangers that confront the black man in America and Africa are very great and serious. These dangers cannot be fought with petty personality attacks, nor will they be fought with pretensions. The emancipation of all black people from white domination, oppression, and exploitation will be fought with revolutionary firmness, determination, dedication, honesty, and integrity.

* *Columbia* [University] *Forum,* Spring 1966, p. 7.

Black leaders cannot mobilize the grass roots to fight their oppression and exploitation while plagued with personal ambitions. We must submerge our past differences and create a unified black movement cutting across the United States and South America with deep roots in the African soil. Africans abroad can thus through such a movement exert pressure on their governments in the formation of their foreign policies in regard to Africa. They can also form lobby groups such as other ethnic groups do in Washington to force the United States Government to accept the representation of African-Americans in all organs of government including those in charge of decisions. In short, in order that African-Americans must become free they must first reidentify themselves with Africa as do Jews, Irish, Germans, and Italians with the respective countries of their origin.

The following were his remarks regarding black scholars and their role in the liberation of the African people at home and abroad:

Very often our people have been led to believe that a black man can only be considered an intellectual or scholar if he has been to Oxford University or Harvard University. This is not true. This approach to education has only helped to produce black Europeans out of our educated people and false black scholars who have been a liability to the black race in Africa and America over the period of one hundred years.

What is actually meant by theoretical or academic education? The unity of theoretical education and the application of this wealth of knowledge to the practical requirements and demands of our liberation is a difficult challenge. In a freedom struggle such as the one that exists in Africa and America today the unity of thought and action must be the cornerstone of all of us who desire to work for the total emancipation of the black race.

There is a wide superficial tendency among some of our intellectuals that reading quotations from Marx, Lenin, and Mao Tse-tung can make them masters of revolutionary theories developed by these great men. Intellectualism in my view is not merely the recitation of Marxism, Leninism, and Mao Tse-tung theories. Anyone who goes about misusing the works of these great men or attributing to himself their progressive phrases for his own ends is committing a serious crime against the black race. A scholar in my opinion constitutes a guiding light in a revolutionary period and is the bond that unites the abstract and the concrete.

In order to remedy this problem Brother Malcolm believed that a new form of education relevant to the black people in America and Africa and their heritage and experience must be urgently devised to enable black people to comprehend the nature of their problem and to know their enemy. A new black consciousness must be developed, fashioned according to the needs and circumstances of black people to wage a resolute struggle against the oppressive Establishment. This new black consciousness must not instill in the black youth a worship of diplomas but must emphasize the contribution that the education must make to the cause of the black people and must by all means deglorify the false "Negro" identity imposed upon African-Americans by their slave masters. The black youth must be made to learn that education does not grant special privileges but imposes a duty and an obligation because it is obtained through sacrifice.

This new African-American consciousness must be woven into the African continental unity through the Organization of African Unity. Hence, the creation of the Organization of Afro-American Unity by Malcolm X became the logical conclusion of his dream. He looked to that day when the African-American brothers and sisters will be united with their family in Africa by occupying a respectable place in the Organization of African Unity. He had great confidence in many of the African revolutionary leaders on the continent with whom he established personal contact following his homecoming trip to the continent. Though Brother Malcolm did not live to witness the materialization of his dreams, the seeds that he planted have started to germinate. Black men and women in Africa, America, and England are now waging their last struggle for total emancipation and the reconstruction of the societies in which they currently live. Those living in America are only completing the unfinished mess of the American Revolution thus giving a full meaning to the glorified "American dream" that has been the luxury of whites.

What kind of a political leader was Brother Malcolm? This is a question that those who profess to be experts and specialists on Africans and Afro-Americans have never raised in all their inquiries into the life of this great Afro-American leader. As a leader, Brother Malcolm represented the homogeneity and identity of the black people. He was worshiped, followed, and admired because he was what the black people were; hence, he was trusted because he knew what the people needed and what he should do for them. To be such a leader in a revolutionary period such as this, Brother Malcolm had to possess certain indispensable qualities: the fighting spirit; the tremendous concentration of mind and will to break all resistance of the adversaries and dissenting friends and brothers; the elaboration of a new philosophy of life, a new reality and a new meaning, and the action for its realization. These were some of the precious qualities of our martyr. The impact of these attributes upon the black people was the merging of trust and faith in their leader. Hence, the very existence of Brother Malcolm was sufficient on the part of black people to justify his actions and measures regardless of their understanding.

As a humble servant of his people he never failed to refer the sufferings of the masses to the principle of moral requirements as evident to the law of nature and reason. He formulated the ideology of the Black Revolution for the liberation of the Afro-Americans and all black people in the world. During his lifetime he sought ideological strength wherever he found it, in the social and economic teachings of his own religion of Islam, and the economic analysis of Karl Marx. He was inspired by the great achievements of the People's Republics of China and Cuba. He took ideas from all quarters, adding them to the considerable mental capital that he possessed.

MALCOLM X:
THE MINUTES OF OUR
LAST MEETING

BY *Gordon Parks*

DEATH was surely absent from his face two days before they killed him. He appeared calm and somewhat
resplendent with his goatee and astrakhan hat. Much of
the old hostility and bitterness seemed to have left him,
but the fire and confidence were still there. We talked of
those months two years ago when I had traveled with him
through the closed world of Muslimism, trying to understand it. I thought back to the austere mosques of the
Muslims, the rigidly disciplined elite guard called the Fruit
of Islam, the instruction it received in karate, judo, and
killing police dogs. I recalled the constant vilification of the
"white devil," the machinelike obedience of all Muslims,
the suspicion and distrust they had for the outsider. But
most of all, I remembered Malcolm, sweat beading on his
hard-muscled face, his fist slashing the air in front of his
audience: "Hell is when you don't have justice! And when
you don't have equality, that's hell! And the devil is the
one who robs you of your right to be a human being! I
don't have to tell you who the devil is. You know who the
devil is." (*"Yes, Brother Malcolm! Tell 'em like it is!"*)

Malcolm said to me now, "That was a bad scene,
brother. The sickness and madness of those days—I'm glad
to be free of them. It's a time for martyrs now. And if I'm
to be one, it will be in the cause of brotherhood. That's
the only thing that can save this country. I've learned
it the hard way—but I've learned it. And that's the significant thing."

I was struck by the change; and I felt he was sincere, but couldn't his disenchantment with Elijah Muhammad have forced him into another type of opportunism? As recently as December 20 he had yelled at a Harlem rally: "We need a Mau Mau to win freedom and equality in the United States!" There was an inconsistency here. Could he, in his dread of being pushed into obscurity, have trumped up another type of zealotry? I doubted it. He was caught, it seemed, in a new idealism. And, as time bore out, he had given me the essence of what was to have been his brotherhood speech—the one his killers silenced. It was this intentness on brotherhood that cost him his life. For Malcolm, over the objections of his bodyguards, was to rule against anyone being searched before entering the hall that fateful day: "We don't want people feeling uneasy," he said. "We must create an image that makes people feel at home."

"Is it really true that the Black Muslims are out to get you?" I asked.

"It's as true as we are standing here. They've tried it twice in the last two weeks."

"What about police protection?"

He laughed. "Brother, nobody can protect you from a Muslim but a Muslim—or someone trained in Muslim tactics. I know. I invented many of those tactics."

"Don't you have any protection at all?"

He laughed again. "Oh, there are hunters and there are those who hunt the hunters. But the odds are certainly with those who are most skilled at the game."

He explained that he was now ready to provide a single, unifying platform for all our people, free of political, religious, and economic differences. "One big force under one banner," he called it. He was convinced that whatever mistakes he had made after leaving Elijah Muhammad had been in the name of brotherhood. "Now it looks like this brotherhood I wanted so badly has got me in a jam," he said.

Within the last year he had sent me postcards from Saudi Arabia, Kuwait, Ethiopia, Kenya, Nigeria, Ghana, and Tanganyika, and I thanked him for them.

"Everybody's wondering why I've been going back and forth to Africa. Well, first I went to Mecca to get closer to the orthodox religion of Islam. I wanted firsthand views of the African leaders—their problems are inseparable from ours. The cords of bigotry and prejudice here can be cut with the same blade. We have to keep that blade sharp and share it with one another." Now he was sounding like the old Malcolm: "Strangely enough, listening to leaders like Nasser, Ben Bella, and Nkrumah awakened me to the dangers of racism. I realized racism isn't just a black and white problem. It's brought bloodbaths to about every nation on earth at one time or another."

He stopped and remained silent for a few moments. "Brother," he said finally, "remember the time that white college girl came into the restaurant—the one who wanted to help the Muslims and the whites get together—and I told her there wasn't a ghost of a chance and she went away crying?"

"Yes."

"Well, I've lived to regret that incident. In many parts of the African continent I saw white students helping black people. Something like this kills a lot of argument. I did many things as a Muslim that I'm sorry for now. I was a zombie then—like all Muslims—I was hypnotized, pointed in a certain direction, and told to march. Well, I guess a man's entitled to make a fool of himself if he's ready to pay the cost. It cost me twelve years."

As we parted he laid his hand on my shoulder, looked into my eyes, and said, "Asalaam Alaikum, brother."

"And may peace be with you, Malcolm," I answered.

Driving home from that last meeting with Malcolm, I realized once more that, despite his extremism and inconsistencies, I liked and admired him. A certain humility was wed to his arrogance. I assumed that his bitterness must have come from his tragic life. His home in East Lansing, Michigan, was burned to the ground by white racists. He had lived for many years with the belief that whites had bludgeoned his father to death and left his body on the tracks to be run over by a streetcar.

Malcolm's years of ranting against the "white devils" helped create the climate of violence that finally killed him, but the private man was not a violent one. He was brilliant, ambitious, and honest. And he was fearless. He said what most of us black folk were afraid to say publicly. When he told off "a head-whipping cop"—as he described him—his tongue was coupled with a million other black tongues. When he condemned the bosses of the "rat-infested ghetto," a Harlem full of fervid "Amens" could be heard ricocheting off the squalid tenements.

I remember Malcolm's complete devotion to Elijah Muhammad and his words when he was serving as the Muslims' spokesman: "All that Muhammed is trying to do is clean up the mess the white man has made, and the white man should give him credit. He shouldn't run around here calling [Muhammad] a racist and a hate-teacher. White man, call yourself a hate-teacher because you invented hate. Call yourself a racist because you invented the race problem."

Malcolm was not after power in the Muslim organization, but his unquestioning belief in the movement, his personal charm, his remarkable ability to captivate an audience brought him that power. With Elijah aging and ailing, Malcolm became the obvious choice as his successor. But his power and prominence also made him a marked man in the tightly disciplined society. His downfall had started even before his notorious comment on President Kennedy's assassination ("Chickens coming home to roost never did make me sad; they've always made me glad!"). But with that statement he unwittingly made himself more vulnerable.

On the night of Malcolm's death, at the home of friends where his family had taken refuge, I sat with his wife Betty, his two oldest children, and a group of his stunned followers, watching a television review of his stormy life. When his image appeared on the screen, blasting away at the injustices of "the enemy," a powerfully built man sitting near me said softly, "Tell 'em like it is, Brother Malcolm, tell 'em like it is."

The program ended and Betty got up and walked slowly to the kitchen and stood staring at the wall. Six-year-old Attallah followed and took her mother's hand. "Is Daddy coming back after his speech, Momma?"

Betty put her arms around the child and dropped her head on the refrigerator. "He tried to prepare me for this day," she said. "But I couldn't bring myself to listen. I'd just walk out of the room. The other day—after they tried to bomb us out of the house—was the only time I could stay and listen. I just closed my eyes and hung onto everything he said. I was prepared. That's why I'm ashamed I cried over him when he was lying there all shot up."

Only Qubilah, the four-year-old, seemed to understand that her father wouldn't come again. She tugged at her mother's skirt. "Please don't go out, Momma."

"I won't go, baby. Momma won't go out." She gently pushed the child's head into her lap and told her to go to sleep.

"He was always away," Betty went on, "but I knew he would always come back. We loved each other. He was honest—too honest for his own good, I think sometimes." I started to leave and she said, "I only hope the child I'm carrying is just like his father."

"I hope you get your wish," I said.

THE BEGINNING, NOT THE END

──────────────── BY *Shirley Graham DuBois*

RADIO TALK GIVEN OVER GHANA RADIO
MARCH 17, 1965

IN a speech before the American Foreign Service Association in Washington, Carl Rowan, Director of the United States Information Agency, characterized Malcolm X as only "an ex-convict," "ex-dope peddler," and a "racial fanatic." This Negro, Rowan, expressed his amazement that many Africans respected and admired Malcolm X. He stressed that his agency—the United States Information in every country—must "correct" this lack of understanding by zealously disseminating the vilification and slanders of the U.S. press, designed to obliterate every memory of our slain brother.

Malcolm X left Ghana for the United States with the song of unity on his lips. His Organization of Afro-American Unity is a second OAU. "In union there is strength!" He said it loud and clear. And discouraged, oppressed people of America, north and south, east and west, heard his voice and were glad.

So, on a bright Sunday afternoon of the much advertised Brotherhood Week, that voice was silenced. The last words they heard as his bullet-riddled body staggered forward were: PEACE! BE CALM!

To an amazing extent the people of Harlem heeded Malcolm's dying injunction, and, for the first time I know of, Afro-American newspapers separated themselves from the powerful, ruling white press. Wrote the *Amsterdam News,* New York's largest Afro-American newspaper: "From the moment of Malcolm's death at 3:30 P.M., February 21, until late Saturday, Harlem remained under a virtual police siege as hundreds of extra cops were rushed into the area. They lined the rooftops, searched people on the streets, and blocked street corners. It was perhaps the tensest week in the community's history."

Disregarding controls and pressures, heedless of economic reprisals and castigations, a united Afro-American press has mourned the death of Malcolm X. Wrote the *Herald-Dispatch* of Los Angeles:

When Malcolm X died, a little bit of thirty million Negroes died with him. . . . And finally, Malcolm X, the young man whose thirst for knowledge was comparable only to that of a camel's thirst for water after a long trek over the desert, was the most promising and effective leader of American Negroes in this century. Could the Black Muslims have influenced Charles de Gaulle to prevent Malcolm X from entering Paris to speak? The order of President de Gaulle came from top-level State Department officials. Malcolm X was in Los Angeles ten days ago organizing throughout this nation to teach black people unity, organization, and authentic Islam. Malcolm X was assassinated because he was teaching the black man the Arab is your brother. "Don't fight the Arab! Don't allow yourself to be drawn into a bloody war in the Middle East, which is inevitable!" Malcolm X died because of this teaching. But there are a thousand other Malcolms. They will rise! A thousand Malcolms that will carry on the battle.

New York dailies and radio mocked the funeral of Malcolm X. "The expected crowds did not show up," they jeered; "empty seats for foreign visitors who failed to materialize," and so forth. I give you excerpts from an account in the Afro-American press:

Dressed in the white linen robes of a Muslim, his head facing the east in accordance with Islamic tradition, Malcolm X, militant black nationalist leader, was laid to rest Saturday in a quiet grave in Ferncliff Cemetery as El-Hajj Malik El-Shabazz. . . . An estimated 30,000 persons from all walks of life in the metropolitan area had walked or waited in line at the Unity Funeral Home last week to view the remains of one of the nation's most articulate critics of the white power structure in what funeral director Joseph Hall said was the largest funeral in Harlem's colorful history. Late Friday the viewing was halted while Sheik Ahmed Hassoun Jaaber, who came here from Egypt with Malcolm to assist in organizing the Mosque, prepared the slain Malcolm's body for burial. . . .

Only the Afro-American press gave the full text of the eulogy delivered by Ossie Davis, foremost Afro-American playwright and actor-director.

Only Afro-American papers printed Osagyefo's message of condolence which was read at the funeral. From the solitude of the wilderness, Osagyefo wrote:

I have received with profound shock the news of the death of your husband at the hand of assassins. Your husband lived a life of dedication for human equality and dignity so that the Afro-American and people of color everywhere may live as men. His work in the cause of freedom will not be in vain. . . .

As Malcolm was leaving Accra for the United States three months ago some of us warned him that his life would be in danger. He smiled that gentle smile, that unforgettable smile, and said, "Your president, Osagyefo, has taught me the true meaning and strength of unity. If I can pass this on to my people, if I can show them the way —my life will be a small price to pay for such a vision."

Malcolm has paid this price! And in the unanimous coming together of the Afro-American press one glimpses the beginning of Malcolm X's victory.

He may well rest in peace! A salaam Alaikum!

WHY I EULOGIZED
MALCOLM X *

————————————————————— BY *Ossie Davis*

You are not the only person curious to know why I would eulogize a man like Malcolm X. Many who know and respect me have written letters. Of these letters I am proudest of those from a sixth-grade class of young white boys and girls who asked me to explain. I appreciate your giving me this chance to do so.

You may anticipate my defense somewhat by considering the following fact: no Negro has yet asked me that question. (My pastor, Reverend Samuel Austin, of Grace Baptist Church where I teach Sunday school, preached a sermon about Malcolm in which he called him a "giant in a sick world.") Every one of the many letters I got from my own people lauded Malcolm as a man, and commended me for having spoken at his funeral.

At the same time—and that is important—most all of them took special pains to disagree with much or all of what Malcolm said and what he stood for. That is, with one singing exception, they all, every last, black, glory-hugging one of them, knew that Malcolm—whatever else he was or was not—Malcolm was a man!

White folks do not need anybody to remind them that they are men. We do! This was his one incontrovertible benefit to his people.

We used to think that protocol and common sense required that Negroes stand back and let the white man

* A number of people, most of them newspapermen, asked Ossie Davis why he eulogized Malcolm X. This is his answer.

speak up for us, defend us, and lead us from behind the scene in our fight. This was the essence of Negro politics. But Malcolm said to hell with that! Get up off your knees and fight your own battles. That's the way to win back your self-respect. That's the way to make the white man respect you. And if he won't let you live like a man, he certainly can't keep you from dying like one!

Malcolm, as you can see, was refreshing excitement; he scared hell out of the rest of us, bred as we are to caution, to hypocrisy in the presence of white folks, to the smile that never fades. Malcolm knew that every white man in America profits directly or indirectly from his position vis-à-vis Negroes, profits from racism even though he does not practice it or believe in it.

He also knew that every Negro who did not challenge on the spot every instance of racism, overt or covert, committed against him and his people, who chose instead to swallow his spit and go on smiling, was an Uncle Tom and a traitor, without balls or guts, or any other commonly accepted aspects of manhood!

Now, we knew all these things as well as Malcolm did, but we also knew what happened to people who stick their necks out and say them. And if all the lies we tell ourselves by way of extenuation were put into print, it would constitute one of the great chapters in the history of man's justifiable cowardice in the face of other men.

But Malcolm kept snatching our lies away. He kept shouting the painful truth we whites and blacks did not want to hear from all the housetops. And he wouldn't stop for love nor money.

You can imagine what a howling, shocking nuisance this man was to both Negroes and whites. Once Malcolm fastened on you, you could not escape. He was one of the most fascinating and charming men I have ever met, and never hesitated to take his attractiveness and beat you to death with it. Yet his irritation, though painful to us, was most salutary. He would make you angry as hell, but he would also make you proud. It was impossible to remain defensive and apologetic about being a Negro in his presence. He wouldn't let you. And you always left his presence with the sneaky suspicion that maybe, after all, you *were* a man!

But in explaining Malcolm, let me take care not to explain him away. He had been a criminal, an addict, a pimp, and a prisoner; a racist, and a hater, he had really believed the white man was a devil. But all this had changed. Two days before his death, in commenting to Gordon Parks about his past life, he said: "That was a mad scene. The sickness and madness of those days! I'm glad to be free of them."

And Malcolm was free. No one who knew him before and after his trip to Mecca could doubt that he had completely abandoned racism, separatism, and hatred. But he had not abandoned his shock-effect statements, his bristling agitation for immediate freedom in this country not only for blacks, but for everybody.

And most of all, in the area of race relations, he still delighted in twisting the white man's tail, and in making Uncle Toms, compromisers, and accommodationists—I deliberately include myself—thoroughly ashamed of the urbane and smiling hypocrisy we practice merely to exist in a world whose values we both envy and despise.

But even had Malcolm not changed, he would still have been a relevant figure on the American scene, standing in relation as he does, to the "responsible" civil rights leaders, just about where John Brown stood in relation to the "responsible" abolitionist in the fight against slavery. Many disagreed with Brown's mad and fanatical tactics which led him to attack a Federal arsenal at Harpers Ferry, to lose two sons there, and later to be hanged for treason.

Yet today the world, and especially the Negro people, proclaim Brown not a traitor, but a hero and a martyr in a noble cause. So in future, I will not be surprised if men come to see that Malcolm X was, within his own limitations, and in his own inimitable style, also a martyr in that cause.

But there is much controversy still about this most controversial American, and I am content to wait for history to make the final decision.

But in personal judgment, there is no appeal from instinct. I knew the man personally, and however much I might have disagreed with him from time to time, I never doubted that Malcolm X, even when he was wrong, was always that rarest thing in the world among us Negroes: a true man.

And if, to protect my relations with the many good white folks who make it possible for me to earn a fairly good living in the entertainment industry, I was too chicken, too cautious, to admit that fact when he was alive, I thought at least that now, when all the white folks are safe from him at last, I could be honest with myself enough to lift my hat for one final salute to that brave, black, ironic gallantry, which was his style and hallmark, the shocking *zing* of fire-and-be-damned-to-you, so absolutely absent in every other Negro man I know, which brought him, too soon, to his death.

MALCOLM X AS A
HUSBAND AND FATHER

BY *Betty Shabazz*

I FIRST saw Malcolm at a Black Muslim meeting. I was
a student at the time and not yet a Muslim, but I had
gone to the meeting with a friend. He didn't speak that
night but appeared at the end of the meeting to make a
few closing remarks. I recall that during the speech I was
leaning back in my seat, but when Malcolm walked onto
the platform—he was just standing there—I sat straight up.
I don't know what it was—his air of authority or what,
but I was very impressed. My reaction was somewhat akin
to respect or maybe even fear. When I met him after the
meeting I was surprised that he was so friendly. He was
very easy to talk to and had a quick smile. He had a way
of making people feel relaxed and close and at the same
time, had a way of holding them at a distance.

We had known one another for about a year before we
married, and up to that time we were "friends," nothing
more. He always said that he liked to talk to different
sisters, to get their opinion about certain things, and he
would always apologize for asking such questions. But he
used to ask me questions about my background—personal
things—and I just said, when he began his apologies for
asking, "Oh, yes, brother. I realize that you're just interested in me as a person, as a sister." I remember him
saying that there were so many women who, if you opened
the door for them or bought them dinner or sent them a
card, before you knew it they'd have their wedding dress
all ready. He wanted me to know that his interest in me

was no more than a brotherly interest. Of course, I knew different.

Occasionally we discussed marriage. He once asked me if I had ever been married and I said, "No." But once, while teasing him I said, "I lied to you and I want to tell you the truth now: I was married before." I'll never forget the way he looked at me! I quickly told him that I was only kidding and he said to me, "That is something you never kid about." It was obvious that he had a serious regard for marriage.

He had said he didn't want to marry anybody; he wanted to dedicate his life to helping black people. He felt that marriage was a responsibility and he didn't know if he could live up to it. He wondered how he could even begin to tell a female where he would be at every minute of the day. (He was thirty-two years old then and a confirmed bachelor.) After we were married, though, it was the easiest thing to do. He would say, "I'll be here and if anyone wants me he can call me there." But at this point in our friendship it was about the hardest thing for him to imagine.

So we were "just friends." We would have dinner at the Black Muslim restaurant in New York almost every Sunday. Actually we never really courted as such; we were just friends until the day we married, although it was obvious to many in the movement what the result of our friendship would be. Everyone had begun to watch the pattern and many people in the movement—men and women—didn't like it. The men seemed to feel that he belonged to the movement and resented the idea of a woman taking up time he might have spent with them. Many of the women were just plain jealous. When I entered the restaurant every man and woman—old, young, fat, whatever—would offer me a seat to prevent Malcolm and me from sitting together. I would say politely, "No, thank you," but they weren't so polite in their replies or in their looks.

I too had concluded that Malcolm wanted to marry me. I never acted as if I knew though, and maintained the relationship on the same level that he did: We had things in common—I was born in Detroit and he still had family in Lansing, Michigan. That was about it. One day, though, I got a call from Malcolm from Detroit; he asked me to marry him. So I flew out to Detroit and we got married in Lansing about four days later.

I guess Malcolm was still a little apprehensive about marriage. He would tell me from time to time that the only thing he could remember about his mother and father's marriage was argument, but I told him that the one thing I wouldn't do was argue. I could see that his apprehension lessened as our marriage continued and we began to have children. He seemed to appreciate having a home and children to come back to.

Because of his own background and because he realized that different people have different temperaments, he felt that there should be some sort of mutual cooperation and understanding within the family. So we would have little family talks. They began at first with Malcolm telling me what he expected of a wife. But the first time I told him what I expected of him as a husband it came as a shock. After dinner one night he said, "Boy, Betty, something you said hit me like a ton of bricks. Here I've been going along having our little workshops with me doing all the talking and you doing all the listening." He concluded that our marriage should be a mutual exchange. He thought that communication and understanding would give each of us an assurance that one wouldn't do anything to violate the trust of the other.

One of the things he often said was that he didn't spend enough time with the children or with me, but I felt that the time that he did have was spent constructively. Looking back now, I remember that whenever Daddy was home the whole house was happy. It wasn't a time for a lot of big, knockdown, drag-out fights that some people have. Daddy would be home tomorrow and there was always something special cooked, little extra touches added to the house. Measuring it in terms of quality, I think he spent as much time with his family as any other man.

Sometimes he would take us to the beach and while he wrote his speeches, the baby and I would either sit on the sand or play in the water. He used to read poetry to us too, and was very good at it. He was also very complimentary in an offhanded kind of way. If I were to cook something especially good, he used to say, "I can cook, you know, Betty. If necessary, I'll cook in a minute." But he never cooked the entire time we were married.

At times funny things would happen when he was home. When the children were quite young and saw Daddy on television, they couldn't quite put the two things together, since sometimes Daddy was there watching himself on the screen. One of the children would look at the picture, go to the television to take a closer look, and then come back and look at Daddy.

There were times when he would say something that he thought was funny but that I never took the same way. He used to tell me, "Betty, none of our children will ever be singers." You see, I used to sing in the choir when I was growing up and I thought I could sing. And he knew I thought I could sing; he'd say, "I can't sing and you sure can't sing." I used to get kind of angry but he was a warm person and deep down I knew he wasn't trying to be malicious.

He also used to do tender, little things that I suppose every woman looks for in her husband. When he was gone for long intervals he used to leave money in different places around the house. I used to get a letter that said, "Look in the top desk drawer in the back. There's some money there for you to buy something, and a love letter too." I would go look and maybe he'd have the money in an envelope with a picture of himself. Sometimes there would just be money and sometimes there really would be a love letter. It got so that as soon as he left the house, I would start looking in all the secret places, but I never found anything. A few days later, though, I'd get a letter telling me where to look—and it was never in a place he'd used before.

I suppose people who only knew Malcolm from his public appearances and fiery speeches couldn't even imagine what he was like as a father. Malcolm had a very beautiful reaction to becoming a father. I don't think he really accepted the fact that I was going to have a baby until she arrived, but once she was here and he realized that he'd made the baby and the baby looked like him—

the gentleness he showed was really so profound. At first it bothered him that Attallah was so light (Malcolm didn't want any light children) and we both wondered what in the world we'd done wrong for this little girl to come out looking like that.

Since Attallah was the first child for each of us, we both learned about child-rearing with her, which is kind of hard and cruel for a first baby. Now, I was the one who had been trained to be a nurse but I was more nervous than Malcolm; he would tell me things to do for the baby that were perfectly correct. And Attallah was very healthy, very robust; we never had any major problems at all.

Although Malcolm was gentle with the children, he also had a philosophy about how a child should be raised. He felt that I should be very strict with Attallah because he could see a lot of wildness in her that needed strictness and proper direction: He saw in her a lot of traits that he himself had possessed. He felt that children should have proper training and education, that they should be able to function with supervision. Basically he wanted the children prepared to accept themselves, to function in a community, and to be able to support themselves. He also wanted them to be aware that it was a spiritual as well as a moral duty to help their brothers and sisters. This was how all the children were to be reared.

Some people have asked me if Malcolm ever expressed a desire to have a son, since we had six girls. Actually, I wanted a son for him more than he wanted one for himself and I think that's why we ended up with six girls. I would say that he would like to have had a son but he only talked about it when I brought the subject up. As long as we had healthy children, he felt that I should be grateful; and he would always add that we could have more children—and more.

Once we went to visit a couple who had two children— both mentally retarded and both at home. I think that's when it finally came across to me that I really do have a lot to be grateful for. All six of my children are healthy, even my twins, who were never even in an incubator.

I did want a son but now I think it's best that I don't have one. I think about the war and about how things in this country are so designed to break the back of a black man. Any black man today who strives to be a man among men is singled out and accused of everything except what he is trying to do. I feel that I am not capable now of accepting or tackling this problem. That could perhaps be a rationalization on my part, I don't know, but sometimes I do feel that it's best that I don't have a son now.

If Malcolm were still alive, though, we just might have a boy. Believe it or not, all of our children were planned. Malcolm said he was going to have six girls before he had a boy. My reply was that he was going to have them by himself. He used to joke about it but if he had lived, we probably would have had a son. According to the sequence of things in our house I would be pregnant or have given birth by now.

Although I didn't take to the idea of having six or seven children in the beginning, I must say that I enjoyed all of my pregnancies. Malcolm seemed to have such a high regard for motherhood: He used always to paraphrase a quote from the Quran that paradise was at the feet of the mother, that man must always remember his mother, that he was born from her womb and she suffered much on his account. He used to talk about the honor of being a mother and how the key to the future and the key to humanity, actually, was through the woman.

During my pregnancies Malcolm always made certain that he was the one who took me to see the doctor. If he was going to be out of town on the day of my appointment, he'd tell me I had to cancel the appointment. When we did see the doctor, Josephine English (who delivered all of our children), it was usually early in the morning, before office hours. Malcolm would then drop me off at home and go about his day's work. He treated me with such tender care and consideration when I was pregnant that I was just plain happy.

My pregnancies have had a reaction on the girls, too. I've had so many babies in my house at one time that all the girls ever thought of was, "I want to have babies like Mommy." So I have to tell them that they shouldn't have any more children than they can afford to take care of.

I loved Malcolm for the traits he displayed as a husband and a father, and I admired and respected the drive, the dedication, and the unselfishness he showed in his work.

When I became a Black Muslim, one of the first projects that I was involved in was a fund-raising drive. Malcolm had started to raise enough money so that Elijah Muhammad's sons could work with their father. They all had menial jobs and Malcolm felt that Elijah Muhammad and his work could be further ahead if he had his sons around him to help. Supposedly they would serve in administrative capacities—form a cadre around their father. But it didn't work out that way.

As I reflect on it, Malcolm's evaluation of the sons wasn't exactly correct. Perhaps these men were in menial jobs because they didn't have the ability to do anything else. Malcolm used to say that one of the worst things to do is to give an ignorant man power, but he never applied this rule to Elijah Muhammad's family. And I think a lot of the things that happened to Malcolm happened because of the family. Of course, he didn't see it at the time, but he had a hand in setting up his own doom through the very people he helped.

I myself was very subjective at the time; I guess my feeling was that who else should you be concerned with other than yourself? I think this is the way a lot of black people feel: "Let me help myself and then if I have time, I'll look back and help." But Malcolm helped me to see things in a different perspective. Malcolm's whole program was for black people collectively: He felt that if black people collectively improved their condition, then all black people become beneficiaries.

But his unselfish, total concern for black people had certain drawbacks because it left him with practically nothing of his own. Elijah Muhammad also must have seen that Malcolm's unselfishness wasn't too good a thing, because on many occassions he would say to Malcolm, "Brother, you should have the house put in your name." And Malcolm would say, "No, sir, dear Holy Apostle. If anything ever happened to me, I know that the Nation [of Islam] will take care of my family." However, this was not the way things turned out.

His profound trust in Elijah Muhammad made him say —and believe—things like that. Sometimes, at the mosque, Malcolm used to teach that Elijah Muhammad could do no wrong because Allah had gone into him, taken his heart out, overhauled and cleansed it, and then put it back in so he could do no wrong. Elijah Muhammad was a little lamb without spots or blemishes. This is what Malcolm actually believed at that time.

He joked about that in his last year because Elijah Muhammad really did have him fooled. But people must remember that Malcolm never had a father from the time he was six years old. He really grew up by himself, so that this need for a father image probably had a lot to do with his profound faith in Elijah Muhammad. And Elijah Muhammad did, in a way, take him on as a son, because he realized the potential that Malcolm had for the movement.

Whatever Malcolm's emotional ties or needs may have been, I'm sure he himself knew that he had eventually to face up to the fact that Elijah Muhammed was indeed a human being who possessed all the human weaknesses that are part of us all. I think he thought about this for a long time, but perhaps was afraid to explore it too deeply since it was a good movement and there were a lot of good people in it. He finally came face to face with this when he allowed himself to see that Elijah Muhammad wasn't practicing what he was preaching. Then he remembered things that had been told to him previously but that he had forgotten (or just put out of his mind).

As far as Malcolm's suspension from the movement was concerned, if it hadn't happened because of the remarks he is supposed to have made about John Kennedy, it would have occurred for some other reason. Malcolm was told two years before this happened that they were trying to get rid of him. At that time he was also told several other things they were planning to do. Certain people in the movement felt that he had gotten too big, that he was trying to get a power base for himself. One of Malcolm's supporters said to the officials, "How can you say this when everything the man does is for the Nation?" They said, "Well, regardless of what he does or who he does it for, we are going to get rid of him whenever we can."

One man traveling in Africa told Malcolm about eight months before the suspension that he had heard the same things over there. But all of these things he never believed. He believed that certain people were trying to break up the movement because it was growing. Then he began to remember all of the little things.

The time of his suspension was one of confusion and reassessment. At that time, he still had that faith and trust in Elijah Muhammad and was still willing to do his bidding. At one point during those ninety days he was sent a letter asking him to do certain things. He carried out the instructions and was then reprimanded for doing what he had been instructed to do. I think this was the breaking point.

Malcolm's entire philosophy was based on morality. He felt that religiously the movement was a vacuum, politically it was a vacuum. It didn't get involved in any of the things most black people were getting involved in. So the only thing left was the moral code. Then he found that the leader wasn't practicing his own preachings. He said he wouldn't be a party to any organization that was designed to get money out of black people because this was all that anybody else had ever done and he wanted no part of it. He vowed that he would undo all that he had done.

I think this was one of the things that I admired about him: Whenever he was wrong he would always admit it and go from there. It never stopped him.

They began teaching at the mosque how all hypocrites should be destroyed and this sort of thing. I think it was at this point that he realized he was not going to be accepted back into the movement. When the letter finally came saying just that, it was no surprise, no shock. There was no reason for any tears because he had already begun to set other things into motion.

However, there was one thing that he felt he had to do as a preparation for the organization he hoped to build. He wanted to make the pilgrimage to Mecca, as all orthodox Muslims try to do at least once in their lifetime. And he wanted to clear up certain unanswered questions about Islam and to see if it held any solution to the black man's problem.

When he returned he did have a new perspective. Part of it, I think, was the human experience of seeing people from different countries functioning together because of a common philosophy. It had more of an effect on him because people who had never seen him before were treating him so graciously while the very people he had given his all to for sixteen years were persecuting him.

A lot of people say that Malcolm changed after that trip, but they never look at the totality and see that the man's entire scope had been broadened. They look at every individual change and say that Malcolm had changed from one thing to another. Many people base this on his denunciation of racism and they misinterpret this statement to mean that now he endorsed the principles of integration as a solution to America's racial dilemma. He had said he saw white people who were also Muslims and who were gracious and friendly, but many people fail to see that Malcolm was only reporting what he saw—it was an observation.

Malcolm's basic goal or objective never changed: He was totally committed to freedom for oppressed people. And when he came back he could see how narrow-minded many groups in America were. The Methodists or the Baptists or the Democrats or whatever all looked at the problem from their particular eye. They would help those who belonged to their group, but no one joined for the sake of humanity—forgetting about politics or religion—to solve the problem of all oppressed people. Malcolm's feeling was that if a group has an answer to the problems of black people, then they should help solve the problem without having all black people join that group. In this sense his scope had been broadened.

When he was first with the Black Muslim movement it was, "Join Elijah Muhammad. He can solve the problem of the black people here in America." And when he came back he had the view of, We will have to solve the problem: leaders from all walks of life. Not in this country alone, but all over the world. It was primarily a non-white problem, but it was the white man's problem too.

Although Malcolm knew that his break with the Black Muslims was final and complete—in the physical sense—

psychologically the final cord had yet to be broken. He would never have said the things he said after he returned from Africa if the Black Muslims had been intelligent enough to let things lie as they were. But they were constantly telling the believers that Malcolm was insane and that Allah was going to chastise him: a psychological brainwashing, in other words.

What Malcolm had begun in Africa and was setting in motion after his return to the United States was an expansion of the black American's struggle from one of civil rights to that of human rights, and thereby an internationalization of the problem. The concept frightened many people, particularly the middle class and those who have certain vested interests in things remaining as they are. Everyone has used the black problem to get support for their own cause. But once they get the support, the black man's freedom has been left at the back door. And while black people in this country are fighting for mere existence—to stay alive—all the white liberals have not put the black man's problem at the top of their list. I think this is why it will have to be a collective fight among all of the black leaders and whoever else will join them.

Malcolm was committed to such an extent that he embarrassed a lot of middle-class people. As a black man in America his focus was the plight of black people in America, but he wanted to strengthen an alliance with all the non-white people in the world. Other people began to see what a dangerous man he could be if he ever achieved his goals. This became most evident when he wasn't allowed to enter Paris. It was obvious that some very powerful forces were beginning to move against him.

As time went on, it gradually became clear what the result of Malcolm's work would be. I, too, was aware of the inevitable and Malcolm tried to prepare me for it, but I'll never say that I was totally prepared: I could never be totally prepared to raise six daughters alone.

I suppose I couldn't give in to my grief for a prolonged period because I had four children—and twins on the way—to think about. My three oldest daughters were very much aware of what had happened and they took it **very** hard, especially Attallah. We can talk and laugh now at some of her actions but they were difficult to know how to cope with at the time. She used to go to school and just sit there without even taking off her hat and coat. It took more than a year and a half before we could put up a picture of him. There was a time when we would avoid even looking at pictures of him on display on the street or in store windows. Now we have pictures all over the house.

Our life together was short but abundant with experiences more rich than most people enjoy in a lifetime. Thinking of this has been of some consolation to me but although I have sincerely tried, I question whether I will ever completely adjust to the fact that he will never return. Whatever Malcolm did and wherever he went, he always knew that I loved him and that whatever he said I would do—not blindly, but because over the years he had proven that he had my best interests at heart.

Malcolm was the greatest thing in my life and he taught me what every female ought to learn: to live and to love as a woman, to be true to myself and my responsibilities as a mother. And to use my spiritual, material, and intellectual capacities to help build a better human society.

PART III

DIALOGUES WITH
MALCOLM X

PREFACE TO PART III

The four dialogues with Malcolm X presented here represent four different stages of his development. Malcolm X was a master debater and defender of his ideas and his movement. He was particularly sharp in debating ideas and issues affecting the freedom of black Americans.

In the "Open Mind" program of Sunday, October 15, 1961, he was on a panel consisting of two college professors, a social scientist (Dr. Kenneth Clark), and a woman lawyer who is now a federal judge. He was not less than equal to the best of this lot. The quickness of his mind and the sharpness of his articulation is well demonstrated here, and the academicians of this panel seem to fall somewhat behind him.

At the time of this dialogue, the Black Muslim movement was growing rapidly and Malcolm X had fully emerged as its public spokesman.

When Dr. Kenneth Clark interviewed Malcolm X about two years later, his respect for the sharp mind of Malcolm X had grown considerably. In referring to this interview and the public personality of Malcolm X, Dr. Clark has said: "Although Minister Malcolm X seems proud of the fact that he did not go beyond the eighth grade, he speaks generally with the vocabulary and the tone of a college-educated person. Happy when this is pointed out to him, he explains that he has read extensively since joining the Black Muslim movement. His role as the chief spokesman for this movement in the New York-Washington region is, *he insists, to raise the level of pride and accomplishment in his followers."*

Dr. Clark further says of him: "He shows the effects of these interminable interviews by a professional calm, and what appears to be an ability to turn on the proper amount of emotion, resentment, and indignation, as needed."

A transcript of a visit to Malcolm X by the FBI is included verbatim because it is self-explanatory and once more shows how well Malcolm X could handle himself in relation to ideas and pressures. It also shows that Malcolm X was a prize that the power establishment in the United States wanted to capture. This establishment that has been successfully buying men and governments the world over, or destroying them, could not believe that this man was not for sale, at any price. In or out of the Black Muslim movement, his ultimate objective was the freedom of his people, by any means necessary.

During the early part of February 1965, Malcolm X stopped in Paris on his way home from his last visit to Africa. He was shocked to discover that he would not be permitted to enter the city. This event, more than anything else during that last period of life, made him believe that there were forces with international motives and connections moving to destroy him. The telephone conversation between Malcolm X and Carlos Moore was Malcolm's last contact with the black community in Paris, which had built a program of action around his teaching.

Malcolm X had planned to address audiences in London and in Paris during the month of February 1965, and to inform the African and Afro-American residents of these cities about the denial of human rights suffered by Afro-Americans—about the brutal treatment inflicted upon them as they attempted to exercise those rights guaranteed by the American Constitution. He had already elevated the civil rights struggle to a human rights struggle, and he had already internationalized it.

J. H. C.

WHERE IS THE
AMERICAN NEGRO HEADED?

"OPEN MIND" NBC TELEVISION
SUNDAY, OCTOBER 15, 1961

MODERATOR: Eric P. Goldman
GUESTS: Mr. Morroe Berger
Mr. Kenneth B. Clark
Mr. Richard Haley
Mrs. Constance B. Motley
Mr. Malcolm X

ANNOUNCER   The open mind, free to examine, to question, to disagree. Our subject today: "Where Is the American Negro Headed?" Your host on "Open Mind" is Eric P. Goldman, Professor of History at Princeton University and the author of *Rendezvous with Destiny* and *The Crucial Decade*.

MR. GOLDMAN   In the years since World War II, unquestionably the most dramatic and most important development in internal American affairs has been the upward lunge of the Negro. In no uncertain terms these 20 million Americans have been making themselves heard.

As the agitation and as the advances have gone on, observers have more and more joined in one type of comment. They've been saying there is a new Negro in America, a new mood, a new emphasis in the programs and demands of the Negro. Today we're going to inquire into statements of this kind, and, I hope, in the course of the inquiry, we will answer candidly such questions as, What does the Negro really want today? Is he, to any significant degree, dissatisfied with the leadership of organizations like the NAACP? And is he really developing a new

149

identity, both in terms of his inner reactions and in terms of his relationships with Africa?

Our panel, here to my right: Mrs. Constance Baker Motley, associated with Thurgood Marshall as assistant counsel of the Legal Defense Fund of the NAACP, who is just back from defending civil rights cases in Mississippi.

Mr. Richard Haley, Field Secretary of CORE, the Congress of Racial Equality, which has led the sit-ins and Freedom Rider activities in the South.

Mr. Morroe Berger, Associate Professor of Sociology at Princeton University, whose expertness in the subject under discussion today is a double one. He wrote the volume entitled *Equality by Statute,* a highly praised study of efforts to bring more equality into American life by legislation. Mr. Berger's sociological studies have also taken him into the Middle Eastern field where he has been interested in the ties that are being asserted today between the American Negro and the Muslims of Africa.

Mr. Malcolm X, Minister of the Temple of Islam No. 7 in New York City, and one of the national leaders of the Black Muslim movement in America.

And Mr. Kenneth B. Clark, Professor of Psychology at the College of the City of New York, author of a historic study on which the Supreme Court, in part, rested its 1954 school desegregation decision, consultant to the NAACP, and winner of the 1961 Spingarn Medal for his work in advancing race relations.

Mr. Clark, would you begin us with a comment on this general question. Is there, to your mind, a really "new Negro" in America?

MR. CLARK   Well, I think the term "new Negro" is a catch phrase and one that catches the imagination of people, but actually, I don't think there's a new Negro. I think the Negro in America today is pretty much the way he has been in the past. In terms of his desires, his wants, I think the Negro today wants exactly what the Negro in the Reconstruction period wanted, namely, full, unqualified equality as an American citizen.

There are some differences today. I think that the Negro today is more direct, more forthright, more impatient, if you will, as he approaches his goal. He becomes much less patient with things which hold him back.

MR. GOLDMAN   Matters of mood rather than of program?

MR. CLARK   And of goal. I think that there is no question that the Negro today has exactly the same goal that the Negro had fifty years ago, seventy years ago, a hundred years ago, probably during slavery, namely, a desire to be free.

MR. GOLDMAN   Mrs. Motley?

MRS. MOTLEY   I think that's about it, Kenneth. I think also that what's new today are the techniques that Negro groups have developed for speeding their full participation in American life. The techniques of the sit-ins and the Freedom Rides have helped to accelerate the pace toward full participation on the part of American Negroes in American life. And I think that these techniques have been dramatic and successful and give the appearance of presenting a new Negro.

MR. GOLDMAN   Mr. X, you seem to be a little restless with all this.

MR. X   Yes, I think there is a new so-called Negro. We don't recognize the term "Negro" but I really believe that there's a new so-called Negro here in America. He not only is impatient. Not only is he dissatisfied, not only is he disillusioned, but he's getting very angry. And whereas the so-called Negro in the past was willing to sit around and wait for someone else to change his condition or correct his condition, there's a growing tendency on the part of a vast number of so-called Negroes today to take action themselves, not to sit and wait for someone else to correct the situation. This, in my opinion, is primarily what has produced this new Negro. He is not willing to wait. He thinks that what he wants is right, what he wants is just, and since these things are just and right, it's wrong to sit around and wait for someone else to correct a nasty condition when they get ready.

MR. GOLDMAN   Does he want anything different in your opinion, Mr. X?

MR. X   In the past he wanted to identify himself with the American way of life, but after a hundred years of begging and a hundred years of waiting, I think there's a growing tendency on the part of the so-called Negro to have reached the conclusion that he can never be recognized as a human being in America as other humans are recognized. So in my opinion, and according to the teachings of the Honorable Elijah Muhammad, I think a growing number of Negroes today are beginning to see, since they can't get it here, that they might as well try elsewhere or try some other form of solution than the ones that have been put in front of us.

MR. GOLDMAN   Mr. Haley, do I note puzzlement over there?

MR. HALEY   Puzzlement, no. But I'm not altogether in agreement. It is unfortunately true, I think, as Mr. X says, that the history of the Negro in America, particularly since Reconstruction, has given us every reason to feel that we can never be accepted in America as human beings. There's a great deal to make one feel this way. Nevertheless, I'm not so quick, even after a hundred years, to give up my belief in man's potentiality to overcome his biggest obstacle, himself. And this is what both the whites and to some extent the Negroes too must overcome.

MR. GOLDMAN   Mr. Berger?

MR. BERGER   If we look back historically to the early period, we find that there's a great deal to be said for the possibility of the Negro becoming a full citizen in this country and I mean in the most intimate relations with white people. If you look at the periods during slavery and especially immediately afterward, you will find that there were extraordinarily intimate relations between the Negroes and white people, a tendency almost immediately to accept in some places the advances of the Negro. But the defeat of this effort just after the Civil War pushed the whole movement in a rearward direction. If we look at what has happened since then, if we think of American Negro-white relations only in the last forty or fifty years when this consolidation of segregation has taken place, we might be pessimistic. If we look at an earlier period, far from becoming pessimistic, I think we have reasons to be optimistic.

MR. GOLDMAN   Whether we're pessimistic or optimistic, I detect a fundamental clash here in the area of what the Negro wants. Am I correct in saying that everyone around the table except Mr. X is saying that the Negro wants integration into American life, and that you are not saying that? Is that fair, Mr. X?

MR. X   It is not a case of integration into the American way of life, nor is it a question of *not* integrating. The question is one of human dignity and integration is only a method or tactic or role that many of the so-called Negroes are using to get recognition and respect as human beings. And many of these Negroes have gotten lost on the road. They're confusing the objective with the method. Now if integration is the objective, then what will we have after we get integration?

I think that the black man in America wants to be recognized as a human being and it's almost impossible for one who has enslaved another to bring himself to accept the person who used to pull his plow, who used to be an animal, subhuman, who used to be considered as such by him—it's almost impossible for that person in his right mind to accept that person as his equal.

MR. CLARK   Mr. X, you sound to me as if you are preaching a doctrine of complete and utter despair. Are you?

MR. X   No, I'm facing facts. If you try and swim the Atlantic Ocean and after several attempts you find you don't make it, well, if your objective is the other side, what are you going to do? It's not a case of having utter despair. You have to go back to shore and try and find another method of getting across if that's where you want to go. Now the so-called Negro in America, a hundred years after Lincoln issued the so-called Emancipation Proclamation, is still knocking on the White House door and still begging practically every white politician who is running for office to pass legislation to bring about an opportunity for the so-called Negro in America to be recognized as a human being—not as a citizen, but as a human being. They can't get recognition as human beings, much less as citizens.

MRS. MOTLEY   You recognize, don't you, that they have made some progress and that there has been greater dignity accorded the American Negro? We don't disagree on that, do we? Don't you think that the Negro today is substantially better off than he was at the end of slavery and that through our own efforts and the efforts of other members of our society we have made progress, and we are continuing to make progress?

MR. X   As a lawyer, I'm sure you'll agree that if you put a man in prison illegally and unjustly, one who has not committed a crime, and after putting him there you keep him in solitary confinement, it's doubly cruel. Now if you let him out of solitary into the regular prison yard, you can call that progress if you want, but the man was not supposed to be put in prison in the first place.

Now you have 20 million black people in America who are begging for some kind of recognition as human beings and the average white man today thinks that we're making progress. He cannot justify the fact that he made us slaves in the first place, which was contrary not only to man's law, contrary not only to God's law, but also contrary to nature's law. I don't call that progress until we have gotten everything we originally had. If a man robs a bank he can't jump up and say: "Well, I'm sorry I've been a robber." He has to make restitution. Here you have 20 million black people who have worked for nothing for 310 years and then for the past hundred years we have been deprived of practically everything a human being needs to exist and keep his morale up. I just can't bring myself to accept the few strides that we've made as any kind of progress. And I think—

MR. GOLDMAN   May I get this discussion off Mr. X specifically and off the Black Muslim movement specifically for a few minutes. I was much struck, on an "Open Mind" program on which Mr. X appeared earlier, by some remarks of Mr. James Baldwin, the well-known Negro nov-

elist. Let me read to you a few of the statements Mr.
Baldwin made on that program.

Mr. Baldwin speaking: "I *do* realize from my own vantage point—I'm a boy from Harlem too—how desperately
and how deeply Negroes hate white people." He went on
to emphasize the point. "Most Negroes, most black people, do not trust white people and most Negroes hate
white people." And then, on the basis of that, he said,
"I personally, speaking only for myself now, I can't
imagine anything this country can offer me that I any
longer want." Now I take all this to be a skepticism about
the value of integration, even if you could get it. Is there
a real trend among Negro intellectuals toward this kind
of thinking?

MR. CLARK   I think we must put statements of that sort,
and Mr. X's statements, in a broader perspective. As a
psychologist, I feel that hate is an extremely difficult
emotion to sustain over a prolonged period of time. Certainly, I myself have felt a great deal of bitterness many
times. Every time I observe an arbitrary form of racial injustice I feel bitter, but like most emotions hate cannot be
sustained longer than my organism can tolerate it.

Negroes, like other human beings, naturally feel hate,
despair, bitterness. This, however, has not stopped the
Negro from the kind of intelligent planning, organization,
and exploitation of all the resources of this government
to obtain his goal, namely, fully and unqualified equality
as an American citizen.

The thing that bothers me, Mr. X, is that you put me
in a position that requires me to take a position—defending the American system—which I'm not particularly
comfortable with. I would like—

MR. X   Why aren't you comfortable taking that position?
If it's a just position, if it's even psychologically just, why
be uncomfortable?

MR. CLARK   Because it's not complete. And neither is
your position complete.

MR. X   I think, sir, you'll find that when you have two
different people, one sitting on a hot stove, one sitting on

a warm stove, the one who is sitting on the warm stove thinks progress is being made. He's more patient. But the one who is sitting on the hot stove, you can't let him up fast enough. You have the so-called Negro in this country, the upper-class Negro or the so-called high-class Negro or, as Franklin Frazier calls them, the "black bourgeois." They aren't suffering the extreme pain that the masses of black people are. And it is the masses of black people to-day, I think you'll find, who are the most impatient, the most angry, because they're the ones that are suffering the most.

MR. BERGER   That's interesting. I don't know if they're the most angry of all the Negroes but certainly I think there's a new Negro in the sense that these are people who have never articulated their demands or made themselves heard to the extent that they are doing now. This is what gives the impression of great militancy, the idea of the new Negro, that is, people lower down in the socioeconomic scale, people of low incomes, are fighting. They are fighting for two things, it seems to me, and I would say that, although there may not be a new Negro in the sense that they're looking for new things, I think they have a different priority and a different urgency about the things that they want.

Two of the things they definitely want are jobs and housing. The important thing that the masses of Negroes now feel is they have got to break out of this box of discrimination and employment and they've got to break out of the Negro ghettos, and these two things have got to happen quickly. This is what I believe is meant when I hear about the new Negro.

MR. GOLDMAN   Mrs. Motley?

MRS. MOTLEY   I think we're in basic agreement, Mr. X, that the condition of the Negro here has been very bad and is still bad in many areas. I think the only respect in which we might disagree is whether there is any need to continue the struggle which we have been making to equalize the situation in our country and we probably disagree on the techniques for achieving this.

MR. GOLDMAN   There's one thing that's coming out in

this discussion, an agreement on the impatience of the Negro. But does this not include impatience with organizations with which you, Mrs. Motley, and you, Mr. Clark, are associated? For example, Mr. X is quoted as calling your colleague, Mr. Thurgood Marshall, "a twentieth-century Uncle Tom." And Mr. Louis Lomax, the Negro journalist, says that there is a Negro "revolt in America, swelling underground for the past two decades, which means the end of the traditional Negro leadership class," which I suspect means you, and you, and you.

MR. CLARK   I think these are exaggerated statements and I think that the present impatience of the Negroes is paradoxically a function of the effectiveness of Negro leadership in the past. I'd like to point out that Mr. X says that the masses of Negroes are in the vanguard of the present civil rights movement. I frankly don't think this is true.

MR. X   Not in the civil rights movement—

MR. CLARK   It might be sentimental and it might play up to the masses to say that the masses are in the vanguard of the movement, but I think accuracy requires us to recognize that the Negro who has been trained, the Negro who has been exposed to more advantages than the average Negro has been permitted to have in America, is the one you are likely to find in the vanguard of the movement. I say this with all due respect to our—

MR. X   You mean eleven students in a school in Atlanta, Georgia, that's progress—

MR. GOLDMAN   Let me be unpleasant here for a moment, let me bore in on this point. There's an article in the current *Harper's* by a woman writer about the young Negro rebels. What the article says is that we really have two Negro groups in America—I'm paraphrasing—one group, the less educated, the socially lower class, who are very much behind the Freedom Riders and similar activities. They're the agitators. And then there are the successful, professional bourgeois, the lawyers and professors and so forth, with a quite different attitude. The author talks about going to Howard University with Freedom Riders (she says Howard is the Harvard of Negro colleges) and she says there wasn't much interest in the Freedom Riders there, which surprises her a great deal. A very suave young Negro student said that his group entirely lacked Negro radicalism. Here you see the Negro elite. These students couldn't care less how Negroes travel on buses. After all, they drive home in their cars.

MR. CLARK   I find that incredible. I think that's a woeful oversimplification and I personally think it's fabrication. I'm glad I don't know the name of the lady who wrote the article. I'm an alumnus of Howard University and I'm now on its board and I go to Howard quite frequently. I would personally like to find the student who would say that to a reporter. I think these attempts to simplify the problem by saying this group of Negroes believes this, that group of Negroes believes that, I think all of this misses the point.

MR. GOLDMAN   Mr. X, don't you agree with some of this, though? I recall your saying on "Open Mind" that, after all, the traditional Negro leadership is always in the Waldorf-Astoria. That's where you see Roy Wilkins, Thurgood Marshall, and so forth. You suggested that they're not out among the Negro people and perhaps don't understand them.

MR. X   I couldn't dispute you because the opportunities I've had to shake their hands would be in that vicinity.

MR. CLARK   Then you were there too, weren't you, Mr. X?

MR. X   Definitely.

MRS. MOTLEY   I think you shook Mr. Marshall's hand in a courtroom.

MR. X   In the courtroom corridor—

MRS. MOTLEY   He's usually found—

MR. X   And I would like to comment on the remark Mr. Goldman made earlier about my saying that Marshall was a twentieth-century Uncle Tom. At the time, a few years back, Marshall made a speech at Princeton, at which time he allowed others to put words in his mouth, very derogatory words, about the Muslims. So that what I said was a reply, but I think that the main thing that all of the black people in America today have to do is that which was done in Bandung by the Africans and Asians in 1955. We have to get together and forget our differences. We're not going to agree on everything but we will agree that all of us are oppressed, all of us are exploited, and the only way we're going to get to our objective is to have some kind of cooperation with each other.

MR. GOLDMAN   Suppose a lot of white people agree that Negroes are oppressed. Mr. X, do you agree with the Honorable Elijah Muhammad when he says, "It is impossible for Negroes and whites to live together. I hate the few drops of white blood that is already in me. There is no intelligent black man who wants integration"?

MR. X   Yes, I believe in everything that Mr. Muhammad says, and when he says that in the first part that he hates the few drops of black blood that are in him, or rather the few drops of white blood that's—

MR. CLARK   That's an interesting slip.

MR. X   I think—

MR. GOLDMAN   Do you say that as a psychologist, Mr. Clark?

MR. CLARK   I say it as a psychologist.

MR. BERGER   What color is Mr. Elijah Muhammad?

MR. X   He's light and I think if you go back during slavery, most of the slaves who got white blood got it by having their mothers raped or ravished by the slave master. It would be impossible for me today to carry the blood of a rapist in me and not hate that blood. Secondly, when he said it is impossible for white and black to live together in peace, the history of America proves that. Most of your white liberals who profess to love Negroes and who profess to be pushing for this integration thing, they themselves live as a rule in lily-white neighborhoods and sometimes they're the first ones to put the FOR SALE sign on their door when a Negro who has fallen for this integration thing moves into their neighborhood. I think that it's very hypocritical today for me as a black man and the white man to sit down with each other and profess that there is a great deal of love between us. I have to look at the white man as the son of the man who kid-

napped my people and brought them here and enslaved
them and he has to look at me as someone to whom he
has done wrong. Always his guilt complex will have him
on guard around me.

I think that we can solve our problems better by looking at the condition of the black men in America as a
collective thing, not individual, but collective. We're in this
condition collectively; we're second-class citizens. Collectively, we're the last hired and the first fired. Okay, since
we suffer collectively the one who benefits, the white man,
benefits collectively. If a white individual were to murder a
man he would be a murderer. Lynching is a murder. For
the past four hundred years our people have been lynched
physically but now it's done politically. We're lynched
politically, we're lynched economically, we're lynched socially, we're lynched in every way that you can imagine.
And we look upon the white man, the American white
man, as a criminal. He has committed a crime against
20 million black people. For me to be segregated is a
crime. For me not to have any rights, that's a crime.

MRS. MOTLEY   Mr. X, let me ask you this: Does Mr.
Muhammad mean by integration simply social intermingling with whites? Or does he mean something else?
When you spoke I got the impression that you were
emphasizing merely a sort of social intermingling with
whites in their houses and that sort of thing and intermarriage. But I think integration may have another
definition which ought to be emphasized more today. What
the Negro seeks is not some sort of social intermingling
per se with whites or intermarriage. What they really
seek is to have the situation in the country equalized more
than it is at the present time. Now does Mr. Muhammad
mean this by integration?

MR. X   No. The Honorable Elijah Muhammad teaches
us that you, a poor man, can't integrate with a rich man.
You can't take a man who has factories and tell him he
must hire Negroes. You can't take a man who has schools
that he has set up himself and tell him he must admit
Negroes. Mr. Muhammad says this: The black people of

America should get together among themselves and do for themselves the same things that the white has done for himself. Do you realize white immigrants have come to this country poor and with no education, and they saved their money and handled it wisely? They set up businesses to provide jobs for their children. They set up factories and industry to create opportunity for their children. Now the black man in America has been so-called free a hundred years. The purchasing power of the black people of America is 20 billion dollars a year. If our people are equal, why haven't our leaders, our professional people, gotten together in some way or another like the white man has done, and set up factories to provide job opportunities, set up housing to provide housing opportunities for Negroes, instead of sitting around here begging the white man for a secondhand house in his neighborhood or demanding that the white man give them a job?

MR. GOLDMAN   Mr. Clark, is that frown a psychological or an ideological frown?

MR. CLARK   Well, it's a frown of perplexity. I'm perplexed. As I listen to Mr. X it seems to me he is asking for the ultimate in segregation. He's asking for segregated factories—

MR. X   No, separate. There is a difference between segregation and separation. Segregation is forced upon an inferior community by a superior community. Separation is done voluntarily by two peoples.

MR. CLARK   Let me take up just one point that you're making. You said, why should the black man ask or beg the white man to be admitted into his schools.

I think the question as you pose it is based on a false premise. The schools are not the white man's schools. The schools are public schools. Negroes are an integral part of America's economy. Negroes pay taxes, Negroes are involved in any crisis which faces this nation. Someone has sold you the mistaken notion that white people own the public schools in America. White people do not own the public schools. Public schools are owned by the public. Twenty million Negroes contribute significantly to the vitality of the country and are now asking that they share equally in all of the benefits, just as they've shared in all of the liabilities of the country.

MR. BERGER   I think that what Mr. Clark is saying, is of course, true. But I think, if I may speak for Mr. Malcolm X for a moment—not that he doesn't speak well for himself—I think that his answer would be, how can you call these schools public schools when they're run by and for the whites and the Negroes have been excluded. There is a point to that and I think that this mood of the Negro favors the kind of thing that Mr. Malcolm X is saying. For the first time in a long while, Negro leaders are saying openly what many Negroes have said to one another for a long time. This is the first time in a long while that the white community is able, so to speak, to eavesdrop on what goes on among Negroes. This brings me to the question of hate. I think hate is not only something difficult to sustain but I think it is often very useful. What has happened on this question of hate is that we have gotten a glimpse into the Negro community, whereas the Negro community has always had a glimpse into the white community. They always knew what the whites were thinking from being servants and so on, from being among whites. The whites have not known what the Negroes were thinking and now they're beginning to find out something about this.

The consequence is that white people are beginning to find that Negroes are very critical, very bitter, and many of them hate whites, as Baldwin says. But this is something that we can carry a bit too far. If you eavesdrop on any community and listen to what people are saying to one another, you can get very depressed. If you listen to good friends of yours talk about you, I think you might become depressed. If Jews listen to what Christians say about them, if Christians listen to what Jews say about them, if all these communities heard everything that everybody said about one another in jest or seriously, I think that all of the groups would be at odds with one another. So I'm not sure that although the Negroes speak that way to one another in this mood of hatred—I'm not so sure that this necessarily represents their mood more accurately than the moderate Negro leaders who speak out without hatred. The fact that people say these things, I don't think means that they always believe them.

MRS. MOTLEY   Mr. X, you said a while ago, nobody should tell a white man that he must hire a Negro in his factory. I think that a lot of people have said the same thing in effect with respect to the laws, for example, prohibiting discrimination in employment. What the law does is not to say to the white man, you must hire a Negro in your factory. The law says to the owner of the factory that you should not discriminate against a qualified Negro solely on account of his race and color.

MR. X   But this type of approach of the present so-called Negro leadership keeps the Negro in a begging category. In my contention, the white people have gotten together and established some kind of economy that provides job opportunities and housing for their own kind. And since our leadership has failed to do so, has failed to get together and provide something for the masses of our people, it puts them on a spot today when someone begins to point these factors out.

MR. CLARK   This is the fallacy in your thinking that bothers me. You keep saying white people have gotten together but there is no industry in America that has been built without Negro labor, Negro consumers, Negro money involved. There is no such thing as a white—

MR. X   A horse can pull the plow. A horse is the one that's actually plowing the field. Does the horse get the benefits? No, even the horse can't say that it's his farm. He's a part of the property on that farm. That's the capacity that you and I have been in in America for the past four hundred years. It was subhuman. The United States Constitution classified us as three fifths of a man, subhuman. That is the United States Constitution.

MR. CLARK   The United States Constitution as interpreted, especially by the May 17, 1954, decision, declares that you are a complete man and that no state can make any law which abrogates your rights as an American citizen based solely upon color.

MR. GOLDMAN   We only have about twelve minutes left and I don't want us not to touch on this. Of course, if there is a new Negro, one of the things that people are commenting on most are his supposed ties, intellectual and emotional, to Africa and to what is going on in Africa. Now, is that important? If so, what is it really? What is this influence that Africa is having?

MRS. MOTLEY   I think that the Negro has found Africa as a place with which he might identify in the broadest sense. Negroes have been for years without a country or homeland, so to speak, of which they could be proud, from their point of view.

Africa has always been looked upon as the dark continent. Now Africa is rising and the Negro in America sees young African leaders who are able and articulate and who are leading their people in the struggle for freedom. And so the American Negro can now look to his homeland, so to speak, and identify with people who are strong and who are respected and looked up to. This has given a new impetus, let us say, to the drive on the part of young Negroes in this country to do something.

MR. CLARK   I think it's possible to exaggerate the African impact upon American Negroes. Certainly there are some dramatic aspects of it. The Negro is certainly happy and proud when he sees an articulate Negro from one of these new nations in the UN. But my own feeling is that the impact of the legal staff of the NAACP and the votes that Negroes in large urban centers in the United States use to elect congressmen and senators and to influence national politics are more likely to have a direct effect upon the rapidity of changes in the status of the Negro in America than what happens in Africa. Now it may be that I am speaking only in terms of a personal idiosyncratic inability to identify with Africa. I confess, I identify with America. I'm American and I want my rights as an American.

MR. GOLDMAN   Mr. Haley, are you agreeing with Mr. Clark?

MR. HALEY   It's possible to underrate the impact of

Africa just as it is possible to overrate it. The big problem, I suppose, is how to estimate it accurately since it's so hard to measure. But one can, just on the basis of his own experience, point out what he has seen, and it does seem to me that many Negroes with whom I've had contact tie themselves or feel a tie not just with emergent Africa but with that whole side of the world, which is just bubbling over with all types and colors and sizes and nationalities of various colored peoples.

MR. GOLDMAN   Mr. X, let me hold you back for just a moment. There is of course the possibility that to the extent that the Negro is turning to Africa he is turning to a leadership which, on the one hand, is one of frenetic racism, a possibility that Mr. Louis Lomax raises in his book, and on the other hand, playing into the hands of Nasser. Now, having said that, Mr. X knows where I'm going, namely to the frequent statement made that you and your Black Muslim movement are in close contact with Nasser, are becoming a part of his worldwide machinery, etc., etc. And having said that, I will let you and Mr. Berger take up the—

MR. X   Number one—the distorted picture that the black men in America have had in the past of Africa is all a part of the crime that the American white man has committed in distorting that picture purposely. Number two— it is true that the emergence of African nations probably isn't impressive to the *big* Negro in America, but the masses of black people in America are impressed. Number three—you can't say that the emergence of Africa doesn't affect the condition of the black people here.

John F. Kennedy himself a couple of months ago issued practically an ultimatum to the whites in Maryland and Virginia not to Jim Crow the Africans who are in this country. Despite the fact that the Negroes provided the balance to get him in office, he can open up his mouth and eliminate the barriers that the Africans run into, but the American so-called Negro is still begging for an integrated cup of coffee.

MR. GOLDMAN   Just a minute, Mr. X. May I get directly

to this point? A number of people state that Negro Muslimism is a way of tying a number of American Negroes into Mr. Nasser's imperialist purposes.

MR. X   Number one—we're not Negroes. Number two—there's no such thing as Muslimism. It's Islam, and that religion is practiced by 725 million non-white people in Africa and in Asia. I think it's absurd to connect us with any one geographic area when the Muslim world stretches from China right up to the shores of West Africa. Everyone in the Muslim world is our brother and we are brothers to them and considered brothers by them.

Now because Nasser probably poses a threat to Israel and the people of Israeli descent have a lot of power and influence over the public media in America, they put out the propaganda concerning the danger of our people here getting connected with someone over there. We're not connected with anybody but our feeling is all dark people today should get together and toss aside the shackles of a common oppressor and that common oppressor is that man who has been sitting up there in Europe.

I think you'll find that not only are the Arabs, who are dark people, getting together but they're getting together throughout Africa and Asia. That's why you're having such a problem now in the United Nations. And this is not something that you should blame on the Muslims. The white man should examine his own record and he can see that his record, the seeds that he has sown, are coming up today. He doesn't like the crop that he planted.

MR. GOLDMAN   Mr. Berger, do you want to comment on this potential tie?

MR. BERGER   I don't believe that the Black Muslims in this country are or will be deeply involved with the propaganda machine of any foreign country. I don't believe that that's so from what I've been able to observe. I do think also that Nasser particularly would have a great deal of difficulty if he tried to associate himself with the Black Muslims. Not only the difficulty that the Black Muslims would give him, but also the difficulty that—to borrow a phrase—the so-called white Muslims in this country might give him. I don't think that they want to be—these so-called white Muslims in this country—want to be associated with the Black Muslims in this country. This is another reason why I would discount those claims of foreign influence on the Black Muslims.

MR. GOLDMAN   Mr. Haley, a word?

MR. HALEY   I must again dissent. I think this preoccupation with Muslims or Africa takes us away from the main point, namely, the Negro in America.

MALCOLM X
TALKS WITH
KENNETH B. CLARK*

MALCOLM X is a punctual man. He arrived at the television studio, with two of his closest advisers, at the precise time of our appointment. He and his friends were immaculately dressed, with no outward sign of their belonging to either a separate sect or the ministry. Minister Malcolm X (and he insists upon being called "Minister Malcolm") is a tall, handsome man in his late thirties. He is clearly a dominant personality whose disciplined power seems all the more evident in contrast to the studied deference paid him by his associates. He is conscious of the impression of power which he seeks to convey, and one suspects that he does not permit himself to become too casual in his relations with others.

Although Minister Malcolm X seems proud of the fact that he did not go beyond the eighth grade, he speaks generally with the vocabulary and the tone of a college-educated person. Happy when this is pointed out to him, he explains that he has read extensively since joining the Black Muslim movement. His role as the chief spokesman for this movement in the New York-Washington region is, he insists, to raise the level of pride and accomplishment in his followers.

Malcolm X has been interviewed on radio, television, and by newspapermen probably more than any other Negro leader during the past two years. He shows the effects of these interminable interviews by a professional calm, and

* June 1963.

what appears to be an ability to turn on the proper amount of emotion, resentment, and indignation, as needed. One certainly does not get the impression of spontaneity. On the contrary, one has the feeling that Minister Malcolm has anticipated every question and is prepared with the appropriate answer, an answer which is consistent with the general position of the Black Muslim movement, as defined by the Honorable Elijah Muhammad.

We began the interview by talking about Malcolm X's childhood:

MALCOLM X   I was born in Omaha, Nebraska, back in 1925—that period when the Ku Klux Klan was quite strong in that area at that time—and grew up in Michigan, partially. Went to school there.

CLARK   What part of Michigan?

MALCOLM X   Lansing. I went to school there—as far as the eighth grade. And left there and then grew up in Boston and in New York.

CLARK   Did you travel with your family from Omaha to Michigan to Boston?

MALCOLM X   Yes. When I was born—shortly after I was born—the Ku Klux Klan gave my father an ultimatum—or my parents an ultimatum—about remaining there, so they left and went to——

CLARK   What was the basis of this ultimatum?

MALCOLM X   My father was a Garveyite, and in those days, you know, it wasn't the thing for a black man to be outspoken or to deviate from the accepted stereotype that was usually considered the right image for Negroes to fulfill or reflect.

CLARK   Of all the words that I have read about you, this is the first time that I've heard that your father was a Garveyite. And, in fact, he *was* an outspoken black nationalist in the nineteen twenties?

MALCOLM X   He was both a Garveyite and a minister, a Baptist minister. In those days you know how it was and how it still is; it has only changed in the method, but the same things still exist: whenever a black man was outspoken, he was considered crazy or dangerous. And the police department and various branches of the law usually were interwoven with that Klan element, so the Klan had the backing of the police, and usually the police had the backing of the Klan, same as today.

CLARK   So in effect your father was required, or he was forced—

MALCOLM X   Yes, they burned the house that we lived in in Omaha, and I think this was in 1925, and we moved to Lansing, Michigan, and we ran into the same experience there. We lived in an integrated neighborhood, by the way, then. And it only proves that whites were as much against integration as they are now, only then they were more openly against it. And today they are shrewd in saying they are for it, but they still make it impossible for you to integrate. So we moved to Michigan and the same thing happened: they burned our home there. And he was—like I say—he was a clergyman, a Christian; and it was Christians who burned the home in both places—people who teach, you know, religious tolerance and brotherhood and all of that.

CLARK   Did you start school in Michigan?

MALCOLM X   Yes.

CLARK   How long did you stay in Michigan?

MALCOLM X   I think I completed the eighth grade while I was still in Michigan.

CLARK   And then where did you go?

MALCOLM X   To Boston.

CLARK   Did you go to high school in Boston?

MALCOLM X   No, I have never gone to high school.

CLARK   You've never gone to high school?

MALCOLM X   The eighth grade was as far as I went.

CLARK   That's phenomenal.

MALCOLM X   Everything I know above the eighth grade, I've learned from Mr. Muhammad. He's been my teacher, and I think he's a better teacher than I would have had had I continued to go to the public schools.

CLARK   How did you meet Mr. Muhammad?

MALCOLM X   I was—when I was in prison, in 1947, I

first heard about his teaching; about his religious message. And at that time I was an atheist, myself. I had graduated from Christianity to agnosticism on into atheism.

CLARK   Were the early experiences in Nebraska and Michigan where, as you say, Christians burned the home of your father, who was a Christian minister—were these experiences the determinants of your moving away from Christianity?

MALCOLM X   No, no, they weren't, because despite those experiences, I, as I said, lived a thoroughly integrated life. Despite all the experiences I had in coming up—and my father was killed by whites at a later date—I still thought that there were some good white people; at least the ones *I* was associating with, you know, were supposed to be different. There wasn't any experience, to my knowledge, that opened up my eyes, because right up until the time that I went to prison, I was still integrated into the white society and thought that there were some good ones.

CLARK   Was it an integrated prison?

MALCOLM X   It was an integrated prison at the prison level, but the administrators were all white. You usually find that in any situation that is supposed to be based on integration. At the low level they integrate, but at the administrative or executive level you find whites running it.

CLARK   How long did you stay in prison?

MALCOLM X   About seven years.

CLARK   And you were in prison in Boston. And this is where you got in touch with—

MALCOLM X   My family became Muslims; accepted the religion of Islam, and one of them who had spent pretty much—had spent quite a bit of time with me on the streets of New York out here in Harlem had been exposed to the religion of Islam. He accepted it, and it made such a profound change in him. He wrote to me and was telling me about it. Well, I had completely eliminated Christianity. After getting into prison and having time to think, I could see the hypocrisy of Christianity. Even before I went to prison, I had already become an atheist and I could see the hypocrisy of Christianity. Most of my associates were white; they were either Jews or Christians, and I saw hypocrisy on both sides. None of them really practiced what they preached.

CLARK   Minister Malcolm—

MALCOLM X   Excuse me, but despite the fact that I had detected this, my own intellectual strength was so weak, or so lacking, till I was not in a position to really see or come to a conclusion concerning this hypocrisy until I had gotten to where I could think a little bit and had learned more about the religion of Islam. Then I could go back and remember all of these experiences and things that I had actually heard—discussions that I had participated in myself with whites. It had made everything that Mr. Muhammad was saying add up.

CLARK   I see.

MALCOLM X   He was the one who drew the line and enabled me to add up everything and say that this is this, and I haven't met anyone since then who was capable of showing me an answer more strong or with more weight than the answer that the Honorable Elijah Muhammad has given.

CLARK   I'd like to go back just a little to your life in prison. What was the basis—how did you—

MALCOLM X   Crime. I wasn't framed. I went to prison for what I did, and the reason that I don't have any hesitation or reluctance whatsoever to point out the fact that I went to prison: I firmly believe that it was the Christian society, as you call it, the Judaic-Christian society, that created all of the factors that send so many so-called Negroes to prison. And when these fellows go to prison there is nothing in the system designed to rehabilitate them. There's nothing in the system designed to reform them. All it does is—it's a breeding ground for a more professional type of criminal, especially among Negroes. Since I saw, detected, the reluctance on the part of penologists, prison authorities, to reform men and even detected that—noticed that after a so-called Negro in prison trys to reform and become a better man, the prison authorities are more against *that* man than they were against him when he was completely criminally inclined, so this is again hypocrisy. Not only is the

Christian society itself religious hypocrisy, but the court system is hypocrisy, the entire penal system is hypocrisy. Everything is hypocrisy. Mr. Muhammad came along with his religious gospel and introduced the religion of Islam and showed the honesty of Islam, showed the justice in Islam, the freedom in Islam. Why naturally, just comparing the two, Christianity had already eliminated itself, so all I had to do was accept the religion of Islam. I know today what it has done for me as a person.

CLARK   I notice that the Black Muslim movement has put a great deal of time, effort, and energy in seeking recruits within the prisons.

MALCOLM X   This is incorrect.

CLARK   It is incorrect?

MALCOLM X   It is *definitely* incorrect.

CLARK   Eric Lincoln's book—

MALCOLM X   Well, Lincoln is incorrect himself. Lincoln is just a Christian preacher from Atlanta, Georgia, who wanted to make some money, so he wrote a book and called it *The Black Muslims in America*. We're not even Black Muslims. We are black people in a sense that "black" is an adjective. We are black people who are Muslims because we have accepted the religion of Islam, but what Eric Lincoln shrewdly did was capitalize the letter "b," and made "black" an adjectival noun and then attached it to "Muslim," and now it is used by the press to make it appear that this is the name of an organization. It has no religious connotation or religious motivation or religious objectives.

CLARK   You do not have a systematic campaign for recruiting or rehabilitating?

MALCOLM X   No, no.

CLARK   What about rehabilitation?

MALCOLM X   The reason that the religion of Islam has spread so rapidly in prison is because the average so-called Negro in prison has had experiences enough to make him realize the hypocrisy of everything in this society, and he also has experienced the fact that the system itself is not designed to rehabilitate him or make him turn away from

crime. Then when he hears the religious teaching of the
Honorable Elijah Muhammad that restores to him his
racial pride, his racial identity, and restores to him also the
desire to be a man, to be a human being, he reforms himself. And this spreads so rapidly among the so-called
Negroes in prison that, since the sociologist and the psy-
chologists and the penologist and the criminologist have all
realized their own inability to rehabilitate the criminal,
when Mr. Muhammad comes along and starts rehabilitating
the criminal with just the religious gospel, it's a miracle.
They look upon it as a sociological phenomenon or psychological phenomenon, and it gets great publicity.

CLARK   You do not, therefore, have to actively recruit.

MALCOLM X   The Honorable Elijah Muhammad has no
active effort to convert or recruit men in prison any more
so than he does Negroes, period. I think that what you
should realize is that in America there are 20 million black
people, all of whom are in prison. You don't have to go to
Sing Sing to be in prison. If you're born in America with
a black skin, you're born in prison, and the masses of black
people in America today are beginning to regard our plight
or predicament in this society as one of a prison inmate.
And when they refer to the President, he's just another
warden to whom they turn to open the cell door, but it's no
different. It's the same thing, and just as the warden in the
prison couldn't rehabilitate those men, the President in this
country couldn't rehabilitate or change the thinking of
the masses of black people. And as the Honorable Elijah
Muhammad has been able to go behind the prison walls—
the physical prison walls—and release those men from that
which kept them criminals, he likewise on a mass scale
throughout this country—he is able to send his religious
message into the so-called Negro community and rehabilitate the thinking of our people and make them conquer
the habits and the vices and the evils that had held us in the
clutches of this white man's society.

CLARK   I think, Minister Malcolm, what you have just
said brings me to trying to hear from you directly your
ideas concerning the philosophy of the Black Muslim movement. Among the things that have been written about this

movement, the things which stand out are the fact that this movement preaches hatred for whites; that it preaches black supremacy; that it, in fact, preaches, or if it does not directly preach, it accepts the inevitability of violence as a factor in the relationship between the races. Now—

MALCOLM X   That's a strange thing. You know, the Jews here in this city rioted last week against some Nazi, and I was listening to a program last night where the other Jew —where a Jewish commentator was congratulating what the Jews did to this Nazi; complimenting them for it. Now no one mentioned violence in connection with what the Jews did against these Nazis. But these same Jews, who will condone violence on their part or hate someone whom they consider to be an enemy, will join Negro organizations and tell Negroes to be non-violent; that it is wrong or im-moral, unethical, unintelligent for Negroes to reflect some kind of desire to defend themselves from the attacks of whites who are trying to brutalize us. The Muslims who follow the Honorable Elijah Muhammad don't advocate violence, but Mr. Muhammad does teach us that any human being who is intelligent has the right to defend himself. You can't take a black man who is being bitten by dogs and accuse him of advocating violence because he tries to defend himself from the bite of the dog. If you notice, the people who are sicking the dogs on the black people are never accused of violence; they are never accused of hate. Nothing like that is ever used in the con-text of a discussion when it's about them. It is only when the black man begins to explode and erupt after he has had too much that they say that the black man is violent, and as long as these whites are putting out a doctrine that paves the way to justify their mistreatment of blacks, this is never called hate. It is only when the black man himself begins to spell out the historic deeds of what whites have been doing to him in this country that the shrewd white man with his control over the news media and propaganda makes it appear that the black people today are advocating some kind of hate. Mr. Muhammad teaches us to love each other, and when I say love each other—love our own kind. This is all black people need to be taught in this country because the only ones whom we don't love are our own kind. Most of the Negroes you see running around here talking about "love everybody"—they don't have any love whatsoever for their own kind. When they say, "Love everybody," what they are doing is setting up a situation for us to love white people. This is what their philosophy is. Or when they say, "Suffer peacefully," they mean suffer peacefully at the hands of the white man, because the same non-violent Negroes are the advocators of non-violence. If a Negro attacks one of them, they'll fight that Negro all over Harlem. It's only when the white man attacks them that they believe in non-violence, all of them.

CLARK   Mr. X, is this a criticism of the Reverend Martin Luther King, Jr.?

MALCOLM X   You don't have to criticize Reverend Martin Luther King, Jr. His actions criticize him.

CLARK   What do you mean by this?

MALCOLM X   Any Negro who teaches other Negroes to turn the other cheek is disarming that Negro. Any Negro who teaches Negroes to turn the other cheek in the face of attack is disarming that Negro of his God-given right, of his moral right, of his natural right, of his intelligent right to defend himself. Everything in nature can defend itself, and is right in defending itself, except the American Negro. And men like King—their job is to go among Negroes and teach Negroes "Don't fight back." He doesn't tell them, "Don't fight each other." "Don't fight the white man" is what he's saying in essence, because the followers of Martin Luther King, Jr., will cut each other from head to foot, but they will not do anything to defend themselves against the attacks of the white man. But King's philosophy falls upon the ears of only a small minority. The majority or masses of black people in this country are more inclined in the direction of the Honorable Elijah Muhammad than Martin Luther King, Jr.

CLARK   Is it not a fact though—

MALCOLM X   White people follow King. White people pay King. White people subsidize King. White people support King. But the masses of black people don't support Martin Luther King, Jr. King is the best weapon that the white man, who wants to brutalize Negroes, has ever gotten in this country, because he is setting up a situation where, when the white man wants to attack Negroes, they can't defend themselves, because King has put this foolish philosophy out—you're not supposed to fight or you're not supposed to defend yourself.

CLARK   But Mr. X, is it not a fact that Reverend King's movement was successful in Montgomery—

MALCOLM X   You can't tell me that you have had success —excuse me, sir.

CLARK   Was it not a success in Birmingham?

MALCOLM X   No, no. What kind of success did they get in Birmingham? A chance to sit at a lunch counter and drink some coffee with a cracker—that's success? A chance to—thousands of little children went to jail; they didn't get out, they were bonded out by King. They had to *pay* their way out of jail. That's not any kind of advancement or success.

CLARK   What is advancement from the point of view of the Muslims?

MALCOLM X   Any time dogs have bitten black women, bitten black children—when I say dogs, that is four-legged dogs and two-legged dogs have brutalized thousands of black people—and the one who advocates himself as their leader is satisfied in making a compromise or a deal with the same ones who did this to these people only if they will offer him a job, one job, downtown for one Negro or things of that sort, I don't see where there's any kind of success, sir; it's a sellout. Negroes in Birmingham are in worse condition now than they were then because the line is more tightly drawn. And to say that some moderate— to say that things are better now because a different man, a different white man, a different Southern white man is in office now, who's supposed to be a moderate, is to tell me that you are better off dealing with a fox than you were when you were dealing with a wolf. The ones that they were dealing with previously were wolves, and they didn't hide the fact that they were wolves. The man that they got to deal with now is a fox, but he's no better than the wolf.

Only he's better in his ability to lull the Negroes to sleep, and he'll do that as long as they listen to Dr. Martin Luther King, Jr.

CLARK   What would be the goals, or what are the goals of the Black Muslim movement? What would the Black Muslim movement insist upon in Birmingham, in Montgomery, and in Jackson, Mississippi, etc.?

MALCOLM X   Well, number one, the Honorable Elijah Muhammad teaches us that the solution will never be brought about by politicians, it will be brought about by God, and that the only way the black man in this country today can receive respect and recognition of other people is to stand on his own feet; get something for himself and do something for himself; and the solution that God has given the Honorable Elijah Muhammad is the same as the solution that God gave to Moses when the Hebrews in the Bible were in a predicament similar to the predicament of the so-called Negroes here in America today, which is nothing other than a modern house of bondage, or a modern Egypt, or a modern Babylon. And Moses' answer was to separate these slaves from their slave master and show the slaves how to go to a land of their own where they would serve a God of their own and a religion of their own and have a country of their own in which they could feed themselves, clothe themselves, and shelter themselves.

CLARK   In fact then, you're saying that the Black Muslim movement—

MALCOLM X   It's not a Black Muslim movement.

CLARK   All right, then—

MALCOLM X   We are black people who are Muslims because we believe in the religion of Islam.

CLARK   —this movement which you so ably represent actually desires separation.

MALCOLM X   Complete separation; not only physical separation but moral separation. This is why the Honorable Elijah Muhammad teaches the black people in this country that we must stop drinking, we must stop smoking, we must stop committing fornication and adultery, we must stop gambling and cheating and using profanity, we must stop

showing disrespect for our women, we must reform ourselves as parents so we can set the proper example for our
children. Once we reform ourselves of these immoral
habits, that makes us more godly, more godlike, more
righteous. That means we are qualified then, to be on
God's side, and it puts God on our side. God becomes
our champion then, and it makes it possible for us to
accomplish our own aims.

CLARK   This movement then, is not particularly sympathetic with the integrationist goals of the NAACP, CORE,
Martin Luther King, Jr., and the student non-violent
movement.

MALCOLM X   Mister Muhammad teaches us that integration is only a trick on the part of the white man today to
lull Negroes to sleep, to lull them into thinking that the
white man is changing and actually trying to keep us here;
but America itself, because of the seeds that it has sown in
the past against the black man, is getting ready to reap the
whirlwind today, reap the harvest. Just as Egypt had to pay
for its crime that it committed for enslaving the Hebrews,
the Honorable Elijah Muhammad teaches us that America
has to pay today for the crime that is committed in enslaving the so-called Negroes.

CLARK   There is one question that has bothered me a
great deal about your movement, and it involves just a little
incident. Rockwell, who is a self-proclaimed white supremacist and American Nazi was given an honored front row
position at one of your—

MALCOLM X   This is incorrect.

CLARK   Am I wrong?

MALCOLM X   This is a false statement that has been put
out by the press. And Jews have used it to spread anti-
Muslim propaganda throughout this country. Mister Muhammad had an open convention to which he invited
anyone, black and white. (And this is another reason why
we keep white people out of our meetings.) He invited
everyone, both black and white, and Rockwell came.
Rockwell came the same as any other white person came,
and when we took up a collection, we called out the
names of everyone who made a donation. Rockwell's name

was called out the same as anybody else's, and this was projected to make it look like Rockwell was financing the Muslims. And secondly, Rockwell came to another similar meeting. At this meeting Mister Muhammad gave anyone who wanted to oppose him or congratulate him an opportunity to speak. Rockwell spoke; he was not even allowed up on the rostrum; he spoke from a microphone from which other whites spoke at the same meeting. And again, the Jewish press, or the Jewish who are a part of the press—Jewish *people* who are part of the press—used this as propaganda to make it look like Rockwell was in cahoots with the Muslims. Rockwell, to us, is no different from any other white man. One of the things that I *will* give Rockwell credit for: He preaches and practices the same thing. And these other whites running around here posing as liberals, patting Negroes on the back—they think the same thing that Rockwell thinks, only they speak a different talk, a different language.

CLARK   Minister Malcolm, you have mentioned the Jews and the Jewish press and Jewish propaganda frequently in this discussion. It has been said frequently that an important part of your movement is anti-Semitism. I have seen you deny this.

MALCOLM X   No. We're a—

CLARK   Would you want to comment on this?

MALCOLM X   No, the followers of Mr. Muhammad aren't anti-anything but anti-wrong, anti-exploitation, and anti-oppression. A lot of the Jews have a guilty conscience when you mention exploitation because they realize that they control 90 per cent of the businesses in every Negro community from the Atlantic to the Pacific and that they get more benefit from the Negro's purchasing power than the Negro himself does or than any other white or any other segment of the white community does, so they have a guilt complex on this. And whenever you mention exploitation of Negroes, most Jews think that you're talking about them, and in order to hide what they are guilty of, they accuse you of being anti-Semitic.

CLARK   Do you believe the Jews are more guilty of this exploitation than are—

MALCOLM X   Jews belong to practically every Negro organization Negroes have. Arthur B. Spingarn, the head of the NAACP, is Jewish. Every organization that Negroes— When I say the head of the NAACP, the *president* of the NAACP is Jewish. The same Jews wouldn't let you become the president of the B'nai B'rith or their different organizations.

CLARK   Thank you very much. You have certainly presented important parts of your movement, your point of view. I think we understand more clearly now some of your goals, and I'd like to know if we could talk some other time, if you would tell me a little about what you think is the future of the Negro in America other than separation.

MALCOLM X   Yes. As long as they have interviews with the Attorney General and take Negroes to pose as leaders, all of whom are married either to white men or white women, you'll always have a race problem. When Baldwin took that crew with him to see Kennedy, he took the wrong crew. And as long as they take the wrong crew to talk to that man, you're not going to get anywhere near any solution to this problem in this country.

A VISIT FROM THE FBI *

AGENT   Morning, how do you do. We are with the FBI. You have a couple minutes, we'd like to talk to you.

MALCOLM   Come on in.

AGENT   I am sorry, did we get you . . .

MALCOLM   I was on the telephone. Your name is . . .

AGENT   Beckwith.

MALCOLM   And your name is . . .

AGENT   Fulton.

MALCOLM   Which office are you from?

AGENT   From New York. There's only one out here. We have two problems we would like to talk to you about. One, . . . why don't you take the article and read it. You might have been called by a couple of reporters, is that right?

MALCOLM   Yes.

AGENT   What did they quote you saying, nonsense?

MALCOLM   I cussed them out. What paper is this from?

AGENT   One of the New York ones, I don't know, I think the *Times,* I am not sure. The problem in this connection is that we have every reason to believe that this fella lied to us when he gave us the original.

MALCOLM   You should . . .

* May 29, 1964. Malcolm X was expecting this visit from the FBI. He set up the tape recorder, under a couch, before they arrived.

AGENT   Now, of course, that is a violation of the Federal law, so he is in jail awaiting trial. Now the U.S. attorney up there preparing the case wanted you interviewed to disprove part of his story which isn't here; that he attended a meeting, I believe Monday or Tuesday, the fourteenth, in Rochester—from about seven or eight until ten or ten-fifteen at night, at which you were there. Of course, you were very well known, naturally, and how he got your name, I don't know. It is part of our proof, see, showing that you in fact were not there. And, if that is the case, that was on Tuesday night, wasn't it?

MALCOLM   Yes, on January 14. Ordinarily, I could have been anywhere, but it just so happens that on that night I was at the International Hotel, out here at the airport, Kennedy Airport, with a writer, Alex Haley, who writes for the *Reader's Digest*. You can get his number from the *Reader's Digest*, he lives in Rome, New York.

AGENT   Yes, I have heard his name. Doubleday is doing a book. He wrote us a letter.

MALCOLM   Right, he wrote a letter.

AGENT   In fact, copies are right here. When that letter came in, he said that Egypt was trying to interview him about something. No, they had been down to where he formerly lived. We had no information on it other than the person who got the letter. So you were with him that night?

MALCOLM   Yes, I was with him, and strange as it may seem, I got a call the next day from a lawyer downtown. Someone had apparently gotten hit over here on Junction Boulevard and Northern Boulevard and my license number had been turned in and he was saying it was I.

AGENT   Do you know the lawyer's name?

MALCOLM   Epstein or something.

AGENT   You didn't get his address or anything?

MALCOLM   No, but as far as I can recall, his name was Epstein. So, luckily, I was able to tell them where I was and Haley was with me until two o'clock in the morning. I picked him up at the airport.

AGENT   That would encompass the entire time. What time did you leave there?

MALCOLM   Must have been around seven o'clock.

AGENT   You said you picked him up at the airport. Had he flown in from Rome?

MALCOLM   No, he flew in from Chicago. He was doing a story on Fuller for the *Digest*, for the *Digest* or *Playboy*, one of the two.

AGENT   You would have no objection to us referring to our conversation if it is necessary to ask him to corroborate your story, would you?

MALCOLM   No. It was quite fortunate, frankly, that I was tied up with him that night, because I could have been anywhere.

AGENT   Well, of course, as you know, we are aware of most of your activities and that is true. That is one reason why we couldn't—on our own—eliminate the fact that you were in fact in or not in Rochester.

MALCOLM   I was here.

AGENT   Had you been in Rochester at any time around this day?

MALCOLM   I haven't been in Rochester in probably six months.

AGENT   Do you know this fella, Booker, by any chance?

MALCOLM   No.

AGENT   Does that name mean anything to you?

MALCOLM   No.

AGENT   Philip Alpert?

MALCOLM   I know a lot of people that I wouldn't know by name.

AGENT   Well, he used the name up there, Alpert Leyton, spelled L E Y T O N, he originally used it.

MALCOLM   I don't know it. What did he say, somebody had a meeting up there . . .

AGENT   Well, basically, his information, when he gave it at first, we couldn't prove or disprove it, so that caused quite a commotion with us. Someone is going to assassinate

the President. I mean, that is of some significance. He
attended a meeting. Now this is his story, briefly. On Tuesday night from, I don't know the times, eight to ten, something like that. A meeting of the Muslims in Rochester. He
couldn't tell us the exact place, he was blindfolded and
taken there, which, of course, is not the way you people,
I know, usually do things. This is his story. Ten were
present, including you, and the assassination was planned—
not the details, but it was planned to the extent that the
ten people would get down in two cars—five each—to
Washington, leaving late that night or early the next morning. Now beyond there, the story fizzles out as to how they
were going to do it. They had no arms as far as he knew.
But, they were definitely going down. Well, of course,
when we got this over the phone, you know, my God, you
know. So when we kept talking to him and he finally admitted, he said no, it was false. Of course, then we threw
him in jail for fraud against the government. That is the
kind of case—that is the statute under which we have
authority to bring him before the commission. He couldn't
make bail, so, of course, he went to trial and the trial is
coming up shortly. I don't know when the trial will be.
Now you'd be put in the position, if necessary—of course,
this is between you and me. In other words, I don't know
that you would even be called, but you would be a government witness in this case. Of course you would be protected
by a subpoena and of course any expenses.

MALCOLM   I shouldn't see where I have to get involved
in something like this. Let me tell you what it is. It is so
ridiculous that what it does, actually what it does . . .

AGENT   I will tell you the first reply that I made was that
it was made up probably for that purpose, to embarrass
your organization.

MALCOLM   Certainly that is what it sounds like to me. It
is so ridiculous, number one, that it sounds like to me
that it was something that was invented even though it
would be denied, it would still serve as a propaganda thing.

AGENT   I agree. My first reaction was that it is possible
that some people are going to do that, but not the Muslims.

MALCOLM   No.

AGENT   Of course, that doesn't relieve us of the responsi-bility of trying to do something about it. This information of yours, seems as how it is a "fraud against the Govern-ment" case, the way we record the information is at your discretion. We, of course, will make a memorandum of our conversation on this point, unless you would prefer to have it written out and you sign it—

MALCOLM   No, I won't sign anything.

AGENT   It is entirely up to you. I will phrase it you prefer not to give any signed statement in this matter. You have no objection to us recording that?

MALCOLM   I don't see why I should have to get in it.

AGENT   You don't, but I have to ask you a few ques-tions. May I take a moment here to get a detail straightened out? Now, as particular to that night of the fourteenth, you said you picked Mr. Haley up?

MALCOLM   Yes.

AGENT   Was that the International Airport you picked him up at?

MALCOLM   Yes.

AGENT   He came into that airport?

MALCOLM   Yes. And then . . .

AGENT   And then you went to the International Hotel?

MALCOLM   Checked in under Alex Haley, under his name. I wasn't checked in there. He had to work. It was about 7 P.M.

AGENT   About 7 P.M.?

MALCOLM   Yes, about 7 P.M.

AGENT   You remained with him until . . .

MALCOLM   About two o'clock in the morning. A waiter came in twice. One time around eight and another time around one o'clock.

AGENT   You didn't know his name.

MALCOLM   No. It would be easy to check.

AGENT   You remained there until two and then you came home?

MALCOLM   Right, I came home.

AGENT   After meeting with Mr. Haley you spent the rest of the night there?

MALCOLM   I haven't been in touch with him since I left. I don't know what time he left the next day.

AGENT   He was scheduled to leave the next day by plane, I presume?

MALCOLM   Most likely.

AGENT   You can see one of the big problems we have on a thing like this. It is trying to prove a negative, so to speak.

MALCOLM   But you know, you have people in Washington who are past masters for making positive out of negative.

AGENT   No comment. In all probability, this is the type of party who is going to go up and say "I plead guilty." But if he doesn't and goes to trial then it is up to us to show that his story was false because that is the charge. He furnished us false information. And, that in fact he knew it was false—which he has already admitted to us.

MALCOLM   What would be his purpose in making a statement like this?

AGENT   I will tell you his reason between us—now I don't know what it is—the reason is that he wanted to test the ability of the government agency. He was worried since President Kennedy's assassination that we may not be on the ball. I don't know.

MALCOLM   Well, was he a Negro?

AGENT   Yes, from Baltimore. He gave us a rather ridiculous story. He wanted to test the capabilities of making any preparations. Now, that is what he said. Of course, we right from the start were pretty much aware that he was wrong—he made up a story. He said he joined the Muslims—and the blindfold bit.

MALCOLM   Has he ever been a Muslim?

AGENT   We don't know for sure. As far as we know, no. He claims that he joined in Baltimore. He said he joined and then became a junior dragon.

MALCOLM   What is that supposed to be?

AGENT   We don't know. Of course, we know better and you know better—and then afterward, after serving his time as a junior dragon, he then became a dragon. He involved you in several different ways in addition to being there on that night. See, he probably knows your name. I would like to bring this out to you. He said in the summer of '63, he was designated by the Baltimore temple as a research specialist to make a study of Negro problems; home, house, family, so fourth, in Baltimore, and as a research specialist in Baltimore it had to have your approval since you were in charge of the entire East Coast of the Nation of Islam at that time. He said you approved his position as a research specialist in Baltimore.

MALCOLM   I have no knowledge of it, although we do need some research . . .

AGENT   Then he said that last summer, with your approval, he was designated the research specialist for the State of New York. That is when he went to Rochester and was doing research of this type in that area. He turned his reports over to Elmer X—he claimed—and then he passed them on to you.

MALCOLM   Elmer X who?

AGENT   He said it was Elmer X up there, and the only Elmer X we were acquainted with was Mr. Grant in Buffalo. As you may well be aware of, he was interviewed as a result of some investigation in that area. All members were contacted. He turned his reports over to Elmer X and that was the last he saw of them. Those are the other two positions where he involved you, being named a research specialist for the State of New York with your approval.

MALCOLM   Has he backed up on that score?

AGENT   Yes.

MALCOLM   He is a nut.

AGENT   Well, not being a psychiatrist . . .

MALCOLM   You wouldn't have to be a psychiatrist. You wouldn't have to be a policeman to know that someone is breaking the law. Common sense. If you have a knowledge of the law, you know once you are breaking it. And this man is even violating laws of intelligence.

AGENT   I think that clears up that. The other problem is probably what you assume we came up for—to obtain any information you want to give us about the Muslims . . .

MALCOLM   I don't assume anything.

AGENT   That is a very general statement on my part. But, as you know, we follow the activities of the Muslims as best we can but we are always looking for new avenues for information, but who better than the head of the Muslims. At least, up until a month ago or something like that. That substantially is the second reason. We used this—this other thing, it came at a very good time as an excuse to push us out here to talk to you. Several of the fellows talked to you several years ago, as I recall.

MALCOLM   I haven't spoken to the FBI since 1956. It was about eight years ago.

AGENT   Yes, about that. How is your suspension status?

MALCOLM   No one knows but Mr. Muhammad, you'd have to ask him.

AGENT   You are still on suspension now? You are not working or teaching now?

MALCOLM   I am still under the suspension.

AGENT   That is a temporary thing as far as you know?

MALCOLM   He is the only one who can give out any information. I couldn't say nothing behind what he would say.

AGENT   I think he said it was a temporary suspension. How soon you resume your duties, we would be—as you sure know—interested in having you help us out.

MALCOLM   Help you out doing what? We are always helping out the government. We have been cleaning up crime . . .

AGENT   Fine, fine, fine . . .

MALCOLM   We help it out more than it helps itself. We are at least able to reform the people who have been made criminals by this society; by the corruption of this society.

And, anyway, to help it out other than that, I wouldn't even know how to begin.

AGENT   What we are interested in, basically, are the people who belong. The names of the members.

MALCOLM   From what I understand, you have all of that.

AGENT   No comment. The teachings, plans, programs.

MALCOLM   No teaching is more public than ours and I don't think you will find anybody more blunt in stating it publicly than we do. I don't think you can go anywhere on this earth and find anybody who expresses their views on matters more candidly than we do.

AGENT   I can only agree with you. You are right. The main thing is there is a certain area of responsibility— this is getting into our angle of it. What we really want are the names of all those who belong, who they are, identification.

MALCOLM   I don't even know them.

AGENT   You keep no records?

MALCOLM   That is not my job. I am just a preacher.

AGENT   But somebody up there keeps the records.

MALCOLM   I don't know who. I don't have any knowledge of those kinds of things. With all the responsibilities that I have had, it is difficult for me to worry about names, plus you would insult my intelligence asking me for them. In fact, you would insult your own because it would mean that your own intelligence isn't heavy enough to weigh me and know in advance what I am going to say when you ask that question.

AGENT   Well, without getting into an argument on semantics, you don't know until you ask . . .

MALCOLM   There is no semantics. That again goes into psychology . . .

AGENT   We have had people that—not this group in particular—who have been just as vociferous against whatever we are investigating. The Communists. Make a good case of it. The Communists for twenty years, you know, they hate everything. We've been told to investigate. I am going to tell you something—you never know until you ask. That has happened so many times. Sometimes you are convinced, but sometimes money brings out the information. I don't intend to insult you here.

MALCOLM   According to the Secretary of the Treasury, this Government's money is in trouble. According to Government economists, the dollar itself is in so much trouble a person would be a fool to sell his soul for one of these decreasing dollars.

AGENT   I couldn't agree with you more. You would be a fool to sell your soul even if the dollar were increasing. This has nothing to do with selling your soul. If you're gonna look at it that way, O.K.

MALCOLM   Depends on how you look at it. I frankly believe that what Mr. Muhammad teaches is 1000 per cent true. Secondly, I believe that everything he has said will come to pass. I believe it. I believe it more strongly today than I did ten years ago because I have seen too much evidence. But, today, all of your world events that are shaping up, total up to too much evidence toward what he said is coming to pass. World events today would make me stronger in my convictions than they would have made me ten years ago.

AGENT   But that is beside the point of what I am trying to get out of you. Fine if that all comes to pass. I have no control of it. All we want to know is the names of the people that are in the organization, and if it is so public and so forth, by your own logic there would seem to be no objection to your saying "I am a Muslim."

MALCOLM   That part of the tree is the root; I mean, the root is always beneath the ground.

AGENT   You don't have to explain that but I don't know what you are talking about . . . Well, would it be fair to say then in answer to a question whether or not you would cooperate with the Government in furnishing pertinent information as I have described?

MALCOLM   I say we have always cooperated with them. The Muslims are the most cooperative group in this country with the Government in that the Muslims are doing work that the Government itself is incapable of doing . . .

AGENT   I say certain information pertinent to our investigation . . .

MALCOLM   You would have to go to Mr. Muhammad for pertinent information. I don't have access to pertinent information.

AGENT   Then it would be fair here again, to say a denial of your desire to furnish information—any information you might—

MALCOLM   I don't know what you mean by that.

AGENT   Well, the names of the members.

MALCOLM   That is not my department.

AGENT   But still you know a lot of names.

MALCOLM   No, I know probably less names than anybody. People I see, I call them brother and sister. I know no names.

AGENT   You have no access?

MALCOLM   I don't ever take on burdens that are not necessary and having names of people that are not necessary to me . . .

AGENT   No, but if you were so disposed to cooperate with us, would you . . .

MALCOLM   What do you mean by cooperate?

AGENT   You giving us any names that you could get . . .

MALCOLM   I am not so disposed.

AGENT   No, that is my point . . .

MALCOLM   As I say, we as an organization . . .

AGENT   Well, that is what I am trying to get out of you, whether or not you . . .

MALCOLM   We as an organization, and I am always an organization—that is why I say we. We cooperate with the Government in that we do what they can't toward correcting the morals of people . . .

AGENT   Of course we are with the FBI, we don't have any jurisdiction or social interest in the morals of anybody . . .

MALCOLM   What I mean collectively, the FBI is supposed to be concerned . . .

AGENT   No, not at all.

MALCOLM   Hoover wrote a book here, not long ago . . .

AGENT   He said the public should be, but we investigate many things. Crimes, anything of interest to the Government and anything that is assigned to us by the executive President or the Attorney General . . . to get information, that is the limit. Now, a citizen, sure, very nice anytime you can keep someone from committing a crime. Very nice. But our interest here in coming to you is not as one citizen to another. I mean we are here as representatives of a Government agency, asking specific things. I am not talking to you as a neighbor. I don't know you and you don't know me.

MALCOLM   There is no Government agency that can ever expect to get any information out of me that is in any way detrimental to any religious group or black group for that matter in this country. No Government agency.

AGENT   Fine.

MALCOLM   Because they should use that same energy to go and find who bombed that church down in Alabama and if these Government agencies spent as much time and energy . . .

AGENT   You know what somebody in the South is saying today—if you people would go up north and investigate the Muslims with the same energy you are trying to find this bomb here . . .

MALCOLM   The Muslims don't bomb churches.

AGENT   I know. I didn't say that . . .

MALCOLM   But still, Muslims don't bomb churches. But still, if we broke the law they would have us in jail tomorrow.

AGENT   Let us hope so. Let us hope so.

MALCOLM   If we were a lawbreaking group—no group is more thoroughly investigated than we. No group is more infiltrated with—I call them stool pigeons—than we. Now, if we were breaking the law, the Government would know about it and they would have us locked up.

AGENT   I wish you were telling the truth. You are partially right. I wish you were entirely right. It would make my job so much easier.

MALCOLM   They need to find the bombers of the church . . .

AGENT   Of course, sure, we need to find a lot of things. We need to find that twenty shiploads of corn oil or soybean oil, but it takes time to do . . .

MALCOLM   No, it doesn't take time if you really want to do it.

AGENT   You think anybody can find that out?

MALCOLM   They should find out who murdered those little girls down in Birmingham, Alabama. I believe some Negro could go down and find out.

AGENT   Well, let's send them down there. We will be glad to pay them.

MALCOLM   They are waiting for the FBI. But, if they stop relying on the FBI, then they would do it themselves.

AGENT   I don't want to take up too much of your time. What I am interested in is if you want to help us. And, I put it to you bluntly, and I feel that I got a candid, blunt answer . . .

MALCOLM   That's the best way to put something like that to me—blunt.

AGENT   I don't want to sneak around the bush and try to trap you into saying anything. There is no point to it, because I have in mind a long-range cooperation between you and me or somebody else.

MALCOLM   Well, see, my religion teaches me that you don't have any long-range anything because time is running out.

AGENT   Well, that is fine. That is all right if you believe it.

MALCOLM   I say that with all due respect.

AGENT   I know almost everything you have said at the meetings over the years, I am very familiar with it . . .

MALCOLM   I think the mistake that white people make when they listen to what we say is they think we are just saying it. We believe it. At least I believe it.

AGENT   Some just go for kicks . . .

MALCOLM   You can put someone on me twenty-four hours a day and they will come back and tell you what I am there for.

AGENT   Frankly, one of the reasons we picked this particular time to contact you is because of the suspension.

MALCOLM   The suspension was brought about by my own doing.

AGENT   Exactly, but who knows what was in your mind when you did receive the suspension. In other words, bitterness could have entered into it. It would not be illogical for someone to have spent so many years doing something, then being suspended.

MALCOLM   No, it should make one stronger. It should make him realize that law applies to the law enforcer as well as those who are under the enforcement of the enforcer.

AGENT   You've taken an attitude toward the thing that's almost unhuman really. You have taken the attitude that Mr. Muhammad wants everyone to take if he chastises them, which is fine. More power to you. But you can see it from our viewpoint, that there is at least a chance and this has happened with other members of the organization suspended for some reason or other that we talked to them.

MALCOLM   Well, I can't get bitter when I know that what I was reprimanded for was something that I actually did. What kind of person would I be to get bitter?

AGENT   Well, that is what we came to find out.

MALCOLM   I know.

AGENT   I have no way of knowing unless I ask. Well, that's all. I don't have any other specific questions. Do you have anything you wish to say?

MALCOLM   No, only what I said. I am still concerned about that church down there in Birmingham.

AGENT   We are too. A lot of men are down there working on it.

MALCOLM   There must be a lot of them down there working on it.

AGENT   Offhand, a bombing is one of the hardest types of things to conduct an investigation on. The bomb is left at the church, you don't know when the bomb was left, you don't know when it was thrown. When the bomb goes off, the evidence is gone. With the Medgar Evers killing, it was a different situation. The rifle was found, you had some evidence, you have a bullet in the man—the bullet itself. We could take the bullet from Medgar Evers and put it in the rifle that was found on the scene.

MALCOLM   I bet if they bombed one of these cathedrals with some little white children in it you would have them the next day.

AGENT   They bombed about a year ago—a bomb went off in St. Patrick's.

MALCOLM   St. Patrick's here in New York.

AGENT   As a matter of fact, not too far from Cardinal Spellman's quarters. They never found it.

MALCOLM   Didn't hurt anybody.

AGENT   Broke a window or two. A bomb is a bomb. It is immaterial to us whether a bomb breaks a window or knocks a house down. We have the same responsibility. The next time you may be standing or we may be standing there.

MALCOLM   I can understand that because now I see why so many of these underworld bombings take place and you never hear anything about it.

AGENT   A man out there recently in Chicago stepped on the starter of his car. A bomb is a very difficult thing to handle unless someone comes forward and gives us some information, like somebody who knew something about it, either one of the perpetrators or somebody who overheard them. I was mentioning there like on the Evers case. The bullet itself you could put in the rifle after it was found. Actually, we could put the Beckwith fingerprints on the rifle itself, we can trace the scope of that rifle, we have things to work with. Just like your wife walks down the street, somebody grabs her purse and runs. Now, by the time you call the policeman and the police get there, it is a very difficult thing to try to work with because there is nothing left in the way of evidence. Your best evidence is to find the purse wherever it is thrown. As you may know, that means somebody takes the valuables out and throws the bag over the fence and that is gone. Somebody breaks into your house, there is a great deal of evidence. You can trace fingerprints. If they spring the lock on your door you can take fingerprints from the door, footprints. After a bombing there is nothing there. The Church is down, you can't even pick the bomb up and trace it.

MALCOLM   It would be dangerous for you to ever say that publicly because your bombings would increase.

AGENT   It has been said before, anybody who knows how to make a bomb knows that. Anybody who has been in the service and gone to their bombing school—of course, there it is used for a different thing. It is one of the reasons why gangland wars have a lot of bombings. Nobody gets killed with a machine gun anymore. You can trace a machine gun. Thirty years ago that was the thing. One thing, machine guns are under regular control now. You can't sell a machine gun and not report it—any guns—machine guns in particular. Then, of course, you don't have complete citizen cooperation. You get a lot of resistance. I'm just glad I don't have to try to find them myself. I am always glad when someone else gets the case.

MALCOLM   When Negroes in the South realize the inability of the law down there to protect them, they are going to start doing something to protect themselves.

AGENT   It is perfectly possible.

MALCOLM   You believe it. They are going to start doing something to protect themselves, not because I say so—it is plain common sense.

AGENT   They are going to do something to protect themselves. Suppose they get some men from their own church group to start a vigilante—stand guard outside their church to make sure no one throws a bomb. That is one thing, but are they going to go down because their church was bombed and bomb some other church, that is a different thing. I cannot blame any Negro church—Baptist church in Montgomery or anywhere else—if they have some of their men stand guard at the church to make sure that no one plants a bomb. It is a chance that they have to do it.

MALCOLM   You would do that with your own family and home.

AGENT   If somebody was blowing up homes and you read that yours was next, you would stand guard and have some of the brothers here stand guard, but if you would go out because your house was blown up and blow the man's house across the street up—

MALCOLM   When one society realizes that what happens to another society will happen to it, then that society will take the measures necessary within itself to see that those criminal elements within it don't go out there and do those things.

AGENT   Unfortunately, most people realize that. If it were not true, of course we would have an anarchy and continued violence. You might have a small portion luckily, by small I mean infinitesimal in numbers. Most of the people even in the South realize that. I don't think you would have gone to Birmingham the Sunday of the bombing and found any white people who were jumping for joy because those four Negro children were killed. Undoubtedly, there would have been some of the perpetrators themselves. Maybe some people who are fanatically inclined with the white citizens and the KKK. But the general run of persons—even those same persons who do not want a Negro to sit beside them on the bus, don't want a Negro to sit beside them at a lunch counter, or don't want a Negro to live in the same neighborhood with them —I don't think even though they felt that way, I don't think you would find many who would jump for joy because those four young girls died in a bombing or that any church itself sustained bombing.

MALCOLM   Perhaps you are right, but I think that when white society realizes that the same thing can happen to it that happens to other socieities because of it, then white society will take measures to see that these other things don't happen.

AGENT   Nobody denies there are injustices in the South and in the North.

MALCOLM   That is my contention. I grew up in white society. I think that they underestimated the feelings of Negroes because Negroes have always shown this long-suffering-type attitude.

AGENT   Until recently, I don't think they so much under-estimated as ignored their feelings. I don't think many white people thirty years ago even thought about Negroes. They say, what do you think about Negroes. I don't know, I never thought about it.

MALCOLM   The reason they never thought about them is because they underestimated them. In their subconscious minds, they don't even give the Negro credit for being independent enough to have feelings about certain things.

AGENT   I think that is changing.

MALCOLM   But it is not changing fast enough.

AGENT   Of course, that is a matter of degree, people will always disagree on that.

MALCOLM   I am not saying the condition is not changing fast enough, the awareness on the part of whites isn't changing fast enough . . .

AGENT   That is probably the root of the problem. Legis-lation, laws, etc. make you like white people, make white people like Negroes. There is nothing, really, except edu-cation . . .

MALCOLM   But they are not trying to educate, they are trying to legislate.

AGENT   Exactly.

MALCOLM   They are not even going about it in sincerity. The only reason they are trying to legislate is for po-litical reasons. If they were really aware of the degree of dissatisfaction among Negroes and the ability of Negroes sooner or later to do something about it themselves, then you wouldn't see the politicians playing around, you would see them making a sincere enough effort to educate, but the only man that you will find doing something along educational lines is Mr. Muhammad. He changes the attitude of the Negro and the average person who has become a Muslim. Although he may appear dogmatic in some of his views on race, you won't find him going out and getting in trouble with whites. The only time there is any trouble is when somebody initiates some kind of trouble with him. The reason I say this is because in my experience, Negroes who become Muslims are more capable of dealing with white society on their intelligence plane, I even might say on a reciprocal plane, than the Negro who hasn't been exposed to Mr. Muhammad's teaching, because the Negro who has been exposed to Mr. Muhammad's teaching faces facts and the facts are this is a white man and this is a black man. This is a fact, there is nothing derogatory, and when you have to deny that you are a white man, you are in trouble. When you have to deal with a man on the basis of a complete denial of what you are and pretend you are denying what he is, you can't even talk on that basis, and this is the impasse that the Negro civil rights movements are jockeying for in this white society. They had a boycott yesterday. What did they accomplish? Let me give you an example: I blame the white man for making these Negroes think they are really leaders and they think they have some kind of program. No, they are jockeying him into such a position that you will be so embarrassed in the sight of the world, and after it is all over, you still haven't solved the problem.

AGENT   No, you don't solve things that way, whether by demonstrations or by laws.

MALCOLM   You notice that we don't demonstrate.

AGENT   My mention of education was on the part of the white people.

MALCOLM   Susskind had a good program last night on Channel 2, about this same thing. But it showed in there that you had some Negroes who moved into a white neighborhood and the repercussions, mental reaction. Many whites tried to band together and act intelligent and they found that they couldn't do it. It isn't prejudice, it is their intelligence that won't enable them to do it. They are not going to let someone live and move into their neighborhood who doesn't know how to keep the neighborhood up.

AGENT   I think that is the big problem rather than the color.

MALCOLM   What programs do you know of going on in the Negro communities now that are showing the Negroes the importance of property and property values? This is not speaking against our people, but you can't come out of slavery overnight and know what to do with your property. There is no program going on among Negroes today that will show Negroes how to act in a higher society or how to act when given access toward the higher things in a higher society, and now no white person can say it without being called a bigot. This is what I mean. The so-called Negro civil rights leader has the white man in a position where he can't even show his intelligence without being called a bigot. But in dealing with a Muslim you can at least say what you think, you wouldn't be called a bigot. If what you say is intelligent, good. If what you say is not intelligent, then it's not. Then until the two can sit down and approach the problem you will have a problem of getting worse rather than getting better. It is going to be worse in 1964 than in 1963, as long as you got these freaks like Rustin who is nothing but a homo who can be projected by the press as a leader of black people, then you are going to have trouble on your hands.

AGENT   That is true, and I wish you were right.

MALCOLM   I know I'm right. All they are going to do is come up with what they call programs to give vent to the frustrations of the Negro and you can't do that but so often. Sooner or later, that Negro is going to be looking for the real thing and then you won't be able to control him and nothing you say will save him, or please him, or even stop him.

AGENT   I agree with you. Not to prolong our talk here, let me ask you this. On occasion, things come up like this of you being in Rochester . . .

MALCOLM   That is once in a lifetime . . .

AGENT   But frequently we get problems. The United Nations about three years ago—you people were accused of being in the line, but I know you weren't because I was down there. But, we get inquiries not only from Washington to determine to what extent, if any, the Muslims were active in picketing of the United Nations. It is important for some people to identify the groups that participate most. Do you have any objection if we contact you on things like that and ask you point-blank are the Muslims involved in this.

MALCOLM   No objection. My telephone number is OL 1-6320.

AGENT   How about that. OL 1-6320.

MALCOLM   That's like telling you the sun shines from the east.

AGENT   I assume we have it, but I will take it down in case we don't. As you know, we haven't called you, so I'm not sure. I will limit this. This will not be once a week or once a month, maybe once a year will be the extent of it. But it will save time and trouble at least.

MALCOLM   We don't picket. If we do picket they know it is us. It is that much difference between us and the others.

AGENT   As I say, we were down there. Here again, we are trying to prove a negative. It is not easy. A man sitting in Washington at a desk, when he calls down he—

MALCOLM   I think Washington is past master. As I said previously, it's making positives out of negatives and negatives out of positives.

AGENT   I will report on my contact with you, for two reasons: One, not to bother you, and two, we clearly indicated that you just wouldn't give us any information.

MALCOLM   Certainly. You can tell them they insult my intelligence, not only, they insult me, period, if they think I will tell them anything.

AGENT   You have the privilege. That is very good. You are not alone. We talk to people every day who hate the Government or hate the FBI. That is why they pay money, you know.

MALCOLM   That is not hate, it is incorrect to clarify that as hate. It doesn't take hate to make a man firm in his convictions. There are many areas to which you wouldn't give information and it wouldn't be because of hate. It would be your intelligence and ideals.

AGENT   I don't know of any, but that is all right.

MALCOLM   It has nothing to do with hate, it is based on my own factual—

AGENT   Disinclination to cooperate with the Government.

MALCOLM   I don't see where it is disinclination. I don't even think it could be worded like that. I am looking for the Government to cooperate with some of these Negroes. I don't see any Government cooperation in Birmingham or any of these other places.

AGENT   Well, you'll have to see your congressman about that. We don't work in that area. It would be good and I think in many ways might be of some benefit to your organization if we can eliminate people now on the other hand, it might possibly get a rumor that you are going to —I don't want to use the wrong word—you say you don't picket, you say you had a little march in Times Square last. Whatever you call it, if we get a rumor on that would you have any objection if I called you?

MALCOLM   No, not at all. I do think you are going to have a lot in 1964, period, of racial disturbances.

AGENT   Of course, I am limiting our relationship to the Muslims, which is the only group you would be able to give an authoritative answer on. The other groups, we will have to get people in the other groups to furnish information.

AGENT (speaking to other agent)   Do you have any other questions?

AGENT   How was your trip to Florida?

MALCOLM   Fine.

AGENT   How do you think Cassius is going to come out? Is he going to win or is he going to lose?

MALCOLM   He can win.

AGENT   I've seen him fight and I think he is a pretty good fighter, but I think he is going to get it knocked off here, come February.

MALCOLM   He lives a clean life, all those things count.

AGENT   Liston does too.

MALCOLM   He might. I don't know as much about him.

AGENT   I don't know either. He's sort of a monster to run into.

MALCOLM   Even a monster, Father Time catches up with them.

AGENT   Right. It got to be that anybody could beat Joe Louis, but if they had fought him six or seven years earlier, they wouldn't have had a chance. You going down to the fight?

MALCOLM   I don't know.

AGENT   I was just wondering.

MALCOLM   Florida is an easy place to go to.

AGENT   Yes, nobody would have to twist your arm to get you to go. Thank you very much for your time.

MALCOLM   You are welcome.

AGENT (speaking to other agent)   You got your folder?

AGENT   We can leave that.

MALCOLM   Oh, that's all right, it would be safe here.

AGENT   All right, thank you very much. Thank you again.

MALCOLM   You are welcome.

TELEPHONE CONVERSATION

T HIS conversation between Malcolm and the Afro-Cuban nationalist Carlos Moore occurred on February 9, 1965. Malcolm X was in London after having been barred from entering Paris. Carlos Moore was in Paris.

MALCOLM   Hello, hello, Brother Carlos?

CARLOS   Malcolm, Malcolm, brother, how are you, man? Look, Malcolm, brother, a whole lot of people turned out at the airport to see you and you know we saw you leaving and everything and we just called off the meeting tonight.

MALCOLM   Mmmm . . . !

CARLOS   You don't think we should have?

MALCOLM   I'd say go ahead and have it.

CARLOS   You say go head and have it. O.K. How are you, brother? Look, brother, we're taping this, so give us a statement. Just talk, we are taping.

MALCOLM   I was surprised when I turned up at Paris and got off the plane and was arrested, since I thought if there was any country in Europe that was liberal in its approach to things, France was it, so I was shocked when I got there and couldn't land. They wouldn't even give me any excuse or explanation. At first I thought it was the American State Department. The only other answer is that France has become a satellite of Washington, D.C. . . . So the other brothers and sisters here in London, they were here when I got back to London. Do I talk like this?

CARLOS   Yes, brother, we want you to talk tonight, so keep talking.

MALCOLM   Yes, one of the first things I tried when I got over here was to try to give the African community living in Europe a full view of the latest development of our struggle in the States and, also, provide the Afro-American community living in Europe with an up-to-date report of *their* struggle for human rights in the States. And since I was down south a few days ago—I was in Alabama just last Tuesday and Wednesday—I thought that I should attempt to give the African and Afro-American community in Europe an up-to-date report on just what was going on.

CARLOS   Yes, well, you know, we are very, very heart-broken and grieved, we saw you at the airport leaving and we called to you but I don't know if you saw us or heard us, but there were a great many people, Afro-Americans, at the airport. There was also a reception committee and the press, there was a press conference right there waiting.

MALCOLM   Well, did they give you any expanations over there?

CARLOS   Well, the French newspapers have come out this evening saying that the French Government did that be-cause of the fact that the speech you gave here in No-vember was "too violent." It's quite ironical because that's one of the, you know . . . Anyhow, that's what the French Government newspaper *Le Monde* has said, but right now we're getting ready to call the meeting for tonight and I would like you to speak at the meeting tonight because we are taping our conversation right now on the phone. So we want you to speak *anyway* tonight at the meeting. So *they are not going to frustrate our plans.*

MALCOLM   Well, just let the meeting go ahead.

CARLOS   Just speak clearly into the phone as it's being taped, brother.

MALCOLM   I don't advocate violence and I'm not a racist, and I'm against racism and against segregation. I'm against anything that is immoral and unjust. I don't judge a person according to the color of his skin, I judge a person accord-ing to what he believes, according to his deeds and his intentions. I do not advocate violence—in fact, the violence I constantly refer to is the violence that the Negro in America is the victim of, and I have never advocated our people going out and initiating any acts of aggression against whites *indiscriminately,* but *I do say* that the Negro in America is a continual victim of the violent actions committed by the organized elements like the Ku Klux Klan and if the United States Government has shown itself unwilling or unable to protect us and our lives and our property, I have said that it is time for our people to organize and band together and protect ourselves, to defend ourselves against this. Now if this is to advocate violence, then I am shocked at the lack of proper understanding on the part of whatever elements over there have this attitude. So by and large, I think that the only way of solving our problems is to realize that *people we think are liberal are not as liberal as they profess and people we think are with us, when we put them to the test they are not really with us, they are not really for the oppressed people as we think,* and I hope that the Afro-American community in Paris, as well as in the whole of Europe, will realize the importance of us sticking together in unity and brotherhood and doing something to solve our own problems and if there are well-meaning whites, also, who are interested in helping, I think they should realize we will accept their help, too, but the *attitude of many elements today makes it doubtful as to the sincerity and the integrity of those who profess to want to help.*

CARLOS   Brother, I will take this opportunity to ask a couple of questions here, because many people are hearing this precisely. Do you feel that the United States Government has definitely something to do with this? What do you feel about that?

MALCOLM   Well, you know, I can't really understand . . . when I asked someone today to call the American Embassy and the American Embassy put out a statement saying they couldn't do anything about it, where, at the same time, the same American Embassy was willing to send troops into the Congo to rescue a man named "Carlson" who was not even a diplomat but one of the missionaries there. They can do something about that. The same American Embassy has troops in South Vietnam and they can do whatever they want to do all over the world, and at the same time they can't do anything about the mishandling of a black man, then I think something is wrong. Whether or not the Embassy had a hand in giving direct orders to the French Government, I don't know.

CARLOS   What is your reaction to the French Government itself?

MALCOLM   Well, as I say, I didn't think I'd ever be barred from entering any country other than South Africa, and when I arrived in Paris this morning, the way they treated me—I thought I'd made a mistake and landed in Johannesburg. I never thought I would be treated in such a manner in Paris, a supposedly liberal country, and as I say, I don't think any other country would have barred me from landing, other than South Africa, or Southern Rhodesia, or perhaps one of the Portuguese protectorates. I didn't think it would happen in Paris. So, as I told the security forces there—I gave them a penny, you know, an English penny, and told them to give this to de Gaulle because from my point of view, *his Government and country were worth less than one penny.*

CARLOS   Brother, as you know, we tried to get in touch with you, the members of the Afro-American community. The members of the Afro-American community tried to get in touch with you at the airport, but they weren't allowed to, but anyway, we want to ask another question because the Afro-American community will be hearing this tonight, and the meeting will go on. We want to ask you about the situation in the United States itself. You were in Selma?

MALCOLM   Yes, I was in Selma last Wednesday. I was supposed to be in . . . At Tuskegee Institute I spoke before three thousand black students on Tuesday night and they insisted I go to Selma the next morning. I went there. I saw the Ku Klux Klan and other elements who were parading in the streets and I saw one little girl named Judy who was about twelve years old whom they arrested and beat, and this morning they told me how they were brutally beating her in the jail and how they took these cattle prods and put them up to her head and she was . . . Therefore, the treatment of black people in Selma, Alabama, is extremely brutal but what I don't understand is that Dr. Martin Luther King, Jr., got out of jail and wanted to go to Washington, D.C. to see Lyndon B. to ask him for some additional recognition concerning the voting rights bill that was passed last year means nothing because already now they are asking for new legislation, which shows the farce in their aims, the sheer hypocrisy on the part of this government as regards the rights of black people in the United States.

CARLOS   Right, brother, and what are the prospects for the struggle in the United States that you have seen for this year?

MALCOLM   Well, 1965 will probably be the *longest, hottest, bloodiest* summer that has yet been seen in the United States since the beginning of the Black Revolution, primarily because the same causes that existed in the winter of 1964 still exist in January, in February, of 1965. Now, these are causes of inferior housing, inferior employment, inferior education. All of the evils of a bankrupt system still exist where black Americans are concerned, and the popular unrest that exists has been increased tremendously now that the African nations themselves have shown overt support for the black struggle in America in our efforts to get our human rights. This gives us added incentive to step up our struggle and, as I said, it will be the *longest, hottest, bloodiest summer of the entire Black Revolution.*

CARLOS   I see, brother. What do you think will be the reaction in the non-white world, mainly the African countries, toward this action of the French Government?

MALCOLM   Well, I don't know—already, as you know, I was in London last night addressing the First Congress of the Council of African Organizations, and when I got back to London, there were representatives of about fifteen different African organizations waiting for me at the airport because they thought I had met with foul play, and they were getting ready to demonstrate. Now, what I do know quite certain, I have already been told that a protest will be launched throughout the European continent and elsewhere around the world in regard to this very criminal and uncouth action on the part of the French Government.

CARLOS   You see, already we have been having a lot of reactions, a lot of phone calls from journalists, from many individuals, Afro-Americans, Africans, who have demonstrated their deep resentment, their deep regret and outrage against this very unprecedented act here in France. We would like to know what do you think the Afro-American community can do in the overall struggle in the United States, because they will be hearing this.

MALCOLM   You mean the Afro-American community in France?

CARLOS   Yes, that's right, the Afro-American community in Europe.

MALCOLM   *The Afro-American community in France and in other parts of Europe must unite with the African community,* and this was the message that I was going to bring to Paris tonight, *the necessity of the black people in the Western Hemisphere realizing for once and for all that we must restore our African cultural roots and heritage; we must re-establish contacts with our African brothers, we must begin from this day forward to work in unity, then we will give our struggle a type of strength in spirit that will enable us to make some real, concrete progress whether we be in Europe, America, or still on the African continent.*

CARLOS   Brother, what else do you have to say on this topic—that was the theme of your talk tonight, right? I would like to know what else you would have liked to have said to the Afro-American community and the African community here in Paris.

MALCOLM   My entire talk would have been based on the importance of unity between the Afro-American and African peoples, black peoples, all over the world for— (interruption)

CARLOS   Operator, operator.

OPERATOR   Have you finished, sir?

CARLOS   No, we have not finished, operator.

OPERATOR   Just a moment, you were cut off by the switchboard. . . .

SWITCHBOARD   Hello! Hello! Why was the phone disconnected?

OPERATOR   I don't know—it was cut off in the hotel.

MALCOLM   Hello, Carlos, I guess we'd better wind it up, brother.

CARLOS   Yes, yes, brother. Then I would like to hear anything you have to say to us.

MALCOLM   Well, just *the importance of unity,* Brother Carlos.

CARLOS   Well, fine, good, brother, and you know our hearts, brother, our hearts, our souls, our bodies and minds are with you—you know we're but one.

MALCOLM   Yes, I know that, brother.

CARLOS   This is the message that I, on behalf of the other brothers here in France, would like to convey to you. (A voice in background: "And sisters.")

MALCOLM   Well, I hope that you, brothers, let the people in France and our friends, and the press, the mass media, and everybody else, know that we were completely indignant today, so that our people in the United States will know they *do* have brothers and allies all around the world.

CARLOS   We will, brother, we will, and right here, right now, we have a room here full of other brothers and sisters who would like to talk to you, but it's not possible, and the brothers and sisters in France send you their love and regards.

(End of recording)

PART IV

MALCOLM X ABROAD

PREFACE TO PART IV

In a few short visits during the last year of his life, Malcolm X did more to enhance the position of the Afro-Americans abroad than any other personality. He single-handedly convinced a large number of Africans, including some heads of state, that the African independence explosion and what was being referred to as the Black Revolution in the United States were events produced by the same historical experience—the Africans were colonized, the black Americans were enslaved. In his speeches in Africa he emphasized the convincing parallels between these two African peoples and their respective freedom struggles.

The expatriate Afro-American communities in Paris, London, and Accra, Ghana, thought of Malcolm X as the one black American worthy of leadership.

In August 1964 Malcolm X addressed a meeting of the Organization of African Unity and first called attention to the plights of the people of African descent in the United States. He called the then recently passed Civil Rights Bill one of the tricks of this century's leading neocolonial power. Then he said: "Our freedom struggle for human dignity is no longer confined to the domestic jurisdiction of the United States Government. We beseech the independent African states to help us bring our problem before the United Nations, on the grounds that the United States Government is morally incapable of protecting the lives and property of 22 million African-Americans. And on the grounds that our deteriorating plight is definitely becoming a threat to world peace.

"Out of frustration and hopelessness our young people have reached a point of no return, we no longer endorse patience and turning the other cheek. We assert the right of self-defense by any means necessary and reserve the right of maximum retaliation against our racist oppressors,

no matter what the odds against us are. From here on in, if we must die anyway, we will die fighting back, and we will not die alone. We intend to see that our racist oppressors also get a taste of death."

Because he wanted his African listeners to know that they shared some of the same dangers as the black Americans, he added: "No one knows a master better than his servants. We have been servants in the United States for over three hundred years. We have a thorough inside knowledge of this man who calls himself 'Uncle Sam.' Therefore you must heed our warning: Don't escape from European colonialism only to become even more enslaved by deceitful, 'friendly' American dollarism. Asalaam Alaikum."

Now the issue had been joined on a broad stage for all the world to see. If the American power establishment wanted a sound reason to kill him, he had boldly given it to them.

Upon his arrival in Cairo to attend this second Cairo conference, a number of African leaders and their various delegations asked him to prepare a memorandum on the real status of black Americans. With the guidance of this memorandum, the thirty-three heads of independent African nations, meeting in Cairo, U.A.R., from July 17 to July 21, 1964, passed a resolution condemning the brutal treatment of the Afro-Americans in the United States.

In the weeks that followed, Malcolm X was invited to visit sixteen African nations and most of these invitations were accepted. In every nation that he visited he made an effort to build a bridge of good will between Africans and Afro-Americans. Unknown to himself, Malcolm X had succeeded where other black men had tried and failed for over a hundred years. From the middle of the nineteenth century, and afterward, every genuine black nationalist has dreamed of a union with Africa and other people of African descent scattered throughout the world.

In a subsequent visit to African nations, Malcolm X continued to build a bridge of good will between Africans and Afro-Americans. This was his best and final contribution to the eventual liberation and union of his people.

J. H. C.

MALCOLM X IN GHANA

—————————————— BY *Leslie Alexander Lacy*

M ALCOLM X came twice to the Republic of Ghana. After his first visit, the black American expatriates there thought that they had seen him for the last time. Most of us had not known Brother Malcolm in America and his stay of four fleeting days and nights in our little community had not been long enough. We heard his message to Africa, and with the Ghanaians had responded with enthusiasm. Some of us, called Malcolm Loyalists by one of the newspapers, had been with him most of those hours, and one, or perhaps two, had felt close enough to love him and feel his strength. But more than anything his first visit made us realize that although we served President Kwame Nkrumah, the tall red man from Harlem was our real leader.

I felt a deep sense of guilt as he boarded his plane. He had asked me how long would it be before I returned to the struggle in America. I had not dared answer him as I had answered others who had asked the same question. That I was helping Kwame Nkrumah achieve a political order that would indirectly help people of African descent achieve social justice in America did not seem like a legitimate reply to a revolutionary who knew better. So I had said, smiling. "Soon, Malcolm."

Also, we felt a small sigh of relief when he left. Malcolm's first coming had interrupted the pleasures of our exile. On very short notice, and without very much knowledge, we had become full-time organizers in preparation for his stay. Presumptuously we called ourselves the Malcolm X Committee. We arranged a busy speaking schedule and contacted our friends in the communication media: They promised us their finest hours. We worked twenty-four hours a day the week prior to his visit. Nothing was left to the innocence of spontaneity. In the spirit of Nkrumah's political mythmaking, we had been prepared to pack the halls with party activists, trade unionists, political opportunists, screaming market women—replete with their baskets and chickens—and Ghana's non-English-speaking street citizens if an overflowing crowd was not apparent for any of Malcolm's scheduled appearances. Our leader had to have the broadest possible exposure; even an audience with the President was not beyond our reach.

And then, of course, there had been the changes of our personal lives. No drinking, especially in the afternoons. No smoking and no pork for the former Muslim advocate. We had to cease and desist all those activities which we considered offensive to our puritan leader. We were like small boys and girls who hurriedly drank orange soda so Father wouldn't smell the tobacco we had happily consumed in his absence. Or better, like unfaithful wives washing our sin away before six P.M.

I had to be especially careful: no non-revolutionary questions. Sitting with my dear friend Julian Mayfield in one of our secret local bars (having our last before the Big Arrival), I had remarked that Malcolm might be pleased with some of the "local action." Julian had pounded his hand firmly and indignantly on the table (but catching his gin glass before it fell): "Malcolm X is a married man with four children," he said with conviction.

His second coming caught us by surprise. Malcolm gave us only twenty-five minutes notice, a call from the airport. But we were ready. Most of us had not gone back to our old lives. Malcolm the man, the father, the person, the revolutionary, and all that we had seen and felt as a result of his first coming, had had a converting effect upon our lives, and he had outlined specific plans on how we could aid our struggle for human rights in America.

Julian, the headman in the Afro-American community since the death of Dr. W. E. B. DuBois, met Malcolm at the Accra airport and brought him directly to my bungalow at the University of Ghana. The university, being close to the airport, was a logical place to form our next move.

I greeted them outside and the three of us returned to my living room. Brother Malcolm looked tired, very tired —like a black man who has looked for a new apartment and is tired and disgusted: first because he did not find a place and second because he has walked for many hours. Or perhaps what I saw on Malcolm's suntanned face was fear. He had been preoccupied with the thought of death and assassination on his first visit, and now as he talked, sometimes incoherently, I felt a strange feeling of finality.

I tried to relax him. I offered him a glass of water. I was sorry that I did not have any Ghanaian food because I knew how much he enjoyed it. I had some oranges in the kitchen so I made him some orange juice. He drank the first glass, and I gave him another.

Malcolm sat down in one of the chairs. It was my best chair. He moved up and down and from side to side trying to find the spot which would allow him to relax. The chair was a product of our local industry, and the Ghanaian carpenters had not yet discovered how to make a seat comfortable. Huge and inviting pillows gave the chair the look of comfort; but like other things in Ghana, outward manifestations were ofttimes misleading. Soon Malcolm gave up his search and settled for a chair that he could at least sit on. There was a mild irritated look on his face, but he smiled and sat down.

Malcolm had not been in Africa long enough to know the meaning of an uncomfortable chair. It was a part of a host of other inconveniences which Westerners, both black and white, had to adjust to: no running water in certain areas, electrity blackouts, hot beer—just to mention a few. Most Westerners were enraged by this inefficiency. Every day you heard their complaints. But the Afro-Americans seldom griped. They hated America so much that they ignored even normal inconveniences which even the Ghanaians complained about. You had the feeling that if you complained, you would be thought disloyal. One member of the Afro-American community was called a CIA agent by another of its members because he had complained to a high-ranking civil servant about his six months' back pay. The accused soon left the country under unexplained circumstances. I asked the accuser several weeks later what had happened to the accused, and I was told: "He was probably deported for spying. He shouldn't have been here anyway. He should go back to the United States and get a job."

"Is there much corruption here?" asked Malcolm innocently. He had picked up a copy of the daily paper, the *Ghanaian Times,* and had seen the headlines, "Down with Corruption."

Malcolm continued to read the ten-page government-controlled newspaper, but after a few moments he looked at Julian for an answer to his question.

"There is some corruption."

"How much?"

"It's difficult to tell."

"How does Mr. Nkrumah deal with it?"

Julian smiled and searched his pockets for a cigarette. Apparently the question had made Julian a little uneasy. Corruption in office was a subject few people wanted to discuss because no one knew to what extent it existed. The Afro-Americans tended to overlook minor forms of corruption in Ghana and only the select political elite knew the workings of the inner kingdom. Julian was especially sensitive on the issue. He was a loyal Nkrumah watcher and an editor of the country's leading magazine, *The African Review.* We always knew that he *knew,* but he never spoke. I knew him well, but much of our relationship was non-political. The only thing which he had ever said to me about the government was: "We don't need a lot of party loyalists. What we really need are committed men and women who are willing to live on their own salaries."

Julian lit his cigarette and said, "The President has taken several steps to crack down. Three months ago he set up a commission to investigate corruption in public office. But if he were to shoot a few of his ministers, other crooks would soon get the point."

Julian then told us a long story about another Nkrumah watcher who had gone to see the President about the "guilty men" in his government. According to Julian, this watcher had told the President: "Mr. President, there are men in your government who are stealing. They are stealing every day. We know they are stealing, and we think you know they are stealing; and since they are not arrested, some of us think that you are stealing too." The next week this party loyalist told Julian: "I have been reduced to the status of a caterer. I am no longer in politics. I am now in charge of the state bakery."

Malcolm seemed perplexed by the whole account. Like most of us before coming to Ghana, he admired Kwame Nkrumah for his militant policies and his strong advocacy of black solidarity. "I guess Mr. Nkrumah knows how to best deal with his people," Malcolm said with a shrug.

Julian remained silent.

Suddenly there was a knock on the door, and Julian went to open it.

"Is Mr. Lacy here?" asked a soft voice from outside.

"Yeah, man." Julian said with disgust. He stood at the door in his stockinged feet with his hands belligerently thrust in his pockets and a scowl on his face for several minutes before letting the young Ghanaian enter.

Julian had little love for the students. He thought that most of them were "right-wing reactionaries." He often stated: "The President should close down the university and put all those elite thinkers to work in the fields." Julian was also disturbed by the way many of these students approached the foreign staff. When they knocked on your door, you could barely hear the sound. Once they came in, their speech was hardly above a whisper. And they were usually docile or even subservient, like an apologetic servant who felt he had disturbed his master.

I did not share all of Julian's views about the students. Certainly, I did not like their obvious docility, but then I also disliked his New York male hysteria. As far as their political attitudes were concerned, well, Julian was badly informed. Sure the students were conservative—that was their English education. But I did not accept his argument —the ruling Convention People's Party argument—that the students were "reactionary," "black English," or "ivory towerists." Needless to say, some of these attitudes existed; but as a general characterization, it had to be rejected. In fact, the students were very concerned about their country; they were pro-Westernization but anti-Westerners. And if the ruling party had had an iota of political astuteness in its dealing with them, most of the students would have been more open to it. What the students really needed was clear direction. But like some nationalist parties elsewhere, the CPP feared disagreeing intellectuals.

"Mr. X," the student said with surprise. "We thought you had gone." The student paused. He seemed overcome by elation. "Mr. X, I'm so glad to see you."

Julian smiled cynically and went into the kitchen.

Malcolm seemed touched by the student's concern. His elation was so completely revealed. Even Julian could not deny it. He was genuinely happy to see our leader. By now Malcolm was on his feet. He gave the student the brotherhood handshake, which other students had taught him on his first visit.

"What is your name?" requested Malcolm.

"Kwame," the student replied in a very manly voice. "I come from Kumasi. I am Ashanti."

"Very good. What are you studying?"

"I'm reading law."

Malcolm did not understand "reading law." The student explained that it was the same as studying law, but that the English say "reading" rather than "studying."

"How is the struggle in America?" the student asked excitedly.

"There are always problems."

"What kind of problems?" the student asked with concern.

"Well, the white man has poisoned the minds of black people in America for so long that it will be hard to organize our people and teach them black nationalism."

"Well, if we can help, let us know," he said authoritatively. "Mr. X, will you be able to speak to us again? I'm sure the Marxist Forum could arrange it."

"I don't know yet, but we'll see. I hope so, Kwame."

The student got up, gave Brother Malcolm the handshake, and left running to tell his friends that Malcolm had returned.

Malcolm was pleased. He loved students. Kwame and hundreds of other students who had heard his historic speech at the University of Ghana seemed to sense that. In my two years at the University of Ghana at Legon, I had never before seen the students in such total agreement. They had talked about Malcolm for days after he left. One folk singer had created a song in his honor called "Malcolm Man."

> Malcolm Man, Malcolm Man
> You speak your tale of woe
> The red in your face like our
> blood on the land
> You speak your tale of woe
> Malcolm Man, Malcolm Man
> The anger that you feel
> Will one day unite our people
> And make us all so real
> Malcolm Man, Malcolm Man

Malcolm Man had also inspired the students to political action. To the surprise of everyone, ten students at Legon had formed a Malcolm X Society. And, of course, the question which no one, especially party activists, could answer was: "Why had 'reactionary' students cheered and applauded a revolutionary?"

Then came another knock on the door. More students, I thought.

"Kwame, did you forget something?" I asked as I opened the door. I remembered that he had originally come to see me but had been distracted upon seeing Malcolm.

"No . . ." he said in a very soft voice.

We could tell that he had something on his mind, but he seemed afraid to speak. He paced the length of the living room twice, and then stood near Malcolm's seat.

"Speak, man, speak," Julian shouted impatiently. "Mr. X has other appointments."

"Is there something you have to tell me?" asked Malcolm sympathetically.

"Yes, Mr. X," the student replied as he looked into

Malcolm's face. "I want to say that the students do not believe what Mr. Basner said about you in the *Ghanaian Times*. None of us here like him. We wish he would go back to South Africa."

"Who is Mr. Basner? What article do you mean?"

"Hasn't Mr. Mayfield told you about it? He wrote a reply to those vicious remarks."

Malcolm was still cool, but he looked worried.

"Mayfield, what is this about?" Malcolm demanded.

The student excused himself hurriedly, and left the house.

Julian answered Malcolm's question. Mr. Basner, H. M. Basner, was a professional Marxist from South Africa. He was white. He had practiced law in South Africa before coming to Ghana, and he had always been known to be on the right side of the freedom struggle in South Africa. There was a warrant for his arrest awaiting him in Cape Town. Like other South Africans, both white and black, Basner had obtained a job in Nkrumah's government. But unlike his other South African compatriots, he held an extremely important job. He wrote a column, "Watching the World from Accra," for the *Ghanaian Times,* and he sometimes served as an adviser and aid to President Nkrumah. Without a doubt he was one of the most, if not the most, important expatriate on Nkrumah's payroll. So what he wrote was relevant.

Two days after Malcolm's first visit, H. M. Basner had written a highly critical article in the *Ghanaian Times* attacking the speech Malcolm had made at Legon. Basner had stated that our leader was a nationalist, and therefore a racist. In New Left Marxist terminology, he attempted to expose the weaknesses of Malcolm's political philosophy, and of course, concluded that there was but one hope: blacks and whites working together; or to use Basner's words, the only hope for the races was "the army of the oppressed."

Julian had replied to Basner in the same paper the next day, but Basner had had the last word.

We had all known Basner's private political sentiments, but they had appeared in a government-controlled newspaper. Had Nkrumah approved of his views? Did that mean that the Ghanaian Government would support Basner's African Nationalist Congress, a predominantly white communist freedom movement in South Africa, in preference to the black nationalist breakaway group called the Pan-African Congress? Did that mean that Nkrumah was leaning more toward the Russians than toward the nationalistic Chinese? And, more importantly, what implications would this have on the black-nationalist-oriented black community in Accra?

Malcolm listened closely to Julian as he developed all of his arguments. I had wanted to ask Malcolm questions about his trip, questions about Africa, questions concerning the use of these experiences upon his return to America. But when Julian stopped finally, nothing came.

Malcolm stood and stretched his arms. "I guess Mr. Nkrumah knows what he is doing. I've got 20 million other black people to think about right now, and I guess I should get back to them soon."

Malcolm looked slowly around the room, letting his eyes linger on that invitingly stuffed chair he had earlier strugged with. He still looked tired. Thanking me for everything, he left with Julian for Accra. Two days later he left the country.

His second coming, unlike his first, was quiet and uneventful. On his first coming he had received a hero's welcome, speeches all over the country, addresses to parliament, excellent press coverage; he had met the President. And of course, there had been Mr. Basner.

On his second go-round, Malcolm was pensive, preoccupied, searching. He had new ideas and strategies. He was hurrying back to Harlem.

MALCOLM X IN EUROPE

BY *Lebert Bethune*

IT was November 27, 1964, and a typical Parisian wintry day—not cold enough to hunch your shoulders against it, but wet and gray and jive enough for you to wish the season would settle into its thing, so you could get into yours and confront it.

A group of about eight black men—most of us from the New World—were sitting in the apartment of a Jamaican writer. And we were listening to him trying to pit his green Caribbean vision and not all hopeless rage against the unremitting acid screams of John Coltrane coming from a phonograph in one corner of the room. 'Trane was shaking the very foundations of that ancient French apartment building, something terrible (the locomotive he was chasing). And most of us there, while we knew the music to speak true, were glad for it to be mingling with the calypso cadences and gay dancing of the young writer. Because he was no less true for being joyous and full of vibrant hope. And with the screaming, this was all about our black reality, too. Anyway, there we were, eight black men—eight expatriates twice removed from home, drinking the ancient bittersweet brew which marks the last four hundred years of our history—yes, joy in spite of pain.

And just about then somebody knocked at the door, and the visitor turned out to be an Afro-Cuban brother. He stood there panting, gleaming with sweat and something that looked a little like fear; he must have run all the way with his message. And he whispered it only to two of us. He said, "Malcolm is in town, let's go."

The silence following those six words was loud enough for everybody to hear above the music, but before anyone could ask questions, we slipped through the door and down five flights. And three of us were running through the labyrinth of the sixth arrondissement in the Latin Quarter as if slavery was abolished—running to meet our man.

I say *our* man, because Malcolm X was by no means the man for all the Afro-Americans living in Paris at that time. Just as he wasn't for all the Afro-Americans in the United States. The range of opinion among black Parisians with regard to the best strategy for lifting the yoke of black people's oppression ran from "by any means necessary" through loving one's enemy; down to those who believed there was no need for any strategy since "France was free from racism."

Faced with the fact of French discrimination against Arabs, many of those holding this latter view would struggle and point out that Arabs were the first foreigners to enslave black Africans. Faced with the occasional personal experience of racial discrimination, some Afro-Americans living in France blamed it more on the spread of American influence than on indigenous racism. In any case, many of them reasoned, half a loaf of freedom with an occasional pebble in the bread was better than no loaf at all.

But as I was saying, Malcolm was our man. And we? We were writers and artists and musicians and drifters with one or two things in common. Firstly, we were most of us young, and pretty much aware of those realities which a black man's existence in any part of the Western world meant. Secondly, while we may have profoundly feared discovering those consequences which our existence in any other part of the world might have meant, we told ourselves that Paris was but a way station in a quest which could only end in Africa. There was something else, too, which we held in common, and that was a sense that our quest might never end in Africa, but that resignation to such a likelihood meant a pain that not even the blues could relieve.

We arrived breathless before the door of the apartment where Malcolm was waiting. None of us had any idea of what we would say to him, far less of what he might say to us. But as we paused to catch breath and perhaps a little composure outside the door of that place, we had an initial surprise. On the nameplate was printed the name of a famous Afro-American writer, second in our admiration to Richard Wright; a man who'd lived in France for almost as long as Wright; an old, venerable man—tough, honest, hip, and the most exciting and vivid chronicler of Harlem alive today.

Perhaps we should not have been surprised. Yet whenever we had met him at one of his favorite haunts, it seemed as if seventeen years in Europe had crystallized his gaunt brown face, but for the affectionate gray eyes, into a mask of weariness and resignation, perhaps loneliness as well—the living blues. However, the presence of Malcolm X within this man's apartment meant suddenly for us the discovery, naïve though it may have been, of an old accomplice to a fiery cleansing hope which was nothing if not a common heritage, and whose reasurrance we felt Malcolm symbolized. So when the old man opened the door to our laughter and our repeating his name like something new we had discovered, we embraced him, all three of us. And he presented us like sons to Brother Malcolm, who was sitting there smiling quietly with amusement (for he instinctively divined what had happened), as human as we somehow never imagined him to be. Yet there was this stillness around him, the steady fire of a man who had attained the zenith of human personality. It irradiated the small room and gathered all of us into it, burning us free from fear.

As I look back on that room now, I realize how much like small boys we were, plying our father with a hundred questions. "How is the movement going?" "How many people are in your organization?" "Why did you leave the Muslims?" A hundred questions, many of them staggeringly naïve, but which simply reflected our remove from the immediate American reality, our innocence vis-à-vis conspiracy, and the total fraternal security we felt in that place.

Brother Malcolm smiled at our questions, answering most of them with parables and adages; others he replied to with silent laughter. "You don't expose the roots of a tree, or you kill it—it's the same with a movement," he said. But above all he wanted to tell us about Africa, about his hopes for increasing solidarity between Africans and Afro-Americans. Someone of us mentioned the name Nyerere in the context of glowing Western press reports about him being a "moderate." Malcolm chuckled and said, "Brother, let me tell you something; you hear a lot of talk in the Western press about moderate this and moderate that, but I have had conversations with some of these so-called moderates recently, and some of the things they said to me would make the hair stand up on the back of your neck." So much for so-called moderate leaders.

We wanted to go on talking within the secure ambience of that small room. In fact, it was less our wanting to talk than to listen to a man who seemed to take for granted so much of what we hungered for—the beauty of black people, the potential strength if we unite, the truth of human community in Africa. But Brother Malcolm wanted to hit the streets and to visit every nook and cranny of Paris where Afro-American brothers hung out. There were news conferences to be held, and by now the French radio was announcing the presence of "the hater of white men" in the City of Light.

However, Malcolm felt that his confrontation with the French press could wait. After all, they were welcome to hear the public speech he was scheduled to give on the following evening. What little time he had, he wanted to spend with brothers and sisters—Afro-Americans and Africans.

Once we hit the streets, we headed straight for a café on Rue St.-André-des-Arts, which was a favorite meeting place of African students. We went in, sat, and somehow immediately the din of voices quieted down. Some of the students standing at the counter turned, regarding us with hesitant smiles and quizzical expressions.

"Mais c'est Malcolm X," somebody said finally, pronouncing the letter X as it is in French—gx. Immediately, we were surrounded by all of the Africans in the café. They all wanted to shake his hand. There were no questions, just warm smiles of brotherhood and recognition, within a throbbing hubbub of black voices calling his name with every nuance of surprise and pleasurable expression. Malcolm's own pleasure was only mitigated by his annoyance at himself for not being able to speak French. "You all speak French," he said, turning to us. "Tell them about the meeting tomorrow night." So we told them of the meeting sponsored by Présence Africaine scheduled for the following night.

His meeting with Africans and Afro-Americans in various cafés followed much the same pattern the rest of the afternoon. In fact, as we walked through the streets, Malcolm was almost invariably recognized and greeted by nearly every African we met in the Latin Quarter. One Senegalese opened his battered wallet to show "Brother Malcolm" that he carried a picture of him along with his family's.

Later that evening we had dinner at a restaurant in Pigalle run by an Afro-American. It was the favorite hangout for the show business branch of the Afro-American community in Paris. Our group had now expanded to around six, and as we sat around him, Malcolm seemed to become more and more relaxed, with much of the wariness about him gone. His presence was much stronger for it. He talked about some of his own days in the show business milieu, and related parables about leadership.

We were drinking wine, and he was drinking orange juice. "You know what you are drinking, don't you?" he observed. "The blood of the lamb." He said a good leader was like a good cook, and we all laughed. "No, I'm serious . . . a good cook has got to know how to use various ingredients in the pot, and it's the same with a good leader. He's got to be able to mix together a lot of different elements to make a meal come out tasting right . . . like that food you all are eating there."

Throughout the rest of the evening he talked with unflagging affability, answering questions asked and many more unasked. He talked, investing every word, every tale, with a profundity which defied boredom and which lit up corners of our minds like flares in a dark night.

At one point, perhaps surprised by his own relaxation and openness, he remarked, with his light brown eyes twinkling, "I'm talking so much here, you'd think I had a taste of the blood of the lamb."

The climax of Malcolm's trip to Paris came on the following night. For my own part, it was a twofold climax. The first involved his major public address at the Salle de la Mutualité. The second took place during those hours following the speech, and lasted into the early hours of the morning while we filmed an interview which was to become the core of the movie *Malcolm X—Struggle for Freedom*.

Malcolm delivered his speech to a capacity audience consisting mainly of African, Afro-American, and French students, and including a number of French workers, intellectuals, and even some of the staid French bourgeoisie, come to hear the man billed by the French press as *"l'avocat de la violence."*

The occasion was a personal triumph for Malcolm, as much for the charming and irresistible but uncompromising style of his manner as for the moral and ideological truth which his demands for freedom at all cost drove home to the audience. The French, regarding even the truth as credible only when it is stylishly presented, succumbed to Malcolm's presence and power. It was a testament to their acceptance of his credibility less than two months later, when he was on a return trip to speak again in Paris, they refused him entry into the country.

Malcolm had not slept from the time we first met him till now. Thirty-eight hours later, as we loaded the last magazine of film and turned the harsh lights on him for yet another take of a statement on the destiny of the black man, he seemed tired, but he kept talking between takes, more urgently now. He was leaving sometime the next day for America, after a long sojourn in Africa. Madame Siné, wife of the French cartoonist in whose home we were shooting, served tea at 4:00 A.M. I have a tape—Malcolm is talking about organizing—"You all should learn how to organize. You got to pull in everybody . . . naturally you know you'll be pulling in danger, too, but you must learn how to handle danger. . . ." The tape ends there.

Altogether Malcolm X visited Europe on at least three occasions. His first visit, the one I've been trying to give some sense of, was in November of 1964. His second visit was to Britain in December of the same year. The third and final trip he made to Europe was in February of 1965, a week and a half before his murder. It was during this last visit, after fulfilling a speaking engagement in London, that he attempted to enter France to speak at a mass rally arranged by the Federation of Black African Students in France, together with the Afro-American community, and found himself declared a prohibited immigrant.

Of the three visits, I would say that the first and second were of greatest significance in terms of exposure, especially the second. The highlight, in fact the *raison d'être*, for this visit, was the Oxford Union Society's annual debate, which was being nationally televised by the BBC on this occasion. The question for debate was "Extremism in the Defense of Liberty Is No Vice, Moderation in the Pursuit of Justice Is No Virtue." The speakers in the debate included the Earl of Longford, Humphry Berkeley, a liberal Tory M.P., and the student president of the Oxford Union Society that year, Christie Davies, all speaking against the motion.

I was lucky to be in London at the time, and apart from wanting to see Malcolm again, I couldn't resist the rich feast of irony which seemed to me inherent in this visit by Malcolm X to Oxford, one of the most sacred of European institutions. However, I should confess also to a desire at the time to see the sacrosanct image of Oxford shattered by the fist of revolutionary logic. So I took a train to Oxford just to be there for that blow.

The irony of his being at Oxford in a debate against, of all people, the Earl of Longford, Privy Councillor to the Queen (whatever that might mean), wasn't lost on Malcolm. But while smiling at that, he pointed out to me that the office of presidency of the Oxford Union was held then by a black Jamaican, who was proposing the motion for debate. He also pointed out that the incoming president for the following term was a Pakistani. I didn't believe then, nor on reflection, that Malcolm was rejoicing in the symbolic "domination" of Oxford by men of color, but it was a matter of more than simple irony for him.

The debate was the occasion for one of the most stirring speeches I have ever heard delivered by Malcolm X. He had been angered by the flippant drawing room comedy manner of Humphry Berkeley, who attempted to compare him with Verwoerd of South Africa. It took an effort of will to keep from trembling, he confided to me later on. However, when he rose to speak slowly, gracefully, a model of black power and beauty, the giggling undergraduates subsided into silence, and Malcolm spoke. It would be an injustice to try to summarize the content or atmosphere of the speech. Suffice it to say that he ranged back and forth through the bloody history of Europe and revolution, finding nowhere the idea of liberty and justice meaningfully supported by anything but uncompromising and total sacrifice in its defense. When it was ended, there was more silence before the audience rose thirty seconds later to an overwhelming response. Try to imagine the Earl of Longford, if you can, limping after, in every way.

The influence of Malcolm X in Europe was a profound one. I ought to say *is* a profound one. He was and is an influence, primarily on the radical youth of Europe, where he holds a place in the pantheon of contemporary revolutionary heroes inspiring them; with Che Guevara and Mao Tse-tung and Lumumba. What specifically about him inspires them?

First of all, Malcolm was a very explicit man, and his analysis of the spiritual and material condition of his people was nothing if not searing in its objectivity and explicitness. Secondly, his grasp of the history of revolution in Europe made it easy for him to relate the situation of the Afro-American to a revolutionary modality which certainly has European as well as Asian antecedents. No longer sufficient for European youth concerned with the destiny of the planet and their place in it are the ambiguities and verbal conundrums of Camus and Sartre. They know they cannot hold this out to the victims of European power and arrogance when explanations for the record, if nothing else, are demanded. Frantz Fanon and Malcolm X made sure of that. Finally, I believe that Malcolm X was influential in Europe because it was easier to identify with him than to sympathize with him. The most articulate Afro-American voices in Europe before him, with the exception of Garvey, engendered sympathy much more readily than identification or fear.

Fear! Elderly Europe, weary-liberal, as well as reactionary, feared Malcolm. They feared him because he was credible. And his credibility stemmed from the moral force of his presence, the clarity of his revolutionary rhetoric, and the clear, blazing evidence of his influence in white America. Today they fear their black children.

MALCOLM X:
AN INTERNATIONAL MAN

────── BY *Ruby M. and E. U. Essien-Udom*

ON January 7, 1965, or about forty-five days before his assassination, Malcolm X spoke in New York City on the topic "Prospects for Freedom in 1965." [1] This address as well as others he made and his public activities in the period following his rupture with the Nation of Islam in March 1964 till the time of his assassination on February 21, 1965, clearly mark him out as "an international man," a leader and spokesman of the oppressed and exploited peoples of the world. In that address there was something of world leader about his survey of international affairs in 1964, something of an intellectual in his analysis of the prospects for freedom and peace in 1965, and something of a convinced and committed world revolutionary. For Malcolm 1964 was important because of the measure of progress he believed the oppressed people in Africa, Asia, Latin America, and the Caribbean had made. Comparing the progress made by the oppressed elsewhere in the world with that of Afro-Americans, he said 1964 was for the latter the "Year of Illusion and Delusion," although in official American circles it was regarded as the "Year of Promise" for them. In Africa, Zambia and Malawi had gained political independence and were admitted to membership of the United Nations, a revolution had swept out

─────────

[1] "Prospects for Freedom in 1965," in *Malcolm X Speaks,* edited by George Breitman (New York: Merit Publishers, 1965). The address was given under the auspices of the Militant Labor Forum.

a reactionary, neocolonialist government in Zanzibar, and the Union of Tanganyika and Zanzibar—named the Republic of Tanzania—was a reality. He spoke of the treacherous repression and defeat of the revolution of the People's Republic of the Congo at Stanleyville by Moise Tshombe aided by "hired killers from South Africa" and the combined Belgium-United States paratroop assault of 1964. In spite of American military might, the oppressed of South Vietnam had continued their resistance to United States imperialism in 1964. He was especially delighted over the fact that the Chinese people who had been oppressed for many centuries, generally regarded as poor and backward, had made a scientific breakthrough with the explosion of the atomic bomb. Concluding this review of world affairs in 1964, he acknowledged that these were "tangible gains," and these gains, he said, were possible because the oppressed had realized that "power in defense of freedom is greater than power in behalf of tyranny and oppression, because power, real power, comes from conviction which produces action, uncompromising action." [2]

By the time of his untimely death Malcolm X had moved from black nationalism to internationalism, and had completely identified himself as well as the Afro-American struggle with the revolution of the "wretched of the earth" [3] —the exploited people of the Third World. He had become a foe of the international capitalist system and a staunch Pan-Africanist. Internationally he had gained in stature and he was widely accepted in Africa and the Middle East and probably in Asia and Latin America as a legitimate leader and spokesman of black Americans. In this essay an attempt is made to describe some of the experiences which shaped Malcolm X's world view, and to analyze the intellectual and ideological transformations he underwent. In the light of this analysis Malcolm's stature as an international man clearly emerges.

The break with Elijah Muhammad's Muslim movement was the necessary precondition for this intellectual and

[2] *Ibid.*, pp. 155–64.
[3] The expression is used in the same broad sense as Frantz Fanon uses it. See *The Wretched of the Earth* (Baltimore: Penguin Books, 1967).

ideological transformation because it released Malcolm from the constrictive doctrines of a religio-racial nationalistic mystique that had been a straitjacket to both his ideological growth and his nationalistic activities. It is very likely that if Malcolm had not been forced out of the Nation of Islam, he might eventually have withdrawn anyway because of the pressure building from both within and without for the Muslims to participate actively in the black freedom movement beyond their largely accommodationist program. In his *Autobiography*, Malcolm records in retrospect a gnawing dissatisfaction with the Nation of Islam which he had begun to feel in 1961:

> If I harbored any personal disappointment whatsoever, it was that privately I was convinced that our Nation of Islam could be an even greater force in the American black man's overall struggle—if we engaged in more *action*. By that, I mean I thought privately that we should have amended or relaxed our general non-engagement policy.[4]

Once he had made the break, Malcolm passed successively from a narrowly defined black nationalist outlook[5] to a Pan-Africanism that merged into a Third World political perspective. And at the time of his death he was on the verge of becoming a revolutionary socialist.

A great deal of prominence has been given to the impact of the African and Middle Eastern experiences of 1964 on Malcolm's thinking, and rightly so because the experience abroad strengthened his convictions and enabled him to sharpen his perspective on the relationship of the Afro-American community to Africa and the international community. We should recall that Malcolm had been subjected to two nationalistic experiences that predisposed him to a larger world view of the racial conflict. Malcolm's father was a Garveyite, and Garveyism has always had as

[4] Malcolm X and Alex Haley, *The Autobiography of Malcolm X* (London: Hutchinson and Collins Ltd., 1966), p. 367.

[5] This may be defined briefly as the preoccupation with the need for Afro-Americans to control the political, economic, and social life of their communities in America. It may also include notions of separation from the dominant white society.

an objective the linking up of the problems of the blacks throughout the world—in Africa, America, Latin America, and the Caribbean. From 1952 when he joined the Nation of Islam until he broke away, Malcolm was exposed to the interconnections between the Afro-American problem and those of the "Asiatics," as Elijah called all non-white peoples. While he was a minister in the Nation of Islam he had also had quite a bit of contact with Middle Eastern and African officials and students, and had visited Egypt and a number of West African countries in 1959 as a representative of Elijah Muhammad. These previous experiences and his earlier ideological orientation are important for understanding the broad international outlook which characterized his latter-day nationalist activities. During the last phase of his life the ideological strands of Garveyism merged with a modified version of Elijah Muhammad's doctrine of the Black Nation to form the core of Malcolm's thinking about the Afro-American's struggle and its relationship to Africa and the world.

The seeds of Malcolm's Third World view were actually contained in the doctrine of the Black Nation as taught by Elijah Muhammad. In Muhammad's teaching the world is divided into two groups of people: the Caucasian race and the Black Nation. The latter comprises the entire world population of the "black, brown, red and yellow races." The Nation of Islam, which consists of the black people of the United States, is an integral part of the Black Nation.[6] It is clear when one compares Malcolm's speech given at the Grass Roots Leadership Conference in Detroit in November 1963, when he was still a minister in the Nation of Islam, with his speech on "The Black Revolution," given in Cleveland on April 8, 1964, after his break with Elijah Muhammad, that Malcolm had retained the basic doctrine about the Black Nation. At the Grass Roots Leadership Conference, Malcolm urged his Afro-American audience to unite as the "Nations of Bandung" had done in 1955:

[6] See E. U. Essien-Udom, *Black Nationalism: A Search for an Identity in America* (Chicago: University of Chicago Press, 1962).

In Bandung back in, I think 1954, was the first unity meeting in centuries of *black* people. . . . At Bandung all the nations came together, the dark nations from Africa and Asia . . . despite their economic and political differences they came together. All of them were *black, brown, red* or *yellow.* [Emphasis added.]

. . . They realized all over the world where the dark man was being oppressed, he was being oppressed by the white man; where the dark man was being exploited, he was being exploited by the white man. So that they got together on this basis —they had a common enemy.[7]

Five months later in Cleveland, after he had severed relations with Elijah Muhammad, Malcolm explained to his audience who the participants of the Black Revolution were and what the objective of the Revolution was:

Now the black revolution has been taking place in Africa and Asia and Latin America; when I say black, I mean nonwhite—black, brown, red or yellow. Our brothers and sisters in Asia who were colonized by the Europeans, and in Latin America, the peasants who were colonized by the Europeans, have been involved in a struggle since 1945 to get the colonialist or the colonizing powers, the Europeans off their land, out of their country.[8]

The Black Nation as conceived by Muhammad was part of a religio-racial mystique involving notions of racial superiority combined with a prophetic struggle that would restore the Black Nation to its rightful place of predominance in the world. In spite of the ahistorical claims of Elijah Muhammad, the peoples conceived as comprising the Black Nation correspond in reality to the colonized and recently independent peoples of the world. In this view the Black Nation is currently engaged in a worldwide revolution to overthrow an international political and economic system which enriches the white world of Europe and America and leaves the darker peoples underdeveloped and impoverished. Largely because Malcolm had already been predisposed to think in such terms, he regarded the Afro-American liberation movement as part and parcel of this Black Revolution or the Third World rebellion against

[7] Breitman, *op. cit.,* p. 5.
[8] *Ibid.,* p. 50.

colonialism and imperialism. However, Malcolm's Third World view was not identical with Muhammad's doctrine about the Black Nation. He had sloughed off the ahistorical and irrational claims of the doctrine and looked at international developments from a historical, political, and economic perspective.

The strand of Garveyism in Malcolm's thinking was apparent from a statement he made at the press conference on March 12, 1964, when he announced his break with the Nation of Islam. He still felt then that Elijah Muhammad had the best solution to the race problem in America, and, like Garvey, advocated the return of Afro-Americans to Africa as the long-range solution. He later modified this position and spoke in terms of a cultural and spiritual return to Africa by black Americans while remaining physically in the United States. But his choice of Africa was a distinct departure from Elijah's doctrines, which made the involvement of Afro-American nationalists with Africa sentimental, self-alienating, and escapist. Nevertheless, both his experience with the Nation of Islam and an earlier exposure to Garveyism predisposed him to greater international involvement.

Afro-Americans and the Black Revolution

Malcolm believed that the world was in the throes of a profound revolution; the colonized and newly independent nations were rebelling and were seeking a way out of their economic and political subordination to the Euro-American powers. He felt that the darker nations were losing their fear of the invincibility of the white man and were successfuly engaging him in guerrilla warfare, as attested by the French defeat in both Indo-China and Algeria, and the indecisive military contests of America in Korea and South Vietnam. For Malcolm not only were the colonial powers threatened with losing all their colonies, but they were aware of being minorities in a world sharply divided between the haves and have-nots. In his view the European monopoly of power was not only being challenged, but the balance of power was shifting in favor of the numerically superior darker nations.

In the light of the above analysis of the balance of forces in the world, Malsolm saw the necessity of linking up the Afro-American freedom struggle with those of the colonized and newly independent peoples of the world. He felt that the problem of the subordination of the Afro-American community to the dominant white majority could be resolved by linking it to this worldwide struggle. This shift in tactics was stressed in a speech entitled "The Ballot or the Bullet" given under the auspices of CORE in Cleveland on April 3, 1964. In this speech Malcolm discussed the necessity for black Americans to reinterpret the nature of the civil rights struggle and to seek new allies. He believed that the civil rights struggle should be seen in the context of a worldwide human rights struggle. Accordingly he proposed that the race problem in America should be brought before the United Nations where

. . . our African brothers can throw their weight on our side, where our Asian brothers can throw their weight on our side, where our Latin American brothers can throw their weight on our side. . . .[9]

Malcolm believed that by viewing the race problem in America in terms of the violation of human rights and by seeking understanding and support from countries of the Third World, the Afro-American would strengthen his relative position vis-à-vis the white majority in America. A broader human rights perspective would enable black Americans to realize that they are part of a global majority. Thus their approach to the freedom struggle would be a demanding rather than a supplicating one. He felt that the pendulum of time, that "great subversive," was swinging in favor of the darker people and therefore of the Afro-Americans—provided they had a correct understanding of the global balance of forces. As part of the global revolution, Malcolm believed that the Afro-American struggle would take on the same complexion as that manifesting itself in other parts of the world. He warned white America not to presume that the same guerrilla warfare tactics which have been successfully employed by

[9] *Ibid.,* p. 35.

peoples in the Third World were not a distinct possibility in the United States:

Just as guerrilla warfare is prevailing in Asia and in parts of Africa and in parts of Latin America, you've got to be mighty naïve, or you've got to play the black man cheap, if you don't think someday he's going to wake up and find that it's got to be the ballot or the bullet.[10]

When Malcolm left America in April 1964 he thought of himself as a black nationalist in an inclusive racial and political sense of being connected with the darker, underdeveloped world of Asia, Latin America, and particularly Africa. His international activities grew out of his identification with Africa as well as his conviction that any progress that Afro-Americans had made between World War II and 1964 had come about largely because of international pressures on the United States. Malcolm felt that the Afro-American community had been historically and politically isolated from world currents, and that if its struggle was to be effective it would have to be brought in line with the overall global struggle that was taking place. He went to Mecca and Africa, therefore, as a self-assigned ambassador of the Afro-American freedom movement, to establish contacts that might enable him eventually to internationalize the Afro-American struggle by presenting a case of the violation of human rights before the United Nations.

The Roving Ambassador

In his *Autobiography*, Malcolm recalls how he weighed his probable success as a leader in the Afro-American freedom movement after his break with Elijah Muhammad. He realized that one of his assets as a leader was that he had an international reputation which would be of incalculable value in getting his views and activities discussed and publicized. In addition to this, Malcolm had also developed important contacts in the Middle East and Africa during his years in the Nation of Islam. These contacts would later open doors to him to which he might

[10] *Ibid.,* p. 38.

probably not have had access. This point is important because it was one of the rewards which the Afro-American community reaped as a result of his prolonged association and dedication to nationalistic activities in the Nation of Islam. With the exception of the late Dr. Martin Luther King, Jr., it would be hard to think of another Afro-American leader of that time who could have commanded abroad as much attention and respect as Malcolm did. Malcolm could, therefore, serve as a roving ambassador for the Afro-American commuity in its quest for international support and understanding of the racial problem in America. When he came to the Middle East and Africa this time he also had the added advantage of being a truly independent leader; except for his organizational connection with the Muslim Mosque, Inc., which he himself had established, he was in no way dependent on any kind of support from any quarter in America. This enabled him to speak out clearly, consistently, and uncompromisingly about the conditions and the aspirations of the black man in America.

The Hajj and a New Perspective

No one who reads Malcolm's account of his hajj to Mecca will doubt that this was one of the crowning experiences of his life. The magnanimous reception of him and what he was able to accomplish there came about through one of those many contacts that he had made in New York when he was still a minister in the Nation of Islam. When he applied for a visa to go to Mecca at the Saudi Arabia Embassy in Washington, D.C., Malcolm was told that he would have to seek approval from Dr. Mahmoud Yousseff Shawarbi. Dr. Shawarbi, whom Malcolm had met previously, was a professor at the University of Cairo, a United Nations adviser, and while on leave in New York served as the director of the Federation of Islamic Association in the United States and Canada. Dr. Shawarbi gave his approval for the visa and presented Malcolm with a book, *The Eternal Message of Muhammad*, which the author, Dr. Abd ar-Rahman Azzam, had personally sent to Professor Shawarbi to deliver to Malcolm. In addition, he gave Malcolm the telephone numbers of his own son, who lived in Cairo, and Dr. Azzam's son, who lived in Jedda in Saudi Arabia. The very gracious and generous reception of him in Jedda by the Azzam family, both father and son, and later by the royal family and other high dignitaries was rather overwhelming to Malcolm:

> Never have I been so highly honored. Never have I been made to feel more humble and unworthy. Who would believe the blessings that have been heaped upon an *American Negro?* A few nights ago, a man who would be called in America a "white" man, a United Nations diplomat, an ambassador, a companion of Kings, gave me *his* hotel suite, *his* bed. By this man (Dr. Azzam), His Excellency Prince Faisal, who rules this Holy Land, was made aware of my presence here in Jedda. The very next morning, Prince Faisal's son, in person, informed me that by the will and decree of his esteemed father, I was to be a State Guest.
>
> The Deputy Chief of Protocol himself took me before the Hajj Court. His Holiness Sheikh Muhammad Harkon himself okayed my visit to Mecca. His Holiness gave me two books on Islam, with his personal seal and autograph, and he told me that he prayed that I would be a successful preacher of Islam in America. A car, a driver, and a guide have been placed at my disposal, making it possible for me to travel about this Holy Land almost at will. The government provides air-conditioned quarters and servants in each city that I visit. Never would I have thought of dreaming that I would ever be a recipient of such honors—honors that in America would be bestowed upon a King—not a Negro. . . .[11]

In the passage cited, Malcolm emphasized the manner in which he, as a *Negro*, had been treated because it was in this respect that the Muslim world had its greatest impact on him. He told a gathering of Muslims with whom he had completed the hajj that what had impressed him most was the color blindness of the Muslim world, the brotherhood of all races, and people of all colors from all over the world coming together as one. His experience in Mecca reaffirmed his faith in Islam as a religion that nurtured fraternity and fostered human worth and dignity. When he was in Mecca, he wrote that Islam, if understood

---

[11] Malcolm X and Haley, *op. cit.,* p. 420.

in America, might be able to save the United States from the cancer of racism. He also felt strongly that the importance of form which pervaded Islamic life could lend dignity, grace, and order to the lives of Afro-Americans.

Apart from his personal religious duty, Malcolm had a twofold purpose in making the hajj. First, he wished to establish a link between the Muslim Mosque, Inc., which he had founded with the estimated 750 million orthodox Muslims of the world. Secondly, he wished to win support for his effort to bring a charge of the violation of the Afro-Americans' human rights before the attention of the world at the United Nations. The hajj would, of course, offer a very favorable opportunity for making valuable contacts, since important Muslim political and religious leaders from all over the world make this pilgrimage. Consider a brief listing of the men whom Malcolm met besides the Azzam family: He had an audience with His Eminence, Prince Faisal, the absolute ruler of Saudi Arabia; he met Sheikh Abdullah Eraif, the mayor of Mecca; Hussein Amini, the grand mufti of Jerusalem, to whom he had been introduced by a member of the Turkish parliament; he met a cabinet minister from black Africa, an Indian high official, and a Sudanese high official. It seemed to Malcolm that everywhere he went he was asked questions about America's racial discrimination. Needless to say, Malcolm performed his self-assigned duty as ambassador whenever the opportunity was offered:

> In a hundred different conversations in the Holy Land with Muslims high and low, and from around the world—and, later, when I got to Black Africa—I don't have to tell you never once did I bite my tongue or miss a single opportunity to tell the truth about the crimes, the evils and the indignities that are suffered by the black man in America. Through my interpreter, I lost no opportunity to advertise the black man's real plight. I preached it on the mountain at Arafat, I preached it in the busy lobby of the Jedda Palace Hotel. . . .[12]

Malcolm's experience in the Holy Land had a profound impact on his thinking about race, which he publicly admitted. Prior to that time he had identified whiteness with

[12] *Ibid.*, p. 424.

arrogance and presumed superiority. Because of his experience in Mecca and the discussions with learned men in the Islamic world, he came to realize that the problem did not reside in whiteness itself but in the attitudes which the Western world and particularly America had vested in whiteness. As a consequence, Malcolm repudiated racist thinking, but this does not mean that he had in any way altered his awareness of the predominance of white power either on the international or the American scene. White power is a reality, but it has to be understood in terms of the imperialistic economic system of Western Europe and America. He clearly understood that this system is rigged against the political, economic, and cultural interests of the underdeveloped world, including such "internal colonies" as the Afro-America community. This was one of the insights Malcolm had gained and later would try to teach to Afro-Americans in his effort to reshape their orientation and approach to their problems.

When Malcolm left Mecca, he stopped briefly in Beirut, Cairo, and Nigeria. In Beirut, as he had done in Mecca and would do in Nigeria and Ghana, he spoke about the social, political, and economic injustices suffered by the black community in America. The American press reported that Malcolm had caused a near riot in Beirut, but Malcolm definitely denied this when he arrived in Nigeria. He has, however, observed that he was decidedly pleased with the wholehearted acceptance of him by the African students who were studying in Beirut:

> When I was done, the African students all but besieged me for autographs, some of them even hugged me. Never have even American Negro audiences accepted me as I have been accepted time and again by the less inhibited, more down-to-earth Africans.[13]

The Omowale

From the time Malcolm came to Nigeria until he left he generated an unbelievable excitement. For those of us who had known Malcolm in the United States it was a joy to experience once again that rare combination of ora-

[13] *Ibid.*, p. 428.

torical brilliance and fearlessness coupled with naked honesty and a genuine humility that made Malcolm so compelling and disarming. The African staff and students at the University of Ibadan were notably impressed by the forcefulness and the obvious honesty of his account of the black man's conditions in America. In his speech at Trenchard Hall at the University of Ibadan, Malcolm stressed the necessity for the African nations to lend their help in bringing the Afro-American's case before the United Nations. He argued that the Afro-American community should cooperate with the world's Pan-Africanists; and that even if they remained in America physically, they should return to Africa philosophically and culturally and develop a working unity within the framework of Pan-Africanism. Following his speech at Trenchard Hall, the Nigerian Muslim Students' Society had a reception for Malcolm in the Students' Union Hall and made him an honorary member of their society. They endowed him with a new name, Omowale, meaning "the son who has come home." This gesture symbolized the wholehearted acceptance of Malcolm as a person and leader which we clearly observed among the radical youths and intellectuals in Nigeria. In his television and radio appearances in Nigeria, Malcolm stressed the need for African support to bring the charge of violation of Afro-American human rights by the United States before the United Nations. Malcolm also met with highly placed Nigerian officials who lent a very sympathetic ear to his ideas. He reports one of them as saying that when the black people throughout the Americas and Africa link up their struggle, the political picture of the world would undoubtedly change. Such global, Pan-Africanist thinking from a highly placed African official was an added encouragement to Malcolm's internationalist approach to the Afro-American problem.

After leaving Nigeria, Malcolm visited Ghana, which at that time was the political Mecca of the Pan-Africanist movement. Short of a twenty-one-gun salute, Malcolm was accorded a reception in Ghana befitting a head of state. A contingent of the Afro-American expatriate community in Ghana had formed a Malcolm X Committee to receive him and escort him through a calendar-packed seven days.

The members of the press were particularly generous and helpful in making speaking arrangements for Malcolm and publicizing his visit. They offered their Press Club for his use as a headquarters and insisted on paying his hotel expenses. At the press conference they arranged for him, Malcolm stressed the need for establishing a dialogue between the African and Afro-American communities. He observed that if the 22 million Afro-Americans were properly organized and informed, they could be an effective force for Africa's good. On their part, he pointed out, the African nations needed to exert effort on a governmental level on America's racial discrimination and dehumanization of its black population. He pointed out that America had become the last bulwark of imperialism and colonialism, shoring up the Verwoerds and Salazars whose regimes had survived because of American support.

In the largest single audience that he had in Africa, Malcolm addressed the students and faculty of the University of Ghana, Legon, in the Great Hall. Miss Alice Windom, an Afro-American member of the Malcolm X Committee, has recorded the impact Malcolm had on the Legon students, who, on the whole, had an image in Africa of being politically conservative in a progressive political situation:

> I believe it is safe to say, from subsequent reports, that he worked a qualitative change in the attitudes of many shaky and downright reactionary students. For he brought home in vivid language the problems of African countries struggling to free themselves from the psychological and cultural as well as the economic and political legacies of colonialism. He thoroughly destroyed the U.S.I.A. image of America and exposed the plight of the Afro-American in terms new to many of the students.[14]

Malcolm also addressed the students at the Kwame Nkrumah Ideological Institute of Winneba, which was the training ground for the cadres needed to carry forward the ideological revolution in Ghana. At the end of his speech the students presented Malcolm with a set of the then President Nkrumah's works and escorted him on a tour of the school.

[14] Unpublished ms.

On this occasion Malcolm met most of the officials of Ghana. To crown this experience, Malcolm was invited to address the members of the Ghanaian parliament. Miss Windom has observed that to her knowledge this was a unique honor accorded to a foreigner by the Ghanaian parliament. In his address to the members of parliament, Malcolm stressed that it was inconsistent for African states to condemn the colonialism and racism of Portugal and South Africa and remain silent while black people in America were being oppressed. At the end of his talk Malcolm has reported one of the comments he heard: "Yes! We support the Afro-American . . . morally, physically, materially if necessary!"

The pinnacle of honor conferred on Malcolm during his visit to Ghana was an audience with Osagyefo Dr. Kwame Nkrumah. Malcolm has given an account of his experience in his *Autobiography*:

> We discussed the unity of Africans and peoples of African descent. We agreed that Pan-Africanism was the key also to the problems of those of African heritage. . . . My time with him was up all too soon. I promised faithfully that when I returned to the United States, I would relay to Afro-Americans his personal warm regards.[15]

The Chinese ambassador and Mrs. Huang Hua gave a formal dinner in Malcolm's honor. Other guests included the Algerian and Cuban ambassadors and Mrs. W. E. B. DuBois. The search for allies and support was paying dividends in Ghana. On Malcolm's last day there, the Nigerian high commissioner, the late Alhaji Isa Wali, gave a luncheon in his honor. His Excellency spoke of his own experience of discrimination when he lived in Washington, D.C., and stressed the brotherhood of the African and Afro-American people. He presented Malcolm with an African robe and turban worn by Muslims in Nigeria, and a translation of the Holy Quaran. Following the luncheon, Mrs. W. E. B. DuBois, then the director of Ghana Television Service, invited Malcolm to her home so that he could see and photograph the place where Dr. DuBois had spent his last days. That evening Malcolm was the

15 Malcolm X and Haley, *op. cit.,* p. 426.

guest of the Cuban ambassador, His Excellency Mr. Armando Entralgo González. All the African ambassadors in Accra were invited to this occasion. The following morning when Malcolm was leaving Accra, a motorcade accompanying five ambassadors arrived to see him off at the airport. Malcolm was uncharacteristically speechless at this farewell tribute: "I no longer had any words." However, he later recorded his feelings about the reception given him in Ghana:

> I can only wish that every American black man could have shared my ears, my eyes, and my emotions throughout the round of engagements which had been made for me in Ghana. And my point in saying this is not the reception that I personally received as an individual of whom they had heard, but it was the reception tendered to me as the symbol of the militant American black man, as I had the honor to be regarded.[16]

From Ghana, Malcolm briefly visited Liberia and Dakar, Senegal. From Senegal he flew to Morocco for a day, where he visited the famed Casbah, a ghetto area created by the French settlers in Casablanca. The Casbah impressed Malcolm as another Harlem in North Africa. He also made a brief visit to Algeria before returning to the United States on May 21, 1964.

The Impact of Africa on Malcolm

Malcolm's experiences in the Middle East and Africa strengthened his conviction about the necessity to internationalize the Afro-American problem, and underscored the possibility of getting African support at the United Nations for a charge of human rights violation against the United States. When Malcolm arrived at Kennedy Airport, he told a large press audience that it was no longer necessary to continue thinking about the struggle in America purely in domestic terms, and stressed that a precedent had already been established internationally by the cases involving violation of human rights against South Africa and Portugal. He saw no reason why America could not be charged similarly. Malcolm told the

[16] *Ibid.*, p. 433.

reporters that he had ample evidence and was certain that Africans were deeply concerned about the Afro-American struggle for human rights and regarded the Afro-Americans as their long-lost brothers. In reply to a question about his letter from Mecca, he told the reporters that he was satisfied that he had established an affiliation with the 750 million orthodox Muslims of the world. He assured his audience that he had renounced racist thinking, but emphasized that this grew largely out of the climate of brotherhood which he had experienced in the Islamic world. He said—and the Kerner Commission Report on the Riots in America has recently affirmed this—that the seeds of racism were so deep in America that few whites were free of it; those who were not conscious racists were subconsciously so. He said that he had nevertheless withdrawn the blanket indictment of white Americans and would in the future judge a man by his deeds, and expressed a willingness to cooperate with those few whites who did not fall into either of the two categories. Malcolm would later make the observation that those whites who seemed to be free of racist bias were usually socialist because it was impossible to be a capitalist without being a racist. Malcolm observed that the peoples of African heritage were presently in a state of disunity, but raised the specter of Garvey when he wondered over the benefits which might accrue to them if the people of Africa and those of African descent in the New World were to unite for the achievement of their common goals.

Throughout Malcolm's stay in the Middle East and West Africa, reporters had tried to reach him to find out what he had to say about a "blood brother" group that was allegedly connected with Malcolm's organization. The first time Malcolm heard anything about this group was at our home in Ibadan when a lecturer at the university asked him a question about the group. Malclom had known nothing about it, but commented that the conditions in the black ghettos might well engender such groups and that we should be concerned with the *cause* rather than the effect. On May 29, 1964, Malcolm spoke at a symposium sponsored by the Militant Labor Forum on "The Harlem Hate Gang Scare." Malcolm's speech on the "Hate Gang" reflects a synthesis of the insights which he had gained abroad with his understanding of the American situation. His foreign experience had led him to see that the Afro-American problem is a part of a "system," both domestic and international, in which there is a vital relationship between capitalism, colonialism, and racism. He became convinced that the capitalist system fosters racism and uses it as an instrument of economic exploitation and political subjugation. The system establishes a colonial relationship between a dominant and subordinate group that is sustained by police brutality, calculated to keep the subjugated people terrified and psychologically castrated. Malcolm argued that Harlem and all the other black ghetto communities in the United States fall into this pattern. He compared Harlem with the Casbah, and he spoke of how his "blood brothers" in Algeria and Morocco had taken him into the Casbahs of their countries and had shown him the conditions and the suffering which their people had lived through under the French colonialists:

Algeria was a police state. Any occupied territory is a police state; their presence is like occupying forces, like an occupying army. . . . They are in Harlem to protect the interests of the businessmen who don't even live there.[17]

Malcolm argued that the same conditions that prevailed in colonial Algeria exist in all the black communities in America. He refused to apologize for the existence of a blood brother organization if it existed at all and argued that the same common oppression, humiliation, and degradation that had made the Algerians realize they were blood brothers and had forced them to resort to terrorist tactics in order to liberate themselves would band together the frustrated and desperate youth of the black ghettos of America into blood brothers or Mau Mau groups. He warned that the young Afro-Americans were not going to be oppressed by people in either sheets or uniforms.

Malcolm did not present himself as a convinced socialist at this time, but he did say he noticed when he was traveling that some of the formerly colonized countries were turning away from capitalism and moving toward

[17] Breitman, op. cit., p. 66.

socialism. He said he did not quite know what kind of political and economic system could cure America of her racism, but he did know that the Afro-American could not achieve freedom under the present economic and political arrangements in America, and clearly asserted that there is a close connection between capitalism and racism. Two months later when he went to Cairo to attend the summit meeting of the Organization of African Unity (OAU), he summed up his opinion on the "American system" in an article published in the Egyptian Gazette:

> The present American "system" can never produce freedom for the black man. A chicken cannot lay a duck egg because the chicken's "system" is not designed or equipped to produce a duck egg. . . . The American "system" (political, economic, and social) was produced from the enslavement of the black man, and this present "system" is capable only of perpetuating that enslavement.
> In order for a chicken to produce a duck egg its system would have to undergo a drastic and painful revolutionary change . . . or REVOLUTION. So be it with America's enslaving system.[18]

Malcolm and the OAU

On June 29, 1964, the Organization of Afro-American Unity (OAAU) was formed in New York with Malcolm as its chairman. July 1964 saw Malcolm in his role as roving ambassador back in Cairo again, this time to participate in the Head of States Summit Meeting of the OAU. Malcolm's appearance in Cairo caused quite a stir. This was the first time that a black American had made an effort to have the Afro-American's plight treated as an African problem. On his return from the conference Malcolm told one of the present authors in Lagos (Nigeria) that he had found no doors closed to him in any of the countries he had visited. In his highly resourceful way, Malcolm lobbied successfully and was admitted as an observer at the meeting. This was quite a feat! It must be remembered that this was a head of states summit meeting.

[18] Malcolm X, "Racism: The Cancer That Is Destroying America," in the Egyptian Gazette, August 25, 1964.

It was an extraordinary concession to Malcolm and the Afro-American community which he represented since he was neither a head of an existing state nor a leader of a state in exile. In an interview with Milton Henry in Cairo played over the GOAL radio program in Detroit, Malcolm confessed that he had to lobby the various delegates to the conference because the information agencies of the United States Government had almost successfully convinced most Africans that the Afro-Americans did not identify with Africa and that Africans would be foolish to get involved with their problems. However, Malcolm eventually succeeded in making the African delegates understand that any improvements in the position of the Afro-Americans had in fact come about as a result of international pressure on America. He argued that it had taken the pressures of Hitler and then Stalin on the American system to bring about the modicum of economic improvement which the Afro-Americans have had since World War II.

In the memorandum which Malcolm submitted to the Summit Meeting he emphasized that the purposes of his organization, the OAAU, were consistent with the objectives of the OAU. Malcolm's main argument was that there was an identity of purpose and interests between the Afro-Americans and the African peoples; that the Afro-American problem was not just their problem or even an American problem but a world problem that had to be resolved by the international community. He argued that the deteriorating plight of the Afro-American community posed a threat to the peace of the entire world. Malcolm cited specific instances of police brutality and humiliation of African representatives and students in America to demonstrate that the racial problems in Africa would never be solved until racism had been destroyed in America. He contended that Africans would never be fully respected until their brothers in America were also recognized and treated as full human beings. Malcolm argued that if Arthur Goldberg, the former U. S. Supreme Court justice, could threaten to take the Russian Government before the United Nations for violating the human rights of 3 million Jews in Russia, there was no reason why the

African members of the OAU should feel reluctant to bring the United States Government before the UN. He argued that if South African racism is not a domestic issue, then American racism should not be treated as a domestic issue. Malcolm pointed out that after ten years the U. S. Supreme Court's decision on desegregation of school facilities had not been implemented. He said that if the United States Government could not enforce the decisions of the highest court in America there was no need thinking that the passage of the 1964 civil rights law was going to be enforced. Because of U.S. propaganda and pressure which had been brought to bear on the African delegates and because of the likelihood of future pressure, Malcolm ended his memorandum with the warning "Don't escape from European colonialism only to become even more enslaved by deceitful, 'friendly' American dollarism."

For reasons which seem to us obvious the American press did not publicize the resolution which the Head of States Summit Conference passed, deploring racism in the United States. Malcolm's efforts were a decided success. Not only did the Summit pass the resolution, but some of the delegates promised officially to assist the OAAU in its plan and to give their support during the following session of the United Nations. The wording of the resolution, as might be expected from an international body with diffuse and often conflicting interests, was mild, but its intent was clear. The Head of States Summit noted "with satisfaction the recent enactment of the Civil Rights Act designed to secure for American Negroes their basic human rights." The OAU was "deeply disturbed, however, by continuing manifestations of racial bigotry and racial oppression against Negro citizens of the United States of America." The resolution reaffirmed the OAU's "belief that the existence of discriminatory practice is a matter of deep concern to member states of the OAU," and urged "the government authorities in the United States of America to intensify their efforts to ensure the total elimination of all forms of discrimination based on race, color, or ethnic origin." [19]

[19] Quoted in Breitman, *op. cit.*, p. 92.

From Malcolm's point of view his participation at the OAU Summit Meeting had been a rewarding experience in many ways. It had given him contact with the revolutionaries from southern Africa and the Portuguese colonies. He told Milton Henry that he had benefited from the exchange of ideas with them; they had described in detail the brutal atmosphere in which they lived and had enlightened him on the means they were using to bring an end to their sufferings. Malcolm felt that Afro-American leaders should unite in a summit body as the African leaders had done, and go abroad as leaders to make their purposes understood by the African Governments and to exchange ideas with African leaders.

Malcolm's Impact on Africa

It might be difficult to gauge the actual impact Malcolm made on Africa, but a rather clear picture does emerge of a number of achievements. He initiated a dialogue between the Afro-American community and the African peoples on an official and unofficial level. By publicizing the nature of the problems confronting the black community and the worsening conditions in the ghettos of America, Malcolm presented a different image of the black man's outlook and mood in America from the image often portrayed by the information agencies of the United States and their official black representatives in Africa. He exposed the hypocrisy of America's African policies and her neocolonialist interests by underscoring the inconsistency of bypassing the black American and ignoring the conditions that were leading to violent racial conflict in America while sending "aid" and Peace Corps volunteers to the African continent. He received promises of support from a few African officials for bringing a charge of violation of human rights by the United States before the United Nations. It is certainly clear from the receptions he was given in the countries he visited and the access he had to African as well as a few Asian officials that they not only gave him a sympathetic hearing but welcomed the stand he took. To this extent he succeeded in taking the Afro-American problem out of isolation and casting it as an international problem that affected the dignity of African peoples in particular and the peace of the world in general.

John Lewis and Donald Harris, who were making a tour of several African countries as representatives of the Student Nonviolent Coordinating Committee toward the end of Malcolm's second tour of Africa, have observed: "Malcolm's impact on Africa was just fantastic. In every country he was known and served as the main criteria for categorizing other Afro-Americans and their political views." [20]

As would be expected, the United States State Department also began to take an interest in the impact Malcolm was having on Africa. In an article in *The New York Times* (August 13, 1964), M. S. Handler noted official American concern regarding Malcolm's activities in Cairo:

> The State Department and the Justice Department have begun to take an interest in Malcolm's campaign to convince African states to raise the question of persecution of American Negroes at the United Nations. . . .
> After studying it [Malcolm's memorandum] officials said that if Malcolm succeeded in convincing just one African government to bring up the charge at the United Nations, the United States government would be faced with a touchy problem.
> The United States, officials here believe, would find itself in the same category as South Africa, Hungary and other countries whose domestic policies have become debating issues at the United Nations. The issue, officials say, would be of service to critics of the United States, Communist and non-Communist, and contribute to the undermining of the position the United States had asserted for itself as the leader of the West in the advocacy of human rights. . . .
> According to one diplomatic report Malcolm had not met with success, but the report was not documented and officials here today conceded the possibility that Malcolm might have succeeded.[21]

If the State Department grudgingly "conceded" that Malcolm might have been successful in convincing at least one African nation to raise the issue of human rights at

[20] *Ibid.*, p. 93.
[21] *Ibid.*, p. 94.

the United Nations, it did not for a moment doubt that Malcolm had had some influence at the United Nations during the debate over the Congo. The African delegates denounced American policy both at home and abroad and cited as evidence the attitude of the United States Government toward the civil rights struggle in Mississippi. M. S. Handler, writing in *The New York Times* (January 2, 1965), reported that Malcolm had urged the Africans to use "the racial situation in the United States as an instrument of attack in discussing international problems," because "such a strategy would give the African states more leverage in dealing with the United States and would in turn give American Negroes more leverage in American society."

In assessing his own impact on African thinking in December 1964, Malcolm observed that the greatest accomplishment that was made in the Afro-American struggle in 1964 was the successful linking together of the Afro-American and the African problems:

And today you'll find in the United Nations, and it's not an accident, that every time the Congo question or anything on the African continent is being debated, they couple it with what is going on, or what is happening to you and me in Mississippi and Alabama.[22]

When he was asked in a radio interview (January 28, 1965) if he took credit for the African delegates at the United Nations linking up the problems of the Congo with Mississippi, Malcolm would only say that the African states were represented by intelligent men and it was only a matter of time before they saw the obvious connections. Furthermore, his response reflects the broad identification he had achieved with the oppressed peoples of the world and his awareness of racism as an instrument of imperialism and neocolonialism:

And it is a good example of why our problem has to be internationalized. Now the African nations are speaking out and linking the problem of racism in Mississippi with the problem of racism in the Congo, and also the problem of racism in South Vietnam. It's all racism. It's all part of the

[22] *Ibid.*, p. 151.

vicious racist system that the Western powers have used to
continue to degrade and exploit and oppress the people in
Africa and Asia and Latin America during recent centuries.

And when these people in these different areas begin to see
that the problem is the same problem, and when the 22 million black Americans see that our problem is the same as the
problem of the people who are being oppressed in South
Vietnam and the Congo and Latin America, then—the oppressed people of this earth make up a majority—then we
approach our problem as a majority that can *demand,* not
as a minority that has to beg.[23]

Lastly, it should be remarked that Malcolm's honesty,
sincerity, and forthrightness in dealing with the problems
posed by racism, imperialism, and neocolonialism endeared
him to African radicals and gave to many who had seen
or heard him a sense of dignity and pride often so lacking
in many of their leaders.

The Last Days

When Malcolm returned to the United States after his
eighteen weeks abroad, he saw his major task as educative.
The Sunday evening talks at the Audubon Ballroom in
New York were designed primarily to enlarge the consciousness of Afro-Americans and to reshape their sense
of identity so that they would see themselves as an extension of the African peoples and part of the Black
Revolution. The basic perspective and ideas he had espoused in Africa and the Middle East had been reaffirmed
by the receptivity to them of the African peoples and
officials he had met. But Malcolm admits in his *Autobiography* that he had to be honest and frank—he knew that
Afro-Americans were not going to rush to take their
problem before the United Nations. Two of the "big six"
civil rights leaders had already indicated in 1963 that
Chairman Mao Tse-tung's statement of support was not
the kind of assistance they needed or were looking for. It
was also clear from some of the comments of leaders and
ordinary people who asked him about his program that the
Afro-American community by and large did not see what

[23] *Ibid.,* p. 234.

could be gained by going to Africa and the Middle East instead of going into the ghetto and trying to forge some kind of program that would create better opportunities for jobs, housing, and education. Malcolm insisted that unless the Afro-Americans understood their problems in the context of the world struggle, they would not really understand the possibilities open to them. He believed that once a man really understood his problem, he will do whatever is necessary to solve it. Consequently, he spent a great deal of time trying to explain the broad political and economic picture as it affected oppressed people throughout the world, and tried to show the Afro-American the connections between his situation and the Third World struggle for decolonization. It would not be an exaggeration to say that Malcolm's main effort was to transform the consciousness and identity of the Afro-American and to prepare him for a revolutionary struggle in America.

Malcolm was convinced that the Western imperialist system was faced with an "external" rebellion in the colonial and ex-colonial areas that had affected and intensified the rebellion of the colonized peoples inside the imperialist nations. The effect of this rebellion was to intensify the Afro-American's drive for his own freedom. What Malcolm envisioned was the linking up of the external and internal rebellions against the imperialists in as many places as possible to exert pressure both on the domestic and international scene. Thus, when he was in Ghana and in France he formed chapters of the OAAU to function as pressure groups against America's domestic colonialism and her neocolonialism abroad. When Malcolm returned to France in November 1964 on the invitation of the Afro-American community in Paris, he was refused entry. Apparently, the Communist trade unions, alarmed at the threat of racial divisions within the labor ranks, put pressure on willing officials to refuse him entry. The potential coalition of Afro-Americans, Africans, and Arabs had alarmed French officials. This incident was cited by Malcolm as further proof that the "power elite" in France, England, and America were becoming concerned about the oppressed within their countries:

The newly awakened people all over the world pose a problem for what is known as Western interests which are imperialism, colonialism, racism and all these other negative isms or vulturistic isms. Just as the external forces pose a grave threat, they can now see that the internal forces pose an even greater threat only when they have properly analysed the situation and know what the stakes really are.[24]

America, Malcolm felt, was the real bastion of international imperialism, and the Afro-American once he appreciated the overall global revolution and understood his relation to it would realize his strategic position in relation to the international power system. On this regard Malcolm was also concerned with the problem of *method* and insisted that Afro-Americans should employ whatever means were necessary to win freedom. The means Malcolm envisioned seem to have included violence, which he felt had proved effective abroad. On one occasion he invited Sheik Abdul Rahman Muhammad Babu of Tanzania, who had taken part in the 1964 Zanzibar revolution, to speak to the audience at the Audubon. Muhammad Babu addressed the audience, and significantly brought the following greetings from another revolutionary, Che Guevara, who wrote:

Dear brothers and sisters of Harlem, I would have liked to have been with you and Babu, but the conditions are not good for this meeting. Receive the warm salutations of the Cuban people and especially those of Fidel, who remembers enthusiastically his visit to Harlem a few years ago.

After Babu spoke, Malcolm rendered this advice to his audience:

You may say, "Well, how in the hell are we going to stop them? A great big man like this?" Brothers and sisters, always remember this. When you're inside another man's house, and the furniture is his, curtains, all those fine decorations, there isn't too much action he can put down in there without messing up his furniture and windows and his house. And you let him know that when he puts his hands on you, it's not only you he puts his hands on, it's his whole house, you'll burn it down. You're in a position to—you have nothing to lose. Then

[24] *Ibid.*, p. 169.

the man will act right . . . he will only act right when you let him know that you know that he has more to lose than you have. You haven't got anything to lose but discrimination and segregation.[25]

In the summer of 1964 Malcolm predicted that the Afro-Americans would eventually be forced to resort to terroristic tactics as other colonized peoples had done to achieve their freedom. He wrote in the *Egyptian Gazette* that for the black masses, particularly the young people, the American dream had become a racist nightmare. By November 1964 he had become convinced that revolutionary struggle was the only alternative that Afro-Americans had in the face of the continued repression and resistance to their efforts to gain their rights within the established political system. The refusal of the Democratic Party leaders to seat the black representatives of the Mississippi Freedom Democratic Party at the Democratic Convention in August 1964, coupled with the brutalities inflicted on black people during and after the Mississippi elections, underscored the futility of trying to work with a corrupt and morally defunct political system. After listening to Fannie Lou Hamer's account of her experience both in Mississippi and in Atlantic City with the leaders of the Democratic Party, Malcolm concluded that to communicate with white America, Afro-Americans needed to change to the language of force and brutality, and adopt methods such as those used by the Kenya freedom fighters:

. . . you and I can best learn how to get real freedom by studying how Kenyatta brought it to his people in Kenya, and how Odinga helped him, and the excellent job that was done by the Mau Mau freedom fighters. In fact, that's what we need in Mississippi. In Mississippi we need a Mau Mau. In Alabama we need a Mau Mau. In Georgia we need a Mau Mau. Right here in Harlem, in New York City, we need a Mau Mau.
   I say it with no anger; I say it with careful forethought. . . .
   We *need* a Mau Mau. If they don't want to deal with the Mississippi Freedom Democratic Party, then we'll give them something else to deal with; if they don't want to deal with the Student Nonviolent Coordinating Committee, then we have to give them an alternative.[26]

[25] *Ibid.*, p. 111.
[26] *Ibid.*, pp. 114–15.

From Black Nationalism to Internationalism

The most remarkable thing about Malcolm's brilliant but short career of dedicated leadership was his capacity for constructive intellectual development. After his break with the Muslims Malcolm underwent an ideological transformation. He came to understand the latent implications of his basic concept of the Black Revolution. When Malcolm spoke of the Black Revolution prior to his visit to the Middle East and Africa he used the words in the framework of political independence or decolonization. At this time he was an advocate of black nationalism in a racially inconclusive sense of the black, yellow, brown, and red peoples—the colonized of the earth. The shift from black nationalism occurred as a result of his African and Middle Eastern experience, which enabled him to see that the basic problem confronting the unindustrialized or colored world was not race but the disadvantageous economic effects of the international capitalist system. This insight strengthened Malcolm's earlier conviction about the need for the people in the underdeveloped world to unite not only to destroy colonialism but capitalism as well. In August 1964 when Malcolm said that it would take REVOLUTION for the black man to achieve freedom in America, he meant the destruction of the capitalist system both domestically and internationally. It was not a question of winning through the ballot anymore but of using the bullet to destroy an economic system that is nationally and internationally incompatible with freedom for the oppressed peoples of the world. When he was asked in January 1965 whether he still felt that there would be an Armageddon in the United States by 1984, as had been predicted by Elijah Muhammad, Malcolm discounted Muhammad's teachings but said he believed that the world was moving toward a showdown:

I believe that there will ultimately be a clash between the oppressed and those that do the oppressing, I believe that there will be a clash between those who want freedom, and those who want to continue the systems of exploitation.[27]

[27] *Ibid.*, p. 252.

We now suggest that Malcolm's basic perspectives were Pan-Africanist combined with a Third World socialist view which saw the struggle going on in the world as being against capitalism, colonialism, and racism. At the time of his death Malcolm's world view was similar to Frantz Fanon's as exemplified in the latter's book, *The Wretched of the Earth*. It is very likely that Malcolm read this book, as it was presented to him as a gift when he was in Africa, but whether he was influenced by Fanon's thinking or not, he was already predisposed to this kind of ideological development. The trip to Africa and the Middle East enabled him to understand the economic implications of his basic concept of the Black Revolution.

But Malcolm was not thinking solely in racial terms toward the end of his life. He very clearly indicated that the oppressed might find allies both in America and in Europe that were opposed to the capitalist system. Several times he reiterated that he would be willing to cooperate with any person or group that was honestly willing to fight against the American system that oppressed its black citizens at home and other peoples abroad.

The revolutionary struggle in the world, as Malcolm saw it, revolved around *power*—power to control human material resources and to determine the rate and path of economic development so that the peoples in the underdeveloped areas (including all the Harlems in the United States) might extricate themselves from the impoverishing colonial economic relationship whereby they have remained suppliers of raw materials and have in turn served as markets for the finished products of the developed countries. Malcolm denounced the American military intervention in the Congo in 1964, pointing out the strategic geographical position of the Congo as the gateway to the racist imperialist regimes of South-West Africa, South Africa, Southern Rhodesia, and Mozambique, where there are huge Western investments in mineral resources. He frequently argued that unless Afro-Americans understood their relation to the Congo, they would not be able to deal effectively with their problem in Mississippi since the same domestic racist interests are linked up internationally with similar interests that combine to oppress the darker races. He tried to destroy the image of America's invincibility in the minds of the Afro-Americans and make them realize that the American, French, British, and other European imperialist powers were being successfully challenged by formerly colonized peoples. He felt that as these newly independent states assumed control over their own resources they were weakening the international capitalist system. When he was asked in an interview what he thought about the struggle between capitalism and socialism, Malcolm remarked:

> It is impossible for capitalism to survive primarily because the system of capitalism needs some blood to suck. Capitalism used to be like an eagle, but now it's more like a vulture. It used to be strong enough to go and suck anybody's blood whether they were strong or not. But now it has become more cowardly, like the vulture, and it can only suck the blood of the helpless. As the nations of the world free themselves then capitalism has less victims, less to suck, and it becomes weaker and weaker. It's only a matter of time in my opinion before it will collapse completely.[28]

Alone, or almost single-handedly, Malcolm sought to link the Afro-American liberation movement with the liberation movement of the Third World, or what he called the Black Revolution. In his effort to internationalize the Afro-American problem Malcolm added a new and powerful dimension to a worldwide struggle that could take on more meaning as the racial conflict in the United States intensifies. Malcolm initiated the linking up of the black freedom fighters in America with revolutionaries all the way from Cuba to Mozambique. In other words, he sought to foster a worldwide revolutionary fraternity that would grow in strength and size as the conflict between the haves and the have-nots intensifies. The radical wing of the Black Power advocates in the United States appears to be executing the ideas implicit in his geopolitical analysis of the Black Revolution. In May 1967, SNCC declared that it was no longer a civil rights organization but a human rights organization interested in human rights not only in the United States but throughout the world, and declared its support for liberation groups struggling to free people

[28] *Ibid.*, p. 215.

from racism and exploitation. In July 1967, Stokely Carmichael attended the Organization of Latin American Solidarity Conference in Havana. When Carmichael left Cuba, he visted Vietnam, Algeria, Syria, Egypt, Guinea, Tanzania, Scandinavia, and France. He talked with leaders in all these countries, including Fidel Castro, Ho Chi Minh, Sekou Toure, Kwame Nkrumah, and Julius Nyerere. In August 1967, James Forman and Harold Moore, Jr., represented SNCC at a seminar sponsored by the United Nations in Kitwe, Zambia, on "Apartheid, Racial Discrimination and Colonialism in Southern Africa." The position paper of their organization was "The Indivisible Struggle Against Racism, Apartheid and Colonialism." These are but a few examples which suggest Malcolm's influence in reshaping and reorientating the Afro-American's perception of the nature of his struggle.[29]

A logical extension of Malcolm's basic concept of the Black Revolution is revolutionary socialism. He believed that eventually the oppressed peoples of the world must come to grips with the *cause* of their exploitation. The only way out for the "haves and have-nots" cycle is through a radical break by the latter with the colonial economic relationship. The disappointing results of the recent UNCTAD (United Nations Conference on Trade and Development) point up the far-reaching implications and visionary scope of Malcolm's concept of the Black Revolution. After the conference Dr. Raul Prebisch, Argentine general secretary, predicted:

If we do not succeed in effective and vigorous economic development the alternatives are clear. The deteriorating situation in the have-not countries will demonstrate that the extremists are right. Black power—now merely a U.S. phenomenon—will become brown, yellow and black power on a global scale.[30]

The reverberations of the Black Revolution or Black Power have also been heard in Great Britain. In response

[29] The Student Nonviolent Coordinating Committee (SNCC), *Position Paper*, Lusaka, 24 July–4 August, 1967; mimeographed.
[30] "The Haves and Have-Nots," *Newsweek*, April 22, 1968.

MALCOLM X: AN INTERNATIONAL MAN 267

to M.P. Enoch Powell's speech in Parliament in April
1968, advocating a clampdown on colored immigration
and a scheme to encourage one in fifty colored immigrants
to return to their homelands, delegates from twenty-one
organizations representing Africans, Indians, Pakistanis,
and West Indians formed a Black Peoples' Alliance in the
United Kingdom. The meeting was sponsored by Mr.
Jagmohan Joshi, president of the thirty thousand-strong
Indian Workers Association. "For the first time," said Mr.
Joshi, "black people have decided to unite their forces." [31]
Malcolm X would not have expected less!

[31] Quoted in the *Daily Sketch* (Ibadan), 30 April, 1968, p. 2.

PART V

MALCOLM X
IN HIS OWN WORDS

PREFACE TO PART V

The best interpreter of Malcolm X is Malcolm X. He was a man in transition. In his short and eventful lifetime, he made many changes because he learned many things. Most important of all, he learned how to correct himself. He was principally a speaker and his style was one of the most effective of any orator of this century. His language was direct and to the point and could be understood on all educational levels. His speech "Message to the Grass Roots," delivered in November 1963, is a perfect example of his mastery of language and the projection of ideas. It was this kind of creativity in Malcolm X that literally built the Black Muslim movement in the United States. This speech also proves that Malcolm X was an astute revolutionary theoretician.

The speech "God's Judgment of White America" set in motion or brought to the surface the difficulties precipitating the forces and circumstances which caused him to be forced out of the Black Muslim movement.

The speeches of Malcolm X in Africa are bridge-building efforts that were partly successful. The fact that these speeches were made at all is remarkable. Even more remarkable is the fact that they were listened to respectfully by most of the heads of state in Africa, who responded quite favorably to the message of Malcolm X.

The African projection of Malcolm X and his brief travels in Africa, on behalf of the plight of black Americans, showed that he had an insight into the worldwide struggle of black people that was over and above that of any other designated leader. His speech to the domestic Peace Corps, made in December 1964, proves again how effective Malcolm X was in getting his message across to young people. To them he was more than a public orator; he was a great teacher and an intellectual father.

The article "Some Reflections on 'Negro History Week' and the Role of the Black People in History" is an excerpt from the pamphlet Malcolm X on Afro-American History. Malcolm X clearly understood that history is an instrument of both enslavement and liberation, and he was trying to tell his people, especially the young, how to use history affirmatively.

While the untimely death of Malcolm X is tragic and unfortunate, the positive aspect is that he left behind a philosophy of liberation. When seen in total context, it will effect his emergency as the finest revolutionary theoretician and activist produced by America's black proletariat in this century.

J. H. C.

DEFINITION OF A
REVOLUTION *

I would like to make a few comments concerning the difference between the Black Revolution and the Negro revolution. Are they both the same? And if they're not, what is the difference? What is the difference between a black revolution and a Negro revolution? First, what is a revolution? Sometimes I'm inclined to believe that many of our people are using this word "revolution" loosely, without taking careful consideration of what this word actually means, and what its historic characteristics are. When you study the historic nature of revolutions, the motive of a revolution, the objective of a revolution, the result of a revolution, and the methods used in a revolution, you may change words. You may devise another program, you may change your goal and you may change your mind.

Look at the American Revolution in 1776. That revolution was for what? For land. Why did they want land? Independence. How was it carried out? Bloodshed. Number one, it was based on land, the basis of independence. And the only way they could get it was bloodshed. The French Revolution—what was it based on? The landless against the landlord. What was it for? Land. How did they get it? Bloodshed. Was no love lost, was no compromise, was no negotiation. I'm telling you—you don't know what a revolution is. Because when you find out what it is, you'll get back in the alley, you'll get out of the way.

* Except from "Message to the Grass Roots." November 1963.

The Russian Revolution—what was it based on? Land; the landless against the landlord. How did they bring it about? Bloodshed. You haven't got a revolution that doesn't involve bloodshed. And you're afraid to bleed. I said, you're afraid to bleed.

As long as the white man sent you to Korea, you bled. He sent you to Germany, you bled. He sent you to the South Pacific to fight the Japanese, you bled. You bleed for white people, but when it comes to seeing your own churches being bombed and little black girls murdered, you haven't got any blood. You bleed when the white man says bleed; you bite when the white man says bite; and you bark when the white man says bark. I hate to say this about us, but it's true. How are you going to be non-violent in Mississippi, as violent as you were in Korea? How can you justify being non-violent in Mississippi and Alabama, when your churches are being bombed, and your little girls are being murdered, and at the same time you are going to get violent with Hitler, and Tojo, and somebody else you don't even know?

If violence is wrong in America, violence is wrong abroad. If it is wrong to be violent defending black women and black children and black babies and black men, then it is wrong for America to draft us and make us violent abroad in defense of her. And if it is right for America to draft us, and teach us how to be violent in defense of her, then it is right for you and me to do whatever is necessary to defend our own people right here in this country.

The Chinese Revolution—they wanted land. They threw the British out, along with the Uncle Tom Chinese. Yes, they did. They set a good example. When I was in prison, I read an article—don't be shocked when I say that I was in prison. You're still in prison. That's what America means: prison. When I was in prison, I read an article in *Life* magazine showing a little Chinese girl, nine years old; her father was on his hands and knees and she was pulling the trigger because he was an Uncle Tom China-man. When they had the revolution over there, they took a whole generation of Uncle Toms in China. And today it's one of the toughest, roughest, most feared countries on this earth—by the white man. Because there are no Uncle Toms over there.

Of all our studies, history is best qualified to reward our research. And when you see that you've got problems, all you have to do is examine the historic method used all over the world by others who have problems similar to yours. Once you see how they got theirs straight, then you know how you can get yours straight. There's been a revolution, a black revolution, going on in Africa. In Kenya, the Mau Mau were revolutionary; they were the ones who brought the word "uhuru" to the fore. The Mau Mau, they were revolutionary, they believed in scorched earth, they knocked everything aside that got in their way, and their revolution also was based on land, a desire for land. In Algeria, the northern part of Africa, a revolution took place. The Algerians were revolutionists, they wanted land. France offered to let them be integrated into France. They told France, to hell with France, they wanted some land, not some France. And they engaged in a bloody battle.

So I cite these various revolutions, brothers and sisters, to show you that you don't have a peaceful revolution. You don't have a turn-the-other-cheek revolution. There's no such thing as a non-violent revolution. The only kind of revolution that is non-violent is the Negro revolution. The only revolution in which the goal is loving your enemy is the Negro revolution. It's the only revoluton in which the goal is a desegregated lunch counter, a desegregated theater, a desegregated park, and a desegregated public toilet; you can sit down next to white folks—on the toilet. That's no revolution. Revolution is based on land. Land is the basis of all independence. Land is the basis of freedom, justice, and equality.

The white man knows what a revolution is. He knows that the Black Revolution is worldwide in scope and in nature. The Black Revolution is sweeping Asia, is sweeping Africa, is rearing its head in Latin America. The Cuban Revolution—that's a revolution. They overturned the system. Revolution is in Asia, revolution is in Africa, and the white man is screaming because he sees revolution in Latin America. How do you think he'll react to you when you learn what a real revolution is? You don't know what a revolution is. If you did, you wouldn't use that word.

Revolution is bloody, revolution is hostile, revolution knows no compromise, revolution overturns and destroys everything that gets in its way. And you, sitting around here like a knot on the wall, saying, "I'm going to love these folks no matter how much they hate me." No, you need a revolution. Whoever heard of a revolution where they lock arms, as Reverend Cleage was pointing out beautifully, singing "We Shall Overcome"? You don't do that in a revolution. You don't do any singing, you're too busy swinging. It's based on land. A revolutionary wants land so he can set up his own nation, an independent nation. These Negroes aren't asking for any nation— they're trying to crawl back on the plantation.

When you want a nation, that's called nationalism. When the white man became involved in a revolution in this country against England, what was it for? He wanted this land so he could set up another white nation. That's white nationalism. The American Revolution was white nationalism. The French Revolution was white nationalism. You don't think so? Why do you think Khruschev and Mao can't get their heads together? White nationalism. All the revolutions that are going on in Asia and Africa today are based on what?—black nationalism. He wants a nation. I was reading some beautiful words by Reverend Cleage pointing out why he couldn't get together with someone else in the city because all of them were afraid of being identified with black nationalism. If you're afraid of black nationalism, you're afraid of revolution. And if you love revolution, you love black nationalism.

To understand this, you have to go back to what the young brother here referred to as the house Negro and the field Negro back during slavery. There were two kinds of slaves, the house Negro and the field Negro. The house Negroes—they lived in the house with the master, they dressed pretty good, they ate good because they ate his food—what he left. They lived in the attic or the basement, but still they lived near the master; and they loved the master more than the master loved himself. They would give their life to save the master's house—quicker than the master would. If the master said, "We got a good house here," the house Negro would say, "Yeah, we got a good house here." Whenever the master said "we," he said "we." That's how you can tell a house Negro.

If the master's house caught on fire, the house Negro would fight harder to put the blaze out than the master would. If the master got sick, the house Negro would say, "What's the matter, boss, we sick?" We sick! He identified himself with his master, more than his master identified with himself. And if you came to the house Negro and said, "Let's run away, let's escape, let's separate," the house Negro would look at you and say, "Man, you crazy. What you mean, separate? Where is there a better house than this? Where can I wear better clothes than this? Where can I eat better food than this?" That was that house Negro. In those days he was called a "house nigger." And that's what we call them today, because we've still got some house niggers running around here.

This modern house Negro loves his master. He wants to live near him. He'll pay three times as much as the house is worth just to live near his master, and then brag about "I'm the only Negro out here." "I'm the only one on my job." "I'm the only one in this school." You're nothing but a house Negro. And if someone comes to you right now and says, "Let's separate," you say the same thing that the house Negro said on the plantation. "What you mean, separate? From America, this good white man? Where you going to get a better job than you get here?" I mean, this is what you say. "I ain't left nothing in Africa," that's what you say. Why, you left your mind in Africa.

On that same plantation, there was the field Negro. The field Negroes—those were the masses. There were always more Negroes in the field than there were Negroes in the house. The Negro in the field caught hell. He ate leftovers. In the house they ate high up on the hog. The Negro in the field didn't get anything but what was left of the insides of the hog. They call it "chitlings" nowadays. In those days they called them what they were—guts. That's what you were—gut-eaters. And some of you are still gut-eaters.

The field Negro was beaten from morning to night; he lived in a shack, in a hut; he wore old, cast-off clothes; he hated his master. I say he hated his master. He was intelligent. That house Negro loved his master, but that field Negro—remember, they were in the majority, and they hated the master. When the house caught on fire, he didn't try to put it out; that field Negro prayed for a wind, for a breeze. When the master got sick, the field Negro prayed that he'd die. If someone came to the field Negro and said, "Let's separate, let's run," he didn't say, "Where we going?" He'd say, "Any place is better than here." You've got the field Negroes in America today. I'm a field Negro. The masses are the field Negroes. When they see this man's house on fire, you don't hear the little Negroes talking about "our government is in trouble." They say, "The government is in trouble." Imagine a Negro: "our government"! I even heard one say "our astronauts." They won't even let him near the plant—and "our astronauts"! "Our Navy"—that's a Negro that is out of his mind, a Negro that is out of his mind.

Just as the slave master of that day used Tom, the house Negro, to keep the field Negroes in check, the same old slave master today has Negroes who are nothing but modern Uncle Toms, twentieth-century Uncle Toms, to keep you and me in check, to keep us under control, keep up passive and peaceful and nonviolent. That's Tom making you non-violent. It's like when you go to the dentist, and the man's going to take your tooth. You're going to fight him when he starts pulling. So he squirts some stuff in your jaw called novocain, to make you think they're not doing anything to you. So you sit there and because you've got all of that novocain in your jaw, you suffer—peacefully. Blood running all down your jaw, and you don't know what's happening. Because someone has taught you to suffer—peacefully.

The white man does the same thing to you in the street, when he wants to put knots on your head and take advantage of you and not have to be afraid of your fighting back. To keep you from fighting back, he gets these old religious Uncle Toms to teach you and me, just like novocain, to suffer peacefully. Don't stop suffering—just suffer peacefully. As Reverend Cleage pointed out, they say you should let your blood flow in the streets. This is a shame. You know he's a Christian preacher. If it's a shame to him, you know what it is to me.

There is nothing in our book, the Koran, that teaches us to suffer peacefully. Our religion teaches us to be intelligent. Be peaceful, be courteous, obey the law, respect everyone; but if someone puts his hand on you, send him to the cemetery. That's a good religion. In fact, that's that old-time religion. That's the one that Ma and Pa used to talk about: an eye for an eye, and a tooth for a tooth, and a head for a head, and a life for a life. That's a good religion. And nobody resents that kind of religion being taught but a wolf, who intends to make you his meal.

That is the way it is with the white man in America. He's a wolf—and you're sheep. Any time a shepherd, a pastor, teaches you and me not to run from the white man and, at the same time, teaches us not to fight the white man, he's a traitor to you and me. Don't lay down a life all by itself. No, preserve your life, it's the best thing you've got. And if you've got to give it up, let it be even Steven.

The slave master took Tom and dressed him well, fed him well, and even gave him a little education—a little education; gave him a long coat and a top hat and made all the other slaves look up to him. Then he used Tom to control them. The same strategy that was used in those days is used today, by the same white man. He takes a Negro, a so-called Negro, and makes him prominent, builds him up, publicizes him, makes him a celebrity. And then he becomes a spokesman for Negroes—and a Negro leader.

I would like to mention just one other thing quickly, and that is the method that the white man uses, how the white man uses the "big guns," or Negro leaders, against the Negro revolution. They are not a part of the Negro revolution. They are used against the Negro revolution.

When Martin Luther King, Jr., failed to desegregate Albany, Georgia, the civil rights struggle in America reached its low point. King became bankrupt almost, as a leader. The Southern Christian Leadership Conference was in financial trouble; and it was in trouble, period, with the people when they failed to desegregate Albany, Georgia. Other Negro civil rights leaders of so-called national stature became fallen idols. As they became fallen idols, began to lose their prestige and influence, local Negro leaders began to stir up the masses. In Cambridge, Maryland, Gloria Richardson; in Danville, Virginia, and other parts of the country, local leaders began to stir up our people at the grass-roots level. This was never done by these Negroes of national stature. They control you, but they have never incited you or excited you. They control you, they contain you, they have kept you on the plantation.

As soon as King failed in Birmingham, Negroes took to the streets. King went out to California to a big rally and raised I don't know how many thousands of dollars. He came to Detroit and had a march and raised some more thousands of dollars. And recall, right after that Roy Wilkins attacked King. He accused King and CORE (Congress of Racial Equality) of starting trouble everywhere and then making the NAACP (National Association for the Advancement of Colored People) get them out of jail and spend a lot of money; they accused King and CORE of raising all the money and not paying it back. This happened; I've got it in documented evidence in the newspaper. Roy started attacking King, and King started attacking Roy, and Farmer attacking both of them. And as these Negroes of national stature began to attack each other, they began to lose their control of the Negro masses.

The Negroes were out there in the streets. They were talking about how they were going to march on Washington. Right at that time Birmingham had exploded, and the Negroes in Birmingham—remember, they also exploded. They began to stab the crackers in the back and bust them up 'side their head—yes, they did. That's when Kennedy sent in the troops, down in Birmingham. After that, Kennedy got on the television and said, "This is a moral issue." That's when he said he was going to put out a civil rights bill. And when he mentioned civil rights bill and the Southern crackers started talking about how they were going to boycott or filibuster it, then the Negroes started talking—about what? That they were going to march on Washington, march on the Senate, march on the White House, march on the Congress, and tie it up, bring it to a halt, not let the Government proceed. They even said they were going out to the airport and lay down on the runway and not let any airplanes land. I'm telling you what they said. That was revolution. That was revolution. That was the Black Revolution.

It was the grass roots out there in the street. It scared the white man to death, scared the white power structure in Washington, D.C., to death; I was there. When they found out that this black steamroller was going to come down on the capital, they called in Wilkins, they called in Randolph, they called in these national Negro leaders that you respect and told them, "Call it off."

GOD'S JUDGMENT OF
WHITE AMERICA *

WHITE America is doomed! Death and devastating destruction hang at this very moment in the skies over America. But why must her divine execution take place? Is it too late for her to avoid this catastrophe?

All the prophets of the past listed America as number one among the guilty nations that would be too proud and blind to repent and atone when God's last messenger is raised in her midst to warn her. America's last chance, her last warning, is coming from the lips of the Honorable Elijah Muhammad today. Accept him and be saved; reject him and be damned!

It is written that white America will reject him; it is also written that white America will be damned and doomed—and the prophets who make these prophecies are never wrong in their divine predictions.

White America refuses to study, reflect, and learn a lesson from history; ancient Egypt didn't have to be destroyed. It was her corrupt government, the crooked politicians, who caused her destruction. Pharaoh hired Hebrew magicians to try and fool their own people into thinking they would soon be integrated into the mainstream of that country's life. Pharaoh didn't want the Hebrews to listen to Moses' message of separation. Even in that day separation was God's solution to the "slaves' problems." By opposing Moses, the magicians were actually choosing sides against the God of their own people.

* December 1, 1963.

In like manner, modern Negro magicians are hired by the American Government to oppose the Honorable Elijah Muhammad today. They pose as Negro "leaders." They have been hired by this white Government (white so-called liberals) to make our people here think that integration into this doomed white society will soon solve our probelm.

The only permanent solution to America's race problem is the complete separation of these 22 million ex-slaves from our white slave master, and the return of these ex-slaves to our own land, where we can then live in peace and security among our own people.

The American Government is trying to trick her 22 million ex-slaves with false promises that she never intends to keep. The crooked politicians in the government are working with the Negro civil rights leaders, but not to solve the race problem. The greedy politicians who run this Government give lip service to the civil rights struggle, only to further their own selfish interests, and their main interest as politicians is to stay in power.

In this deceitful American game of power politics, the Negroes (i.e., the race problem, the integration and civil rights issues) are nothing but tools, used by one group of whites called liberals against another group of whites called conservatives, either to get into power, or to remain in power.

The white liberal differs from the white conservative only in one way: The liberal is more deceitful than the conservative. The liberal is more hypocritical than the conservative.

Both want power, but the white liberal is the one who has perfected the art of posing as the Negro's friend and benefactor; and by winning the friendship, allegiance, and support of the Negro, the white liberal is able to use the Negro as a pawn or tool in this political football game that is constantly raging between the white liberals and white conservatives.

Politically, the American Negro is nothing but a football, and the white liberals control this mentally dead ball through tricks of tokenism: false promises of integration and civil rights. In this profitable game of deceiving and exploiting the political potential of the American Negro, those white liberals have the willing cooperation of the Negro civil rights leaders. These "leaders" sell out our people for just a few crumbs of token gains. These "leaders" are satisfied with token victories and token progress because they themselves are nothing but token leaders.

According to a New York *Tribune* editorial (dated February 5, 1960), out of 11 million qualified Negro voters, only 2,700,000 actually took time to vote. This means that, roughly speaking, only 3 million out of 11 million Negroes who are qualified to vote actually take an active part, and the remaining 8 million remain voluntarily inactive, and yet this small (3 million) minority of Negro voters holds the decisive edge in determining who will be the next President.

If who will be the next President is influenced by only 3 million Negro voters, it is easy to understand why the presidential candidates of both political parties put on such a false show with the Civil Rights Bill and with false promises of integration. They must impress the 3 million voting Negroes who are the actual "integration seekers."

If such a fuss is made over these 3 million integration seekers, what would presidential candidates have to do to appease the 8 million non-voting Negroes, if they ever decide to become politically active?

The 8 million non-voting Negroes are in the majority; they are the downtrodden black masses. The black masses have refused to vote, or to take part in politics, because they reject the Uncle Tom approach of the Negro leadership that have been handpicked for them by the white man.

These Uncle Tom leaders do not speak for the Negro majority; they do not speak for the black masses. They speak for the black bourgeoisie, the brainwashed, white-minded, middle-class minority, who are ashamed of black, and don't want to be identified with the black masses, and are therefore seeking to lose their black identity by mixing, intermarrying, and integrating with the white man.

The race problem can never be solved by listening to this white-minded minority. The white man should try to learn what the black masses want, and the only way to learn what the black masses want is by listening to the man who speaks for the black masses of America. The one man here in America who speaks for the downtrodden, dissatisfied black masses is this same man so many of our people are flocking to see and hear. This same Mr. Muhammad who is labeled by the white man as a black supremacist, and as a racist.

If the 3 million white-minded Negroes are casting their ballots for integration and intermarriage, what do the non-voting black masses want? Find out what the black masses want, and then perhaps America's race problem can be solved.

The white liberals hate the Honorable Elijah Muhammad, because they know their present position in the power structure stems from their ability to deceive and to exploit the Negro, politically as well as economically.

They know that the Honorable Elijah Muhammad's divine message will make our people (1) wake up, (2) clean up, and (3) stand up. They know that once the Honorable Elijah Muhammad is able to resurrect the Negro from this mental grave of ignorance by teaching him the truth about himself and his real enemy, the Negro learns to think for himself, he will no longer allow the white liberal to use him as a helpless football in the white man's crooked game of "power politics."

The white liberals control the Negro and the Negro vote by controlling the Negro civil rights leaders. As long as they control the Negro civil rights leaders, they can also control and contain the Negro's struggle, and they can control the Negro's so-called "revolt."

The Negro revolution is controlled by foxy white liberals, by the Government itself. But the Black Revolution is controlled only by God.

The Black Revolution is the struggle of the non-whites of this earth against their white oppressors. The Black Revolution has swept white supremacy out of Africa, out of Asia, and is getting ready to sweep it out of Latin America. Revolutions are based upon land. Revolutionaries are the landless against the landlord. Revolutions are never peaceful, never loving, never non-violent, nor are they ever compromising. Revolutions are destructive and bloody. Revolutionaries don't compromise with the enemy;

they don't even negotiate. Like the flood in Noah's day, revolution drowns all opposition . . . or like the fires in Lot's day, the Black Revolution burns everything that gets in its path.

History must repeat itself! Because of America's evil deeds against these 22 million Negroes, like Egypt and Babylon before her, America herself now stands before the bar of justice. White America is now facing her day of judgment, and she can't escape because today God Himself is the judge. God Himself is now the administrator of justice, and God Himself is to be her divine executor!

Is it possible for America to escape this divine disaster? If America can't atone for the crimes she has committed against the 22 million Negroes, if she can't undo the evils she has brutally, mercilessly heaped upon our people these past four hundred years, then America has signed her own doom, and our people would be foolish to accept her deceitful offers of integration into her doomed society at this late date!

How can America atone for her crimes? The Honorable Elijah Muhammad teaches us that a desegregated theater or lunch counter won't solve our problems. An integrated cup of coffee isn't sufficient pay for four hundred years of slave labor, and a better job in the white man's factory or position in his business is, at best, only a temporary solution. The only lasting or permanent solution is complete separation on some land that we can call our own.

The Honorable Elijah Muhammad teaches us that the race problem can easily be solved, just by sending these 22 million ex-slaves back to our own homeland where we can live in peace and harmony with our own kind. But this Government should provide the transportation, plus everything else we need to get started again in our own country. This Government should provide everything we need in machinery, materials, and finance; enough to last us from twenty to twenty-five years, until we can become an independent people in our own country.

If this white Government is afraid to let her 22 million ex-slaves go back to our country and to our own people, then America must set aside some separate territory here in the Western Hemisphere, where the two races can live apart from each other, since we certainly don't get along peacefully while we are here together.

The size of the territory can be judged according to our own population. If our people number one seventh of America's total population, then give us one seventh of this land. We don't want any land in the desert, but where there is rain and much mineral wealth.

We want fertile, productive land on which we can farm and provide our own people with sufficient food, clothing, and shelter. This Government must supply us with the machinery and other tools needed to dig into the earth. Give us everything we need for them from twenty to twenty-five years, until we can produce and supply our own needs.

If we are a part of America, then part of what she is worth belongs to us. We will take our share and depart, then this white country can have peace. What is her net worth? Give us our share in gold and silver and let us depart and go back to our homeland in peace.

We want no integration with this wicked race that enslaved us. We want complete separation from this race of devils. But we should not be expected to leave America and go back to our own homeland empty-handed. After four hundred years of slave labor, we have some *back pay* coming, a bill owed to us that must be collected.

If the Government of white America truly repents of its sins against our people, and atones by giving us our true share, only then can America save herself!

But if America waits for Almighty God Himself to step in and force her into a just settlement, God will take this entire continent away from her; and she will cease to exist as a nation. Her own Christian scriptures warn her that when God comes He can give the "entire Kingdom to whomsoever He will," which only means that the God of justice on Judgment Day can give this entire continent to whomsoever He wills!

White America, wake up and take heed, before it is too late!

SPEECH TO AFRICAN SUMMIT
CONFERENCE—
CAIRO, EGYPT *

Their Excellencies
First Ordinary Assembly of Heads of State and
  Governments
Organization of African Unity
Cairo, U.A.R.

YOUR EXCELLENCIES: The Organization of Afro-American Unity has sent me to attend this historic African Summit Conference as an observer to represent the interests of 22 million African-Americans whose *human rights* are being violated daily by the racism of American imperialists.

The Organization of Afro-American Unity (OAAU) has been formed by a cross section of America's African-American community, and is patterned after the letter and spirit of the Organization of African Unity (OAU).

Just as the Organization of African Unity has called upon all African leaders to submerge their differences and unite on common objectives for the common good of all Africans, in America the Organization of Afro-American Unity has called upon Afro-American leaders to submerge their differences and find areas of agreement wherein we can work in unity for the good of the entire 22 million African-Americans.

Since the 22 million of us were originally Africans, who are now in America, not by choice but only by a cruel accident in our history, we strongly believe that African

* July 17, 1964.

problems are our problems and our problems are African problems.

YOUR EXCELLENCIES: We also believe that as heads of the independent African states you are the shepherds of *all* African peoples everywhere, whether they are still at home here on the mother continent or have been scattered abroad.

Some African leaders at this conference have implied that they have enough problems here on the mother continent without adding the Afro-American problem.

With all due respect to your esteemed positions, I must remind all of you that *the Good Shepherd* will leave ninety-nine sheep who are safe at home to go to the aid of the one who is lost and has fallen into the clutches of the imperialist wolf.

We in America are your long-lost brothers and sisters, and I am here only to remind you that our problems are your problems. As the African-Americans "awaken" today, we find ourselves in a strange land that has rejected us, and, like the prodigal son, we are turning to our elder brothers for help. We pray our pleas will not fall upon deaf ears.

We were taken forcibly in chains from this mother continent and have now spent over three hundred years in America, suffering the most inhuman forms of physical and psychological tortures imaginable.

During the past ten years the entire world has witnessed our men, women, and children being attacked and bitten by vicious police dogs, brutally beaten by police clubs, and washed down the sewers by high-pressure water hoses that would rip the clothes from our bodies and the flesh from our limbs.

And all of these inhuman atrocities have been inflicted upon us by the American governmental authorities, the police themselves, for no reason other than we seek the recognition and respect granted other human beings in America.

YOUR EXCELLENCIES: The American Government is either unable or unwilling to protect the lives and property of your 22 million African-American brothers and sisters. We stand defenseless, at the mercy of American racists who murder us at will for no reason other than we are black and of African descent.

Two black bodies were found in the Mississippi River this week; last week an unarmed African-American educator was murdered in cold blood in Georgia; a few days before that three civil rights workers disappeared completely, perhaps murdered also, only because they were teaching our people in Mississippi how to vote and how to secure their political rights.

Our problems are your problems. We have lived for over three hundred years in that American den of racist wolves in constant fear of losing life and limb. Recently, three students from Kenya were mistaken for American Negroes and were brutally beaten by the New York police. Shortly after that two diplomats from Uganda were also beaten by the New York City police, who mistook them for American Negroes.

If Africans are brutally beaten while only visiting in America, imagine the physical and psychological suffering received by your brothers and sisters who have lived there for over three hundred years.

Our problem is your problem. No matter how much independence Africans get here on the mother continent, unless you wear your national dress at all time when you visit America, you may be mistaken for one of us and suffer the same psychological and physical mutilation that is an everyday occurrence in our lives.

Your problems will never be fully solved until and unless ours are solved. You will never be fully respected until and unless we are also respected. You will never be recognized as free human beings until and unless we are also recognized and treated as human beings.

Our problem is your problem. It is not a Negro problem, nor an American problem. This is a world problem; a problem for humanity. It is not a problem of civil rights, but a problem of human rights.

If the United States Supreme Court justice Arthur Goldberg a few weeks ago could find legal grounds to threaten to bring Russia before the United Nations and charge her with violating the human rights of less than 3 million

Russian Jews, what makes our African brothers hesitate to bring the United States Government before the United Nations and charge her with violating the human rights of 22 million African-Americans?

We pray that our African brothers have not freed themselves of European colonialism only to be overcome and held in check now by American *dollarism*. Don't let American racism be "legalized" by American dollarism.

America is worse than South Africa, because not only is America racist, but she is also deceitful and hypocritical. South Africa preaches segregation and practices segregation. She, at least, practices what she preaches. America preaches integration and practices segregation. She preaches one thing while deceitfully practicing another.

South Africa is like a vicious wolf, openly hostile toward black humanity. But America is cunning like a fox, friendly and smiling, but even more vicious and deadly than the wolf.

The wolf and the fox are both enemies of humanity, both are canine, both humiliate and mutilate their victims. Both have the same objectives, but differ only in methods.

If South Africa is guilty of violating the human rights of Africans here on the mother continent, then America is guilty of worse violations of the 22 million Africans on the American continent. And if South African racism is not a domestic issue, then American racism also is not a *domestic* issue.

Many of you have been led to believe that the much publicized, recently passed Civil Rights Bill is a sign that America is making a sincere effort to correct the injustices we have suffered there. This propaganda maneuver is part of her deceit and trickery to keep the African nations from condemning her racist practices before the United Nations, as you are now doing as regards the same practices of South Africa.

The United States Supreme Court passed laws ten years ago making America's segregated school system illegal. But the Federal Government cannot enforce the law of the highest court in the land when it comes to nothing but equal-rights to education for African-Americans. How can anyone be so naïve as to think all the additional laws brought into being by the Civil Rights Bill will be enforced?

These are nothing but tricks of this century's leading neocolonialist power. Surely, our intellectually mature African brothers will not fall for this trickery?

The Organization of Afro-American Unity, in cooperation with a coalition of other Negro leaders and organizations, has decided to elevate our freedom struggle above the domestic level of civil rights. We intend to internationalize it by placing it at the level of human rights. Our freedom struggle for human dignity is no longer confined to the domestic jurisdiction of the United States Government.

We beseech the independent African states to help us bring our problem before the United Nations, on the grounds that the United States Government is morally incapable of protecting the lives and the property of 22 million African-Americans. And on the grounds that our deteriorating plight is definitely becoming a threat to world peace.

Out of frustration and hopelessness our young people have reached the point of no return. We no longer endorse patience and turning the other cheek. We assert the right of self-defense by whatever means necessary, and reserve the right of maximum retaliation against our racist oppressors, no matter what the odds against us are.

From here on in, if we must die anyway, we will die fighting back, and we will not die alone. We intend to see that our racist oppressors also get a taste of death.

We are well aware that our future efforts to defend ourselves by retaliating—by meeting violence with violence, eye for eye and tooth for tooth—could create the type of racial conflict in America that could easily escalate into a violent, worldwide, bloody race war.

In the interests of world peace and security, we beseech the heads of the independent African states to recommend an immediate investigation into our problem by the United Nations Commission on Human Rights.

If this humble plea that I am voicing at this conference is not properly worded, then let our elder brothers, who know the legal language, come to our aid and word our plea in the proper language necessary for it to be heard.

One last word, my beloved brothers at this African Summit: "No one knows the master better than his servant." We have been servants in America for over three hundred years. We have a thorough inside knowledge of this man who calls himself "Uncle Sam." Therefore, you must heed our warning. Don't escape from European colonialism only to become even more enslaved by deceitful, "friendly" American dollarism.

May Allah's blessings of good health and wisdom be upon you all.

Asalaam Alaikum
MALCOLM X, Chairman
Organization of Afro-American Unity

THE SECOND AFRICAN
SUMMIT CONFERENCE *

Every effort by the American press to play down the importance and the success of the Second African Summit Conference held recently here in the ancient African city of Cairo could well be a drastic mistake for the Western powers, and especially for America.

The entire continent of Africa and her awakening people is the richest prize yet in the key struggle for the "balance of power" currently waged between East and West. Not only her unlimited supplies of untapped mineral resources, but also her strategic geographic position makes her extremely vital in the present world struggle.

Why does the press of the Western powers constantly ridicule and play down the idea of a United States of Africa? They know that a divided Africa is a weak Africa, and they want to keep her a dependent target of Western "philanthropy," or what is being increasingly described here as "benevolent" colonialism. The neocolonialists who would "woo and rule" Africa today must skillfully disguise their selfish aims within their generous offers of unlimited "economic aid, Peace Corpism or crossroadism," all of which is nothing but the modern counterpart of the nineteenth-century "missionaryism."

A united Africa is a strong and independent Africa, an Africa that can stand on its own feet, walk for itself,

---

* This press statement was made by Malcolm X in Cairo, Egypt, on August 21, 1964, on behalf of the Organization of Afro-American Unity.

and avoid the snares and pitfalls devised by the "benevolent" imperialists to keep the mother continent divided,
weak, and dependent upon the "philanthropic" West for
"economic" aid, political "guidance," and military "protection."

During the Second African Summit Conference any un-
biased observer could easily see that Africa is making
every effort today to stand on her own feet and speak with
her own voice. Africa seeks only her rightful place in the
sun. The degree to which the well-meaning element in the
American public realizes that "to be independent and self-
sustaining" is Africa's only aim, will determine the attitude
and the degree of pressure the American public will put
upon the politicians at home in order to keep the American
Government's foreign policy toward Africa a policy of
genuine assistance instead of the thinly disguised "benevolent" colonialism, "philanthropic" imperialism . . . or
what many of the more "cautious recipients" of American
economic aid are beginning to label as *American dollarism*.

I refer to the importance of the well-meaning element of
American society being properly informed and having the
correct understanding of Africa's aims and efforts because
America today is the leading Western power, and the attitude of the American public can play a vital role in
determining whether there will be a positive or negative
reaction of the West in the face of Africa's efforts toward
a united and independent continent.

The American people must be made to understand that
this vast continent is aflame with the spirit of revolution;
not a negative or destructive revolution based on revenge,
but a revolution designed to produce the constructive social changes that will bring positive benefits to the long-
neglected African people.

The *bloodless* revolution here in Cairo that dethroned
and sent into exile the despotic former King Farouk,
and Egypt's steady progress toward positive social changes
during the past twelve years, has made the United Arab
Republic and its militant President Gamal Abdel Nasser
the cornerstone and pattern of the overall African Revolution.

Despite the distorted picture painted of the United Arab Republic by anti-African propagandists, President Nasser and his able assistants have made great progress in his "step by step" program to bring the benefits of modernization to his people. He has skillfully guided them away from the antiquated *liabilities* of their past, while at the same time showing them how to retain and harness the assets of their ancient and glorious civilization.

The successful industrialization of the United Arab Republic in just twelve years since the revolution and the thirst he has since inspired within the Egyptian masses to educate themselves in the free schools set up throughout Egypt since the revolution are only a few of the many revolutionary accomplishments that have served as a cornerstone and pattern for the spirit of economic, political, and intellectual independence that has been sweeping this entire mother continent these past twelve years.

And the revolutionary spirit he has inspired here on this continent among his fellow Africans has leaped across the Atlantic Ocean and entered into the heart and mind of 22 million of our people in America who are also of African origin.

The spirit of brotherly understanding and unity in which President Gamal Abdel Nasser opened and conducted the Second African Summit Conference held recently here in Cairo inspired all others with the same spirit of willingness to recognize the necessity for changes, and successfully laid the groundwork for serious discussions toward the formation of a truly independent and United States of Africa.

The success of this Second Summit Conference is not only an overwhelming victory for the people here on the mother continent, but it is also a victory for the 22 million brothers and sisters in America who are of African origin . . . for we awakening Afro-Americans are well aware today that a united Africa is a strong Africa, and it is only in the *strength* of our African brothers that we in America will ever realize a true solution to our own struggle for independence and the recognition and respect of our own human rights.

The time has come when the awakened voice of Africa

is being heard with a tremendous impact throughout the world, and the ever increasing importance and influence of the voice can be traced to the First African Summit Conference, which was held in Addis Ababa in May of 1963.

It was this First African Summit Conference that laid the foundation for the crushing blow, physically and psychologically, to the schemes of the European and American neoimperialists to weaken Africa by keeping her artificially divided into "Africa above the Sahara and Africa below the Sahara, Arab Africa and 'African,' Muslim Africa and non-Muslim Africa, light-skinned and dark-skinned Africa."

The Summit Conference in Addis Ababa was the first step taken by Africans themselves to destroy these divisive concepts that had been skillfully created and propagated by the American and European neoimperialists. These successful steps toward unity which were set in motion at the First Summit Conference made the enemies of African unity quite ill and desperate to create new countermeasures to forestall African unity. But the fortunes spent by the neoimperialists in their divisive propaganda has been like pouring money down the drain . . . because their former African "concubine" has awakened and the illicit honeymoon between Mother Africa and her former European "lovers" is now over forever.

The sunlight of mutual understanding that shined forth brilliantly from the First Summit Conference created a new climate here on the mother continent, ushering in an atmosphere of brotherliness among the various heads of the independent African states. Personality conflicts that formerly kept some of them narrow-minded, shortsighted, and apart were submerged into the background and de-emphasized; and instead areas and topics of common concern, common benefit, and common agreement were emphasized and discussed. The good of Africa was put above the personal feelings of a few individuals.

Yes, the First Summit was indeed an accomplishment within itself. No one selfishly argued that it should be held in Lagos, Accra, Monrovia, Algiers, Khartoum, or Canakry instead of Addis Ababa. They showed respect for Emperor Haile Selassie, even though he was an absolute monarch and most of the others were from anti-monarchy republics. This first Summit brought together the African monarchs, kings, and presidents on the same level . . . it created a "working atmosphere" between monarchies, kingdoms, and republics, between the big countries and the small ones, those rich in natural resources and those that were almost barren.

Thus, the first Summit created the climate for unity. But it was here in Cairo at the Second African Summit Conference that the real unity of *action* began to take form, when all the heads of the independent African states denounced imperialism and racism in all of its forms including even the passage of a resolution condemning the continued racist oppression of the 22 million Afro-Americans in the United States. And many of them for the first time joined in denouncing Israel as a base and tool of neo-imperialism, and they openly supported the right of the Arab refugees to return to their Palestine homeland. They could easily see that since over 80 per cent of the Arab world is on the African continent, Arab problems are inseparable from African problems.

The spirit of brotherhood was so strong at this Second Summit Conference that the heads of state not only agreed on the necessity of a united Africa, but they vigorously discussed the problems also of restoring liberty and dignity to the mother continent as a whole. They recognized the Government of Zambia and the Government-in-exile of Angola, accepting both heads of state (Kenneth Kaunda and Robert Holden) as full participants at the Summit Conference. They gave full support to the freedom fighters of the Africa Liberation movement, and expressed concrete plans to assist their freedom struggle both morally and materially, even if it necessitated supplying weapons for an open, bloody revolt against the remaining racist diehards.

Although many of them recognized that Israel is nothing but a base here on the northeast tip of the mother continent for the twentieth-century form of "benevolent colonialism," they felt that the most pressing problem facing the continent is the openly racist Government occupying South Africa, the remnant of the nineteenth-century colonialism represented by the forced rule of the European minority over the African majority. The collective decisions and resolutions by the Conference to bring strict sanctions against the racist Government of South Africa were agreed to by all of the African heads of state, and thus there is no doubt that this firm stand to support the African majority's struggle for liberty in that area will step up their efforts to throw out the racist European minority that is forcibly ruling their country.

They also recognized the seriousness of our problem in America, its relationship to the African continent, and their moral obligation to give us their all-out support in our struggle for human rights—and thus my coming to the Summit Conference was not in vain as some elements in the American press have tried to "suggest," but instead my coming proved to be very fruitful for our freedom struggle in America, and especially for our plan to take our problems before the United Nations. I had traveled over six thousand miles from America to attend this African Summit Conference as an observer. The Organization of Afro-American Unity (OAAU) had sent me to present the true plight and the feelings of 22 million Afro-Americans to these heads of independent African states.

Upon my arrival in Cairo I was met with open arms by the African leaders and their various delegations. *I found no doors closed to me.* They asked me to prepare a memorandum on the real status of our people in America, explaining how we are also victimized by neoimperialism in its racist American form, and they urged me to present my memorandum to the Conference so they could take action on it in our behalf.

I tried to summarize our plight in as few words as possible, but my memorandum of continued atrocities against the Afro-American by racists in the United States still stretched into nine pages. It charged America with practicing a worse form of organized racism than South Africa, and described how this racist element in the State Department had skillfully alienated us from the natural sympathy and support of our African brothers in our freedom struggle by using white "liberals" to gain our friendship and confidence in order to "advise" and maneuver us into a twelve-year fight for our civil rights, knowing that as long as our freedom struggle was labeled "civil rights" it would be considered by the African nations as American "domestic" affairs and our plight would remain within the sole jurisdiction of the American Federal Government for a "solution."

My memorandum charged that this same racist element in the State Department knew that our newly formed Organization of Afro-American Unity (OAAU) was planning to internationalize America's race problem by lifting it from the level of *civil* rights to a struggle for the universally recognized *human rights,* and on these grounds we could then bring America before the United Nations and charge her with violating the U.N. Declaration of Human Rights and thereby of also violating the U.N. Charter itself.

In order to keep the Organization of Afro-American Unity (OAAU) from gaining the interest, sympathy, and support of the independent African states in our effort to bring the miserable plight of the 22 million Afro-Americans before the U.N., the racist element in the State Department very shrewdly gave maximum worldwide publicity to the recent passage of the Civil Rights Bill— which was actually only a desperate attempt to make the African states think America was sincerely trying to correct the continued injustices done to us, and thereby maneuver the African Government into permitting America to keep her racism "domestic"—and still within her sole jurisdiction.

This racist element within the State Department realizes that if any intelligent, truly militant Afro-American is ever permitted to come before the United Nations to testify in behalf of the 22 million mistreated Afro-Americans, our dark-skinned brothers and sisters in Africa, Asia, and Latin America would then see America as a "brute beast," even more cruel and vulturous than the colonial powers of Europe and South Africa combined. I was relieved and delighted to learn how easily most of the African heads of state and their advisers could see through the tricks of the American racists. One of them told me he knew the Civil Rights Bill was only a "political maneuver" to capture the

Negro votes in the coming elections, and he stressed that it could hardly have been accidental that passage of the bill came to fruition during this crucial election year.

Another described it as a beautiful document on paper but agreed that it was a document that could never be implemented. Another said it was like the novocain a dentist gives a patient who has a rotten, abscessed tooth without ever pulling the tooth—or treating the condition while ignoring the cause.

All of them with whom I was able to establish personal contact agreed with my contention that our problem was one of *human rights* instead of only civil rights. They also agreed that we needed and deserved the full support of the entire world in our struggle for human rights.

Thus, these enlightened heads of the thirty-three independent African states at the Second Summit Conference passed a resolution condemning the continued brutal treatment of the Afro-American in the United States, and they voiced full sympathy and support in our struggle to break the yoke of American racism. This resolution had so many frightening implications for America's future image and position in the world, especially for her foreign policy in this crucial election year; it is not surprising that the American press completely *smothered* the fact that the Second Summit Conference passed such a resolution, despite the fact that it was sent out over UPI wire services to all the American news outlets. Right up to this moment the American public has never been told that the Second African Summit passed a resolution condemning the mistreatment of the Afro-Americans and voicing full support of our freedom struggle.

The voice of Africa is becoming stronger every day. The spirit of unity here in Cairo during this Second Summit Conference, and their agreement that there is no room here on the mother continent for imperialism any more—in any form—and by the time these heads of state convene their Third Summit Conference in Accra next year, most of the remaining strongholds of imperialism are sure to have fallen under the crushing weight of a rising, *United Africa!*

RACISM:
THE CANCER THAT IS
DESTROYING AMERICA *

I AM not a racist, and I do not subscribe to any of the tenets of racism. But the seed of racism has been firmly planted in the hearts of most American whites ever since the beginning of that country. This seed of racism has rooted itself so deeply in the subconsciousness of many American whites that they themselves ofttimes are not even aware of its existence, but it can be easily detected in their thoughts, their words, and in their deeds.

In the past I permitted myself to be used by Elijah Muhammad, the leader of the sect known as the Black Muslims, to make sweeping indictments of all white people, the entire white race, and these generalizations have caused injuries to some whites who perhaps did not deserve to be hurt. Because of the spiritual enlightenment which I was blessed to receive as the result of my recent pilgrimage to the Holy City of Mecca, I no longer subscribe to sweeping indictments of any one race.

My religious pilgrimage (hajj) to Mecca has given me a new insight into the true brotherhood of Islam, which encompasses all the races of mankind. The pilgrimage broadened my scope, my mind, my outlook, and made me more flexible in approaching life's many complexities and in my reactions to its paradoxes.

At Mecca I saw the spirit of unity and true brotherhood displayed by tens of thousands of people from all over the world, from blue-eyed blonds to black-skinned

* Written for the *Egyptian Gazette*, August 25, 1964.

Africans. This served to convince me that perhaps some American whites can also be cured of the rampant racism which is consuming them and about to destroy that country.

I am now striving to live the life of a true Suni Muslim. In the future I intend to be careful not to sentence anyone who has not first been proven guilty. I must repeat that I am not a racist nor do I subscribe to the tenets of racism. I can state in all sincerity that I wish nothing but freedom, justice, and equality, life, liberty, and the pursuit of happiness for all people.

However, the first law of nature is self-preservation, so my first concern is with the oppressed group of people to which I belong, the 22 million Afro-Americans, for we, more than any other people on earth today, are deprived of these inalienable *human rights*.

But time is running out for America. The 22 million Afro-Americans are not yet filled with hate or a desire for revenge, as the propaganda of the segregationists would have people believe. The universal law of justice is sufficient to bring judgment upon the American whites who are guilty of racism. The same law will also punish those who have benefited from the racist practices of their forefathers and have done nothing to atone for the "sins of their fathers." Just look around on this earth today and see the increasing troubles this generation of American whites is having. The "sins of their fathers" are definitely being visited upon the heads of this present generation. Most intelligent American whites will admit freely today without hesitation that their present generation is already being punished and plagued for the evil deeds their forefathers committed when they enslaved millions of Afro-Americans in that country.

But it is not necessary for their victim—the Afro-American—to seek revenge. The very conditions the American whites created are already plaguing them into insanity and death. They are reaping what their forefathers have sown. "Their chickens are coming home to roost." And we, the 22 million Afro-Americans—their victims— need only to spend more time removing the "scars of slavery" from the backs and the mind of our own people, physical and mental scars left by four hundred years of inhuman treatment there in America at the hands of white racists.

The key to our success lies in *united action*. Lack of unity among the various Afro-American groups involved in our struggle has always been the reason we have failed to win concrete gains in our war against America's oppression, exploitation, discrimination, segregation, degradation, and humiliation. Before the miserable condition of the 22 million "second-class citizens" can be corrected, all the groups in the Afro-American community must form a united front. Only through united efforts can our problems there be solved.

How can we get the unity of the Afro-American community? Ignorance of each other is what has made unity impossible in the past. Therefore we need enlightenment. We need more light about each other. Light creates understanding, understanding creates love, love creates patience, and patience creates unity. Once we have more knowledge (light) about each other we will stop condemning each other and a *united front* will be brought about.

All 22 million Afro-Americans have the same basic goal, the same basic objective. We want freedom, justice, and equality, we want recognition and respect as *human beings*. We are not divided over objectives, but we have allowed our racist enemies to divide us over the *methods* of attaining these common objectives. Our enemy has magnified our minor points of difference, then maneuvered us into wasting our time debating and fighting each other over insignificant and irrelevant issues.

The common goal of 22 million Afro-Americans is respect as *human beings,* the God-given right to be a *human being*. Our common goal is to obtain the *human rights* that America has been denying us. We can never get civil rights in America until our *human rights* are first restored. We will never be recognized as citizens there until we are first recognized as *humans*.

The present American "system" can never produce freedom for the black man. A chicken cannot lay a duck egg because the chicken's "system" is not designed or equipped to produce a duck egg. The system of the chicken was produced by a chicken egg and can therefore reproduce only that which produced it.

The American "system" (political, economic, and social) was produced from the enslavement of the black man, and this present "system" is capable only of perpetuating that enslavement.

In order for a chicken to produce a duck egg its system would have to undergo a drastic and painful revolutionary change . . . or *REVOLUTION*. So be it with America's enslaving system.

In the past the civil rights groups in America have been foolishly attempting to obtain constitutional rights from the same Government that has conspired against us to deny our people these rights. Only a world body (*a world court*) can be instrumental in obtaining those rights which belong to a human being by dint of his being a member of the human family.

As long as the freedom struggle of the 22 million Afro-Americans is labeled a civil rights issue it remains a domestic problem under the jurisdiction of the United States, and as such, bars the intervention and support of our brothers and sisters in Africa, Asia, Latin America, as well as that of the well-meaning whites of Europe. But once our struggle is lifted from the confining civil rights label to the level of *human rights,* our freedom struggle has then become *internationalized*.

Just as the violation of *human rights* of our brothers and sisters in South Africa and Angola is an international issue and has brought the racists of South Africa and Portugal under attack from all other independent governments at the United Nations, once the miserable plight of the 22 million Afro-Americans is also lifted to the level of *human rights* our struggle then becomes an international issue, and the direct concern of all other civilized governments. We can then take the racist American Government before the World Court and have the racists in it exposed and condemned as the criminals that they are.

Why should it be necessary to go before a world court in order to solve America's race problem? One hundred years ago a civil war was fought supposedly to free us from the Southern racists. We are still the victims of their racism. Lincoln's Emancipation Proclamation was supposedly to free us. We are still crying for freedom. The politicians fought for amendments to the Constitution supposedly to make us first-class citizens. We are still second-class citizens.

In 1954, the U.S. Supreme Court itself issued a historic decision outlawing the segregated school system, and ten years have passed and this law is yet to be enforced even in the Northern states.

If white America doesn't think the Afro-American, especially the upcoming generation, is capable of adopting the guerrilla tactics now being used by oppressed people elsewhere on this earth, she is making a drastic mistake. She is underestimating the force that can do her the most harm.

A real honest effort to remove the just grievances of the 22 million Afro-Americans must be made immediately or in a short time it will be too late.

COMMUNICATION AND
REALITY *

FIRST, I want to let you know I am very thankful for the invitation to speak here this afternoon. Number one, before a group such as this, and number two, I always feel more at home in Harlem than anywhere else I've ever been. The topic we are going to discuss in a very informal way is Africa and the African Revolution and its effect on the Afro-American.

I take time to mention that because I am one who believes that what's happening on the African continent has a direct bearing on what happens to you and me in this country: The degree to which they get independence, strength, and recognition on that continent is inseparable from the degree to which we get independence, strength, and recognition on this continent, and I hope before the day is over to be able to clarify that.

First, I would like to point out that since it is my understanding that most of you are training to be leaders in the community, the country, and the world, some advice that I would give is that whenever you occupy a position of responsibility never accept images that have been created for you by someone else. It is always better to form the habit of learning how to see things for yourself, listen to things for yourself, and think for yourself; then you are in a better position to judge for yourself.

We are living in a time when image-making has become a science. Someone can create a certain image and then use

* A speech to the Domestic Peace Corps. December 12, 1964.

that image to twist your mind and lead you right up a blind path. An example: A few weeks ago, I was on a plane traveling from Algiers to Geneva. There were two white Americans sitting beside me, one a male, the other a female. I had met the male in the airport and we had struck up a conversation. He was an interpreter for the United Nations and was based in Geneva. The lady was with the American Embassy in Algeria. So we conversed for about forty minutes between Algiers and Geneva, a nice human conversation. I don't think they were trying to be white and they weren't trying to prove they weren't white. They weren't particularly trying to prove anything. It was just a conversation between three human beings. I certainly wasn't trying to make them think I wasn't black; race just didn't come into the conversation.

So, after we had this quiet, objective, friendly, and very informative conversation for about forty minutes, the lady looked at my briefcase and said, "I want to ask you a personal question. What kind of last name could you have that begins with an 'X'?" This was bugging her. I said, "That's it, 'X,' " like that. So she said, "Well, what's your first name?" I said, "Malcolm." She waited about ten minutes and said, "You're not Malcolm X?" and I said, "Yes." She said, "But you're not what I was looking for." I told her right then and there about the danger of believing what she hears someone else say or believing what she reads that someone else has written and not keeping herself in a position to weigh things for herself.

So I just take time to mention that because it is very dangerous for you and me to form the habit of believing completely everything about anyone or any situation when we only have the press as our source of information. It is always better, if you don't want to be completely in the dark, to read about it. But don't come to a conclusion until you have an opportunity to do some personal, firsthand investigation for yourself.

The American press, in fact the FBI, can use the American press to create almost any kind of image they want of anyone on the local scene. And then you have other police agencies of an international stature that are able to use the world press in the same manner. If the press is able to project someone in the image of an extremist, no matter what that person says or does from then on, it is considered by the public as an act of extremism. No matter how good, constructive, or positive it is, because it's done by this person who has been projected as an extremist, the people who have been misled by the press have a mental block and the press knows that. The person can run and save someone from drowning in the middle of the Hudson, but still the act is looked upon with suspicion because the press has been used to create suspicion toward that person.

I point these things out—especially for you and me, those of us who are trying to come from behind. If we aren't aware, we'll find that all these modern methods of trickery will be used and we will be maneuvered into thinking that we are getting freedom or thinking that we are making progress when actually we will be going backward.

And one of the things that you and I as an oppressed people should be on guard against, as I said, is to be very careful about letting anyone paint our images for us. The world press as well as the American press can make the victim of the crime look like the criminal and can make the criminal look like the victim. You don't think that is possible for someone to do this to your mind, but all you have to do is take a look at what happened in the Congo. The world press projected the scene in the Congo as one wherein the people who were the victims of the crime were made to appear as if they were the actual criminals and the ones who were the actual criminals were made to appear as if they were the actual victims. The press did this, and by the press doing this, it made it almost impossible for the public to analyze the Congo situation with clarity and keep it in its proper perspective.

An example: Here we had African villages in the Congo that had no kind of air force whatsoever, they were completely without defense against air attacks; planes were dropping bombs on these African villages. The bombs were destroying women and children. But there was no great outcry here in America against such an inhuman act because the press very skillfully made it look like a humanitarian project by referring to the pilots as "American trained." And as soon as they put the word American in there, that was supposed to lend it some kind of respectability or legality.

They called them American-trained, anti-Castro Cuban pilots and since Castro is a word that is almost like a curse, the fact that they were anti-Castro pilots made whatever they were doing an act of humanitarianism. But still you can't overlook the fact that they were dropping bombs on villages in Africa that had no defense whatsoever against bombs. But they called this an act of humanitarianism and the public was made to accept it as an act of humanitarianism.

I have to point this out because it is an example of how the press can maneuver and manipulate your mind to make you think that mass murder is some kind of humanitarian project simply by making the image of the criminal appear to be that of a humanitarian and the image of the victim that of the criminal.

So it is good to keep this in mind because you can take it a step further. One of the principal images in that scene over there was Tshombe, who is a murderer. He murdered the rightful prime minister of the Congo; this cannot be denied. The rightful minister of the Congo was Patrice Lumumba. Now, the one who is responsible for having murdered him in cold blood—and the world knows it—was put over the Congo as its premier by the United States Government and this gave him some kind of image of respectability because America sanctioned him. Not only did America sanction him, she supplied him with sufficient funds wherein he could then go to South Africa and import hired killers, mercenaries they call them, but a mercenary is a hired killer.

So this man, Tshombe, who was a murder hired by the United States and placed in a position of authority over the Congo, showed his nature by what he did with American money—he hired some more killers. But because he was appointed by America Tshombe wasn't looked upon as a murderer or a killer, and the American press gave the mercenaries an image of respectability. An image of respectability. Now these mercenaries, under Tshombe's sanction and support, were indiscriminately shooting African women and children as well as African men.

No one got upset over the loss of thousands of Congolese lives; they only got upset when the lives of a few whites were at stake. Because when the lives of the whites were at stake, the press immediately played on your sentiment by referring to these whites as innocent hostages, as nuns and priests and missionaries, and it gave them an image that you would sympathize with.

I must point this out because it shows you how tricky the press can be. The press can make you not have any sympathy whatsoever for the death of thousands of people who look just like yourself, but at the same time, they make tears roll down your face over the loss of a few lives that don't look anything like yourself. They manipulate your feelings.

So my advice to any of you who at any time think that you'll ever be placed in a position of responsibility—you owe it to others as well as to yourself to be very careful about letting others make up your mind for you. You have to learn how to see for yourself, hear for yourself, think for yourself, and then judge for yourself.

Secondly, I would like to say this: It concerns my own personal self, whose image they have projected in their own light. I am against any form of racism. We are all against racism. The only difference between you and me is that you want to fight racism and racists non-violently and lovingly and I'll fight them the way they fight me. Whatever weapon they use, that's the one I'll use. I go for talking the kind of language he talks. You can't communicate with a person unless you use the language he uses. If a man is speaking French, you can talk German all night long, he won't know what you're talking about. You have to find out what kind of language he understands and then you put it to him in the language that he understands.

I'm a Muslim, which means my religion is Islam. I believe in Allah. I believe in all of the prophets, whoever represented God on this earth. I believe what Muslims believe: prayer, fasting, charity, and the pilgrimage to the Holy Land, Mecca, which I've been fortunate to have made four or five times. I believe in the brotherhood of man, all men, but I don't believe in brotherhood with anybody who doesn't want brotherhood with me. I believe in treating people right, but I'm not going to waste my time trying to treat somebody right who doesn't know how to return that treatment. This is the only difference between you and me.

You believe in treating everybody right whether they put a rope around your neck or whether they put you in the grave. Well, my belief isn't that strong. I believe in the brotherhood of man, but I think that anybody who wants to lynch a Negro is not qualified for that brotherhood and I don't put forth any effort to get them into that brotherhood. You want to save him and I don't.

Despite the fact that I believe in the brotherhood of man as a Muslim, and in the religion of Islam, there is one fact also that I can't overlook: I'm an Afro-American and Afro-Americans have problems that go well beyond religion. We have problems that our religious organization in itself cannot solve and we have problems that no one organization can solve or no one leader can solve. We have a problem that is going to take the combined efforts of every leader and every organization if we are going to get a solution. For that reason, I don't believe that as a Muslim it is possible for me to bring my religion into any discussion with non-Muslims without causing more division, animosity, and hostility; then we will only be involved in a self-defeating action. So based upon that, there is a group of us that have formed an organization. Besides being Muslims, we have gotten together and formed an organization that has nothing to do with religion at all; it is known as the Organization of Afro-American Unity.

In this organization we involve ourselves in the complete struggle of the Afro-American in this country, and our purpose in becoming involved with a non-religious group is to give us the latitude to use any means necessary for us to bring an end to the injustices that confront us. I believe in any means necessary. I believe that the injustices that we have suffered and will continue to suffer will never be brought to a halt as long as we put ourselves in a straitjacket when fighting those injustices.

Those of us in the Organization of Afro-American

Unity have adopted as our slogan "by any means necessary" and we feel we are justified. Whenever someone is
treating you in a criminal, illegal, or immoral way, why,
you are well within your rights to use anything at your dis-
posal to bring an end to that unjust, illegal, and immoral
condition. If we do it like that, we will find that we will
get more respect and will be further down the road toward
freedom, toward recognition and respect as human beings.
But as long as we dillydally and try to appear that we're
more moral by taking a beating without fighting back,
people will continue to refer to us as very moral and well-
disciplined persons, but at the same time we will be as far
back a hundred years from now as we are today. So I
believe that fighting those who fight us is the best course
of action in any situation.

Again, if the Government doesn't want Negroes fighting
anyone who is fighting us, then the Government should do
its job; the Government shouldn't put the weight on us. If
the Ku Klux Klan in Mississippi is carrying on criminal
activities to the point of murdering black people, then I
think if black people are men, human beings, the same as
anybody else, you and I should have the right to do the
same thing in defense of our lives and our property that
all other human beings on this earth do in defense of their
lives and in defense of their property, and that is to talk
the language that the Klan understands.

So I must emphasize, we are dealing with a powerful
enemy, and again, I am not anti-American or un-American.
I think there are plenty of good people in America, but
there are also plenty of bad people in America and the bad
ones are the ones who seem to have all the power and be
in these positions to block things that you and I need.
Because this is the situation, you and I have to preserve the
right to do what is necessary to bring an end to that situation, and it doesn't mean that I advocate violence, but at
the same time I am not against using violence in self-
defense. I don't even call it violence when it's self-defense,
I call it intelligence.

So what impact or effect does the African Revolution
have upon you and me? Number one, prior to 1959, many
of us didn't want to be identified with Africa in any way,

not even indirectly or remotely. The best way to curse one of us out was to call us an African; we'd get insulted. But if you've noticed, since 1959 and in more recent years, that's changed. It's changing among us subconsciously faster than we even realize.

The reason for this change is that prior to 1959 the African image was not created by Africans. The image of Africa was created by European powers. These Europeans joined with America and created a very negative image of Africa and projected this negative image abroad. They projected Africa as a jungle, a place filled with animals, savages, and cannibals. The image of Africa and the Africans was made so hateful that 22 million of us in America of African ancestry actually shunned Africa because its image was a hateful, negative image. We didn't realize that as soon as we were made to hate Africa and Africans, we also hated ourselves. You can't hate the root and not hate the fruit. You can't hate Africa, the land where you and I originated, without ending up hating you and me.

And the man knew that. We began to hate African features. We hated the African nose and the African lips and the African skin and the African hair. We hated the hair so much we even put lye on it to change its looks. We began hating ourselves. And you know, they accuse us of teaching hate.

What is the most inhuman or immoral: a man that teaches you to hate your enemies or a man that skillfully maneuvers you into hating yourself? Well, I think teaching a man to hate himself is much more criminal than teaching him to hate someone else. Look at you—who taught you to hate yourself? If you say we're hate teachers, you tell me who taught you to hate so skillfully, so completely, until we have been maneuvered today so that we don't even want to be what we actually are. We want to be somebody else, we want to be someone else, we want to be something else. Many of us want to be somewhere else.

Then after 1959, as Africans began to get independence, they began to change the image of the African. They got into a position to project their own image abroad. The image began to swing from negative to positive and to the same degree that the African image began to change from negative to positive, the Afro-American's image also began to change from negative to positive. His behavior and objectives began to change from negative to positive to the same degree that the behavior and the objectives of the African changed from negative to positive. They had a direct bearing upon the attitude that we here in America began to develop toward each other and also toward the man, and I don't have to say what man.

There were elements in the State Department that began to worry about this change in image. As Africa became militant and uncompromising, you and I became militant and uncompromising, and even the most bourgeois Uncle Tom Afro-American was happy when he heard about the Mau Maus. [Applause.] Yeah, he was happy when he heard it. He wouldn't say so openly because it wasn't a status symbol to identify with it in some quarters. In other quarters, it was. But all of this uncompromising and militant action on the part of the Africans created a tendency among our people in this country to be the same way, but many of us didn't realize it. It was an unconscious effect, but it had its effect.

That racist element in the State Department became worried about this. And you are out of your mind if you don't think that there's a racist element in the State Department. I'm not saying that everybody in the State Department is a racist, but I'm saying they sure got some in there and they got them in powerful positions. And this is the element that became worried about the changing Negro mood and the changing Negro behavior. Especially if that mood and behavior became one of violence, and by violence they only mean when a black man protects himself against the attack of the white man.

When it comes time for a black man to explode, they call it violence, but white people can be exploding against black people all day long and it's never called violence. I have even had some of you come to me and ask if I'm for violence. I'm the victim of violence and you're the victim of violence. In fact, you've been so victimized by it, you can't recognize it for what it is today.

The fear was that the changing image of the African

would have a tendency to change your and my image much too much, and they knew you and I tended to iden- tify with Africa where we didn't formerly do so. Their fear was that sympathy and that identity would eventually de- velop into sort of an allegiance for African hopes and aspirations above and beyond America's hopes and aspira- tions. So they had to do something to create a division between the Afro-American and the African so that you and I and they could not get together and coordinate our efforts and make faster progress than we had been making up to that time.

They don't mind you struggling for freedom as long as you struggle according to their rules. As long as you let them tell you how to struggle, they go for your struggle. But as soon as you come to one of them who is supposed to be for your freedom and tell him you're for freedom by any means necessary, he gets away from you. He's for his freedom by any means necessary, but he'll never go along with you to get your freedom by any means neces- sary.

United States history is that of a country that does whatever it wants to by any means necessary, to look out for its interest by any means necessary, but when it comes to your and my interest, then all of the means become limited. And we can't go along with that. We say what's good for the goose is good for the gander. If we are going to be non-violent, then let America become non-violent. Let her pull her troops out of Saigon and pull her troops out of the Congo and pull back all her troops everywhere and then we will see that she is a non-violent country, that we're living in a non-violent society. But until they get non-violent themselves, you're out of your mind to get non-violent. That's all I say on that.

I'm for peace, but I don't see how any black people can be at peace before the war is over, and you haven't even won a battle yet. If I have to follow a general who is fighting for my freedom and the enemy begins to pin peace medals on him before I've gotten my freedom, I'm afraid I'll have to find another general because its impossible for a general to be at peace when his people don't get no peace. It is impossible to give out peace medals when the people who are oppressed don't have any peace.

The only man who has peace is the man at the top. And I don't think that black people should be at peace in any way; there should be no peace on earth for anybody until there's peace also for us.

As the African nations began to get very nationalistic, very militant, and very uncompromising in their search for freedom, the European powers found they couldn't stay on the African continent any longer. It's like someone in a football game or a basketball game: When he's trapped or boxed in, he doesn't throw the ball away, but he has to pass it to someone who's in the clear. And this is the same thing the Europeans did.

The Africans didn't want them anymore, so they had to pass the ball to one of their partners who was in the clear and that partner was Uncle Sam. Uncle Sam caught the ball and he's been carrying it ever since. All you have to do is go to the African continent, travel from one end of it to the other, and you'll find out that the American position and influence has only replaced the position and influence of the former colonial powers and they did it very skillfully.

They knew that no non-African could stay on that continent against the will of the African, so they had to use a better, more subtle method. They had to make friends with the African. They had to make the African think they were there to help them, so they started pretending like they wanted to help you and me over here. They came up with all these pretty slogans about integration which they haven't produced yet.

They came up with slogans about this kind of program and that kind of program, but when you analyze it very closely, you find that they haven't produced it yet. It hasn't produced what it was supposed to produced. It's so hard for them to produce results that when they get that much of it, it makes headlines.

The law was handed down by the Supreme Court. They said you could go to any school you want, but when you get out there and get ready to go to a school like the law

says, the law is the one busting you upside your head, or
turning the water hose on you, or the cattle prod, so this
kind of shook the Afro-American up. He wondered
whether the Supreme Court was really in a position to say
what the law of the land was supposed to be. They passed
a law they could not enforce. And I don't mean they
couldn't enforce it in Mississippi, I mean they couldn't
enforce it in New York City. They couldn't even desegregate the schools in New York City, so how in the
world are they going to enforce it in Louisiana, Mississippi, and some of these other places?

These were token moves, designed to make you and me
cool down just a little while longer by making us think
that an honest effort was being made to get a solution to
the problem. And then as they began to appear as if they
were for the black man in this country, abroad they were
blown up. Especially the United States Information Service. Its job abroad, especially in the African continent, is
to make the Africans think that you and I are living in
paradise, that our problems have been solved, that the
Supreme Court desegregation decision put all of us in
school, that the passage of the Civil Rights Bill last year
solved all of our problems, and that now that Martin
Luther King, Jr., has gotten the peace prize, we are on our
way to the promised land of integration.

I was over there when all of this happened and I know
how they used it. They don't use it in an objective, constructive way; they use it to trick and fool the African into
thinking that most of their time is spent in loving you and
me and trying to solve your and my problem with honest
methods, and that they were getting honest results.

So I would like to say in my conclusion why we in the
Organization of Afro-American Unity feel that we just
can't sit around and rely upon the same objectives and
strategies that have been used in the past.

If you study the so-called progress of the Afro-American, go back to 1939, just before the war with Hitler,
most of our people were dishwashers, waiters, and shoeshine boys. It didn't make any difference how much education we had. We worked downtown in those hotels as

bellhops and on the railroad as waiters and in Grand Central Station as redcaps. Prior to 1939, we knew what our position was going to be even before we graduated from school.

In those days our people couldn't even work in a factory. In Michigan where all of the factories were, they were primarily shining shoes and working at other menial tasks. Then when Hitler went on a rampage, America was faced with a manpower shortage. This is the only time you and I got a break. Some of you are too young to remember it, and some of you are so old you don't want to remember it.

They let us in the defense plants, and we began to get jobs as machinists for the first time. We got a little skill, made a little more money. Then we were in a position to live in a little better neighborhood. When we moved to a little better neighborhood, we had a little better school to go to and got a little better education. This is how we came out of it; not through someone's benevolence and not through the efforts of organizations in our midst. It was the pressure that Uncle Sam was under. The only time that man has let the black man go one step forward has been when outside pressure has been brought to bear upon him. It has never been for any other reason. World pressure, economic pressure, political pressure, military pressure: When he was under pressure, he let you and me have a break.

So the point that I make is that it has never just been on our own initiative that you and I have made any steps forward. And the day that you and I recognize this, then we see the thing in its proper perspective because we cease looking just to Uncle Sam and Washington, D.C., to have the problems solved and we cease looking just within America for allies in our struggle against the injustices.

When you find people outside America who look like you getting power, my suggestion is that you turn to them and make them your allies. Let them know that we all have the same problem, that racism is not an internal American problem, but an international problem. Racism is a human problem and a crime that is absolutely so ghastly that a person who is fighting racism is well within his rights to fight against it by any means necessary until it is eliminated.

When you and I can start thinking like that and we get involved in some kind of activity with that kind of liberty, I think we'll get some ends to some of our problems almost overnight.

SOME REFLECTIONS ON "NEGRO HISTORY WEEK" AND THE ROLE OF THE BLACK PEOPLE IN HISTORY *

THIS week comes around once every year. And during this one week they drown us with propaganda about Negro history in Georgia and Mississippi and Alabama. Never do they take us back across the water, back home. They take us down home, but they never give us a history of back home. They never give us enough information to let us know what we were doing before we ended up in Mississippi, Alabama, Georgia, Texas, and some of those other prison states. They give us the impression with Negro History Week that we were cotton pickers all of our lives. Cotton pickers, orange growers, mammies and uncles for the white man in this country—this is our history when you talk in terms of Negro History Week. They might tell you about one or two people who took a peanut and made another white man rich. George Washington Carver—he was a scientist, but he died broke. He made Ford rich. So he wasn't doing anything for himself and his people. He got a good name for us, but what did we get out of it?—nothing; the master got it.

Just like a dog who runs out of the woods and grabs a rabbit. No matter how hungry the dog is, does he eat it? No, he takes it back and lays it at the boss's feet. The boss skins it, takes the meat, and gives the dog the bones. And the dog is going right on, hungry again. But he could have gotten the rabbit and eaten it for himself. And boss couldn't even have caught him until later, because he can

* January 25, 1965.

outrun the boss. It's the same way with you and me. Every contribution we make, we don't make it for our people, we make it for the man, we make it for our master. He gets the benefit from it. We die, not for our people, we die for him. We don't die for our home and our house, we die for his house. We don't die for our country, we die for his country. A lot of you all were fools on the front lines, were you not? Yes, you were. You put on the uniform and went right up on the front lines like a roaring hound dog barking for master. And when you come back here—you've had to bark since you came back.

So Negro History Week reminds us of this. It doesn't remind us of past achievements, it reminds us only of the achievements we made in the Western Hemisphere under the tutelage of the white man. So that whatever achievement that was made in the Western Hemisphere that the spotlight is put upon, this is the white man's shrewd way of taking credit for whatever we have accomplished. But he never lets us know of an accomplishment that we made prior to being born here. This is another trick.

The worst trick of all is when he names us Negro and calls us Negro. And when we call ourselves that, we end up tricking ourselves. My brother Cassius was on the screen the other night talking with Les Crane about the word "Negro." I wish he wouldn't have gone so fast, because he was in a position to have done a very good job. But he was right in saying that we're not Negroes, and have never been, until we were brought here and made into that. We were scientifically produced by the white man. Whenever you see somebody who calls himself a Negro, he's a product of Western civilization—not only Western civilization, but Western crime. The Negro, as he is called or calls himself in the West, is the best evidence that can be used against Western civilization today. One of the main reasons we are called Negro is so we won't know who we really are. And when you call yourself that, you don't know who you really are. You don't know what you are, you don't know where you came from, you don't know what is yours. As long as you call yourself a Negro, nothing is yours. No languages—you can't lay claim to any language, not even English; you mess it up. You can't lay claim to any name, any type of name, that will identify you as something that you should be. You can't lay claim to any culture as long as you use the word "Negro" to identify yourself. It attaches you to nothing. It doesn't even identify your color.

If you talk about one of them, they call themselves white, don't they? Or they might call someone else Puerto Rican to identify them. Mind you how they do this. When they call him a Puerto Rican, they're giving him a better name. Because there is a place called Puerto Rico, you know. It at least lets you know where he came from. So they'll say whites, Puerto Ricans, and Negroes. Pick up on that. That's a drag, brothers. White is legitimate. It means that's what color they are. Puerto Rican tells you that they're someone else, came from somewhere else, but they're here now. Negro doesn't tell you anything. I mean nothing, absolutely nothing. What do you identify it with? —tell me—nothing. What do you attach it to, what do you attach to it?—nothing. It's completely in the middle of nowhere. And when you call yourself that, that's where you are—right in the middle of nowhere. It doesn't give you a language, because there is no such thing as a Negro language. It doesn't give you a country, because there is no such thing as a Negro country. It doesn't give you a culture—there is no such thing as a Negro culture, it doesn't exist. The land doesn't exist, the culture doesn't exist, the language doesn't exist, and the man doesn't exist. They take you out of existence by calling you a Negro. And you can walk around in front of them all day long and they act like they don't even see you. Because you made yourself non-existent. It's a person who has no history; and by having no history, he has no culture.

Just as a tree without roots is dead, a people without history or cultural roots also becomes a dead people. And when you look at us, those of us who are called Negro, we're called that because we are like dead people. We have nothing to identify ourselves as part of the human family. You know, you take a tree, you can tell what kind of tree it is by looking at the leaves. If the leaves are gone, you can look at the bark and tell what kind it is. But when you find a tree with the leaves gone and the bark gone, everything gone, you call that a what?—a stump; and you can't identify a stump as easily as you can identify a tree. And this is the position that you and I are in here in America. Formerly we could be identified by the names we wore when we came here. When we were first brought here, we had different names. When we were first brought here, we had a different language. And these names and this language identified the culture that we were brought from, the land that we were brought from. In identifying that, we were able to point toward what we had produced, our net worth. But once our names were taken and our language was taken and our identity was destroyed and our roots were cut off with no history, we became like a stump, something dead, a twig over here in the Western Hemisphere. Anybody could step on us, trample upon us, or burn us, and there would be nothing that we could do about it.

Those of you who are religious, who go to church, [know] there are stories in the Bible that can be used easily to pretty well tell the condition of the black man in America once 'he became a Negro. They refer to him in there as the lost sheep, meaning someone who is lost from his own kind, which is how you and I have been for the past four hundred years. We have been in a land where we are not citizens, or in a land where they have treated us as strangers. They have another symbolic story in there, called the dry bones. Many of you have gone to church Sunday after Sunday and got, you know, the ghost, they call it, got happy. When the old preacher started singing about dry bones, you'd knock over benches, just because he was singing about those bones, "them dry bones" (I know how they say it). But you never could identify the symbolic meaning of those bones—how they were dead because they had been cut off from their own kind. Our people here in America have been in the same condition as those dry bones that you sit in church singing about. But you shed more tears over those dry bones than you shed over yourself. This is a strange thing, but it shows what happens to a people when they are cut off and stripped of everything, like you and I have been cut off and stripped of everything. We become a people like no other people, and we are a people like no other people, [there's] no other people on earth like you and me. We're unique, we're different. They say that we're Negro, and they say that Negro means black; yet they don't call all black people Negroes. You see the contradiction? Mind you, they say that we're Negro, because Negro means black in Spanish, yet they don't call all black people Negroes. Something there doesn't add up.

And then to get around it they say mankind is divided up into three categories—Mongoloid, Caucasoid, and Negroid. Now pick up on that. And all black people aren't Negroid—they've got some jet black ones that they classify as Caucasoid. But if you'll study very closely, all of the black ones that they classify as Caucasoid are those that still have great civilizations, or still have the remains of what was once a great civilization. The only ones that they classify as Negroid are those that they find with no evidence that they were ever civilized; then they call them Negroid. But they can't afford to let any black-skinned people who have evidence that they formerly occupied a high seat in civilization, they can't afford to let them be called Negroid, so they take them on into the Caucasoid classification.

And actually Caucasoid, Mongoloid, and Negroid— there's no such thing. These are so-called anthropological terms that were put together by anthropologists who were nothing but agents of the colonial powers, and they were purposely given that status, they were purposely given such scientific positions, in order that they could come up with definitions that would justify the European domination over the Africans and the Asians. So immediately they invented classifications that would automatically demote these people or put them on a lesser level. All of the Caucasoids are on a high level, the Negroids are kept at a low level. This is just plain trickery that their scientists engage in in order to keep you and me thinking that we never were anything, and therefore he's doing us a favor as he lets us step upward or forward in his particular society or civilization. I hope you understand what I am saying.

Ancient Black Civilizations

Now then, once you see that the condition that we're in is directly related to our lack of knowledge concerning the history of the black man, only then can you realize the importance of knowing something about the history of the black man. The black man's history—when you refer to him as the black man you go way back, but when you refer to him as a Negro, you can only go as far back as the Negro goes. And when you go beyond the shores of America you can't find a Negro. So if you go beyond the shores of America in history, looking for the history of the black man, and you're looking for him under the term "Negro," you won't find him. He doesn't exist. So you end up thinking that you didn't play any role in history.

But if you want to take the time to do research for yourself, I think you'll find that on the African continent there was always, prior to the discovery of America, there was always a higher level of history, rather a higher level of culture and civilization, than that which existed in Europe at the same time. At least five thousand years ago they had a black civilization in the Middle East called the Sumerians. Now when they show you pictures of the Sumerians they try and make you think that they were white people. But if you go and read some of the ancient manuscripts or even read between the lines of some of the current writers, you'll find that the Sumerian civilization was a very dark-skinned civilization, and it existed prior even to the existence of the Babylonian empire, right in the same area where you find Iraq and the Tigris-Euphrates Rivers there. It was a black-skinned people who lived there, who had a high state of culture way back then.

And at a time even beyond this there was a black-skinned people in India, who were black, just as black as you and I, called Dravidians. They inhabited the subcontinent of India even before the present people that you see living there today, and they had a high state of culture. The present people of India even looked upon them as gods; most of their statues, if you'll notice, have pronounced African features. You go right to India today—in their religion, which is called Buddhism, they give all their Buddhas the image of a black man, with his lips and his nose, and even show his hair all curled up on his head; they didn't curl it up, he was born that way. And these people lived in that area before the present people of India lived there. The black man lived in the Middle East before the present people who are now living there. And he had a high culture and a high civilization, to say nothing about the oldest civilization of all that he had in Egypt along the banks of the Nile. And in Carthage in northwest Africa, another part of the continent, and at a later date in Mali and Ghana and Songhai, and Moorish civilization—all of these civilizations existed on the African continent before America was discovered.

Now the black civilization that shook the white man up the most was the Egyptian civilization, and it was a black civilization. It was along the banks of the Nile, which runs through the heart of Africa. But again this tricky white man, and he's tricky—and mind you again, when I say this, it's not a racist statement. Some of them might not be tricky, but all of them I've met are tricky. And his civilization shows his trickiness. This tricky white man was able to take the Egyptian civilization, write books about it, put pictures in those books, make movies for television and the theater—so skillfully that he has even convinced other white people that the ancient Egyptians were white people themselves. They were African, they were as much African as you and I. And he even gave the clue away when he made this movie, *King Solomon's Mines,* and he showed the Watusis, you know, with their black selves, and he outright admitted in there that they looked like the ancient pharaohs of ancient Egypt. Which means that the white man himself, he knows that the black man had this high civilization in Egypt, whose remains today show the black man in that area had mastered mathematics, had mastered architecture, the sciences of building things, had even mastered astronomy.

The pyramid, as the white scientists admit, is constructed in such a position on this earth to show that the black people who were the architects of it had a knowledge of geography that was so vast, they knew the exact center of the earth's land mass. Because the base of the pyramid is located in the exact center of the earth's land mass, which could not have been so situated by its architect unless the architect in that day had known that the earth was round and knew how much land there was in all the directions from where he was standing. The pyramid was built so many thousand years ago that they don't even know the exact time it was built, but they do know that the people who brought it into existence had mastered the science of building, had mastered the various sciences of the earth and had mastered astronomy. I read where one scientist said that the architect of the pyramid had built a shaft that went outward from the center of the pyramid, and the place it marked in the sky was the location where a star, a blue star I think, some kind of a star, made an appearance only once every fifty thousand years. Now they say that this architect's knowledge of astronomy was so vast that he evidently had access to histories or records that spotlighted the existence of a star that made its appearance at a certain spot in the sky only once every fifty thousand years. Now he could not have known this unless he had records going back beyond fifty thousand years. Yet the pyramid is a living witness today that the black people who were responsible for bringing it into existence had this kind of knowledge.

When you read the opinions of the white scientists about the pyramids and the building of the pyramids, they don't make any secret at all over the fact that they marvel over the scientific ability that was in the possession of those people way back then. They had mastered chemistry to such an extent that they could make paints whose color doesn't fade right until today. When I was in Cairo in the summer, I was in King Tut's tomb, plus I saw that which was taken out of the tomb at the Cairo museum, and the colors of the clothing that was worn and the colors inside the tomb are as bright and vivid and sharp today as they were when they were put there some thousands of years ago. Whereas, you know yourself, you can paint your house, and have to paint it again next year. This man hasn't learned how to make paint yet that will last two

years. And the black man in that day was such a master
in these various scientific fields that he left behind evidence
that his scientific findings in that day exceed the degree
to which the white man here in the West has been able to
rise today. And you must know this, because if you don't
know this, you won't really understand what there is about
you that makes them so afraid of you, and makes them
show that they find it imperative for them to keep you
down, keep you from getting up, because if they let you
up one inch, you've got it and gone—just one inch, you've
got it and gone. And you should get it and go.

Just behind the pyramids is a huge statue which many
of you are familiar with, called the Sphinx. The people
who live over there call it Abou Al-hole, which means
"father of everything." This too was put over there so long
ago they don't know who did it, nor do they know how
long ago it was done. And they marvel at it. What causes
them to marvel is the fact that the black man could have
been at such a high level then, and now be where he is
today, at the bottom of the heap, with no outer sign that
he has any scientific ability left within him. And he himself
doesn't believe that he has any of this ability within him;
he thinks that he has to turn to the man for some kind of
formula on even how to get his freedom or how to build
his house. But the black man by nature is a builder, he is
scientific by nature, he's mathematical by nature. Rhythm
is mathematics, harmony is mathematics. It's balance. And
the black man is balanced. Before you and I came over
here, we were so well balanced we could toss something
on our head and run with it. You can't even run with your
hat now—you can't keep it on. Because you lost your
balance. You've gotten away from yourself. But when you
are in tune with yourself, your very nature has harmony,
has rhythm, has mathematics. You can build. You don't
even need anybody to teach you how to build. You play
music by ear. You dance by how you're feeling. And you
used to build the same way. You have it in you to do it.
I know black brickmasons from the South who have never
been to school a day in their life. They throw more bricks
together and you don't know how they learned to do it,
but they know how to do it. When you see one of those

other people doing it, they've been to school—somebody had to teach them. But nobody teaches you always what you know how to do. It just comes to you. That's what makes you dangerous. When you come to yourself, a whole lot of other things will start coming to you, and the man knows it.

European "Civilization"

In that day the black man in Egypt was wearing silk, sharp as a tack, brothers. And those people up in Europe didn't know what cloth was. They admit this. They were naked or they were wearing skins from animals. If they could get an animal, they would take his hide and throw it around their shoulders to keep warm. But they didn't know how to sew and weave. They didn't have the knowledge in Europe, not in those days. They didn't cook their food in Europe. Even they themselves will show you when they were living up there in caves, they were knocking animals in the head and eating the raw meat. They were eating raw meat, raw food. They still like it raw today. You watch them go in a restuarant, they say, "Give me a steak rare, with the blood dripping in it." And then you run in and say, "Give me one rare, with the blood dripping in it." You don't do it because that's the way you like it; you're just imitating them, you're copying, you're trying to be like that man. But when you act like yourself, you say, "Make mine well done." You like cooked food, because you've been cooking a long time; but they haven't been cooking so long—it wasn't too long ago that they knew what fire was. This is true.

You were walking erect, upright. You ever watch your walk? Now you do this to walk erect. You've come up with that other walk. But when you're yourself, you walk with dignity. Wherever you see the black man, he walks with dignity. They have a tendency to be other than with dignity, unless they're trained. When their little girls go up to these, you know, hifalutin schools, and they want to teach them how to walk, they put a book on their head. Isn't that what they do? They teach them how to walk like you. That's what they're learning how to walk like, like you. But you were almost born with a book on your head. You can throw it up there and run with it. I was amazed when I was in Africa to see the sense of poise and balance that these people over there have, all throughout Africa and Asia. They have that poise and that balance. But this is not an accident. This comes from something. And you have it too, but you've been channeling yours in another direction, in a different direction. But when you come to yourself, you'll channel it right.

Also, as I said earlier, at that same time there was another African civilization called Carthage. One of the most famous persons in Carthage was a man named Hannibal. You and I have been taught that he was a white man. This is how they steal your history, they steal your culture, they steal your civilization—just by Hollywood producing a movie showing a black man as a white man. I remember one day I told someone that Hannibal was black—some Negro, he was in college, you understand—I told him Hannibal was a black man, and he had a fit. Really, he did, he wanted to fight me on that. He said, "I know better than that." "How do you know?" He said, "I saw him." "Where'd you see him?" He said, "In the movies." And he was in college, really, he was a highly educated "Negro"— and he had a fit when I told him Hannibal was black. And some of you all right now are having a fit because you didn't know it either. Hannibal was famous for crossing the Alps Mountains with elephants. Europeans couldn't go across the Alps on foot by themselves—no, they couldn't. Hannibal found a way to cross the Alps with elephants. You know what an elephant is—a great big old animal, it's hard to move him down the road. They moved him across the mountains. And he had with him ninety thousand African troops, defeated Rome and occupied Italy for between fifteen and twenty years.

This is why you find many Italians dark—some of that Hannibal blood. No Italian will ever jump up in my face and start putting bad mouth on me, because I know his history. I tell him when you talk about me, you're talking about your pappy, your father. He knows his history, he knows how he got that color. Don't you know that just a handful of black American troops spent a couple of years in England during World War II and left more brown babies back there—just a handful of black American soldiers in England and in Paris and in Germany messed up the whole country. Now what do you think ninety thousand Africans are going to do in Italy for twenty years? It's good to know this because when you know it, you don't have to get a club to fight the man—put truth on him.

Even the Irish got a dose of your and my blood when the Spanish Armada was defeated off the coast of Ireland, I think around about the seventeenth or eighteenth century; I forget exactly, you can check it out. The Spanish in those days were dark. They were the remnants of the Moors, and they went ashore and settled down in Ireland and right to this very day you've got what's known as the black Irish. And it's not an accident that they call them black Irish. If you look at them, they've got dark hair, dark features, and they've got Spanish names—like Eamon de Valera, the president, and there used to be another one called Costello. These names came from the Iberian peninsula, which is the Spanish-Portuguese peninsula, and they came there through these seamen, who were dark in those days. Don't let any Irishman jump up in your face and start telling you about you—why, he's got some of your blood too. You've spread your blood everywhere. If you start to talk to any one of them, I don't care where he is, if you know history, you can put him right in his place. In fact, he'll stay in his place, if he knows that you know your history.

PART VI

APPENDIX

ORGANIZATION OF AFRO-AMERICAN UNITY: A STATEMENT OF BASIC AIMS AND OBJECTIVES *

T HE Organization of Afro-American Unity, organized and structured by a cross section of the Afro-American people living in the United States of America, has been patterned after the letter and spirit of the Organization of African Unity established at Addis Ababa, Ethiopia, May 1963.

We, the members of the Organization of Afro-American Unity gathered together in Harlem, New York;

CONVINCED that it is the inalienable right of all people to control their own destiny;

CONSCIOUS of the fact that freedom, equality, justice, and dignity are essential objectives for the achievement of the legitimate aspirations of the people of African descent here in the Western Hemisphere, we will endeavor to build a bridge of understanding and create the basis for Afro-American Unity;

CONSCIOUS of our responsibility to harness the natural and human resources of our people for their total advancement in all spheres of human endeavor;

INSPIRED by a common determination to promote understanding among our people and cooperation in all matters pertaining to their survival and advancement, we will support the aspirations of our people for brotherhood and solidarity in a larger unity transcending all organizational differences;

* New York, June 1964.

CONVINCED that, in order to translate this determination into a dynamic force in the cause of human progress, conditions of peace and security must be established and maintained;

DETERMINED to unify the Americans of African descent in their fight for Human Rights and Dignity, and being fully aware that this is not possible in the present atmosphere and condition of oppression, we dedicate ourselves to the building of a political, economic, and social system of justice and peace;

DEDICATED to the unification of all people of African descent in this hemisphere and to the utilization of that unity to bring into being the organizational structure that will project the black people's contributions to the world;

PERSUADED that the Charter of the United Nations, the Universal Declaration of Human Rights, the Constitution of the United States of America, and the Bill of Rights are the principles in which we believe and these documents if put into practice represent the essence of mankind's hopes and good intentions;

DESIROUS that all Afro-American people and organizations should henceforth unite so that the welfare and well-being of our people will be assured;

RESOLVED to reinforce the common bond of purpose between our people by submerging all of our differences and establishing a non-religious and non-sectarian constructive program for Human Rights;
DO hereby present this Charter.

I. *ESTABLISHMENT*

The Organization of Afro-American Unity shall include all people of African descent in the Western Hemisphere, as well as our brothers and sisters of the African continent.

II. *SELF-DEFENSE*

Since self-preservation is the first law of nature, we assert the Afro-American's right of self-defense.

The Constitution of the United States of America clearly affirms the right of every American citizen to bear arms. And as Americans, we will not give up a single right guaranteed under the Constitution. The history of unpunished violence against our people clearly indicates that we must be prepared to defend ourselves or we will continue to be a defenseless people at the mercy of a ruthless and violent racist mob.

We assert that in those areas where the government is either unable or unwilling to protect the lives and property of our people, that our people are within their rights to protect themselves by whatever means necessary. A man with a rifle or club can only be stopped by a person who defends himself with a rifle or club.

Tactics based solely on morality can only succeed when you are dealing with basically moral people or a moral system. A man or system which oppresses a man because of his color is not moral. It is the duty of every Afro-American and every Afro-American community throughout this country to protect its people against mass murderers, bombers, lynchers, floggers, brutalizers, and exploiters.

III. *EDUCATION*

Education is an important element in the struggle for Human Rights. It is the means to help our children and people rediscover their identity and thereby increase self-respect. Education is our passport to the future, for tomorrow belongs to the people who prepare for it today.

Our children are being criminally short-changed in the public schools of America. The Afro-American schools are the poorest-run schools in New York City. Principals and teachers fail to understand the nature of the problems with which they work and as a result they cannot do the job of teaching our children. The textbooks tell our children nothing about the great contributions of Afro-Americans to the growth and development of this country. The Board of Education's integration plan is expensive and unworkable; and the organization of principals and supervisors in the New York City school system has refused to support the Board's plan to integrate the schools, thus dooming it to failure.

The Board of Education has said that even with its plan there are 10 per cent of the schools in the Harlem-Bedford-Stuyvesant community they cannot improve. This means that the Organization of Afro-American Unity must make the Afro-American community a more potent force for educational self-improvement.

A first step in the program to end the existing system of racist education is to demand that the 10 per cent of the schools the Board of Education will not include in its plan be turned over to and run by the Afro-American community. We want Afro-American principals to head these schools. We want Afro-American teachers in these schools. We want textbooks written by Afro-Americans that are acceptable to us to be used in these schools.

The Organization of Afro-American Unity will select and recommend people to serve on local school boards where school policy is made and passed on to the Board of Education.

Through these steps we will make the 10 per cent of schools we take over educational showplaces that will attract the attention of people all over the nation.

If these proposals are not met, we will ask Afro-American parents to keep their children out of the present inferior schools they attend. When these schools in our neighborhood are controlled by Afro-Americans, we will return to them.

The Organization of Afro-American Unity recognizes the tremendous importance of the complete involvement of Afro-American parents in every phase of school life. Afro-American parents must be willing and able to go into the schools and see that the job of educating our children is done properly.

We call on all Afro-Americans around the nation to be aware that the conditions that exist in the New York City public school system are as deplorable in their cities as they are here. We must unite our efforts and spread our program of self-improvement through education to every Afro-American community in America.

We must establish all over the country schools of our own to train our children to become scientists and mathematicians. We must realize the need for adult education and for job retraining programs that will emphasize a changing society in which automation plays the key role. We intend to use the tools of education to help raise our people to an unprecedented level of excellence and self-respect through their own efforts.

IV. *POLITICS—ECONOMICS*

Basically, there are two kinds of power that count in America: economic and political, with social power deriving from the two. In order for the Afro-Americans to control their destiny, they must be able to control and affect the decisions which control their destiny: economic, political, and social. This can only be done through organization.

The Organization of Afro-American Unity will organize the Afro-American community block by block to make the community aware of its power and potential; we will start immediately a voter-registration drive to make every unregistered voter in the Afro-American community an Independent voter; we propose to support and/or organize political clubs, to run Independent candidates for office, and to support any Afro-American already in office who answers to and is responsible to the Afro-American community.

Economic exploitation in the Afro-American community is the most vicious form practiced on any people in America: twice as much rent for rat-infested, roach-crawling, rotting tenements; the Afro-American pays more for foods, clothing, insurance rates and so forth. The Organization of Afro-American Unity will wage an unrelenting struggle against these evils in our community. There will be organizers to work with the people to solve these problems, and start a housing self-improvement program. We propose to support rent strikes and other activities designed to better the community.

V. *SOCIAL*

This organization is responsible only to the Afro-American people and community and will function only with their support, both financially and numerically. We believe that our communities must be the sources of their own strength politically, economically, intellectually and culturally in the struggle for Human Rights and Dignity.

The community must reinforce its moral responsibility to rid itself of the effects of years of exploitation, neglect, and apathy, and wage an unrelenting struggle against police brutality.

The Afro-American community must accept the responsibility for regaining our people who have lost their place in society. We must declare an all-out war on organized crime in our community; a vice that is controlled by policemen who accept bribes and graft, and who must be exposed. We must establish a clinic, whereby one can get aid and cure for drug addiction and create meaningful, creative, useful activities for those who were led astray down the avenues of vice.

The people of the Afro-American community must be prepared to help each other in all ways possible; we must establish a place where unwed mothers can get help and advice; a home for the aged in Harlem and an orphanage in Harlem.

We must set up a guardian system that will help our youth who get into trouble and also provide constructive activities for our children. We must set a good example for our children and must teach them to always be ready to accept the responsibilities that are necessary for building good communities and nations. We must teach them that their greatest responsibilities are to themselves, to their families, and to their communities.

The Organization of Afro-American Unity believes that the Afro-American community must endeavor to do the major part of all charity work from within the community. Charity, however, does not mean that to which we are legally entitled in the form of government benefits. The Afro-American veteran must be made aware of all the benefits due him and the procedure for obtaining them. These veterans must be encouraged to go into business together, using GI loans, etc.

Afro-Americans must unite and work together. We must take pride in the Afro-American community, for it is home and it is power.

What we do here in regaining our Self-Respect, Manhood, Dignity, and Freedom helps all people everywhere who are fighting against oppression.

VI. *Culture*

"A race of people is like an individual man; until it uses its own talent, takes pride in its own history, expresses its own culture, affirms its own selfhood, it can never fulfill itself."

Our history and our culture were completely destroyed when we were forceably brought to America in chains. And now it is important for us to know that our history did not begin with slavery's scars. We come from Africa, a great continent and a proud and varied people, a land which is the new world and was the cradle of civilization. Our culture and our history are as old as man himself and yet we know almost nothing of it. We must recapture our heritage and our identity if we are ever to liberate ourselves from the bonds of white supremacy. We must launch a cultural revolution to unbrainwash an entire people.

Our cultural revolution must be the means of bringing us closer to our African brothers and sisters. It must begin in the community and be based on community participation. Afro-Americans will be free to create only when they depend on the Afro-American community. Afro-American artists must realize that they depend on the Afro-American for inspiration. We must work toward the establishment of a cultural center in Harlem which will include people of all ages, and will conduct workshops in all of the arts, such as film, creative writing, painting, theater, music, Afro-American history, etc.

This cultural revolution will be the journey to our rediscovery of ourselves. History is a people's memory, and without a memory man is demoted to the lower animals.

Armed with the knowledge of our past, we can with confidence charter a course for our future. Culture is an indispensable weapon in the freedom struggle. We must take hold of it and forge the future with the past.

When the battle is won, let history be able to say of each one of us:

"He was a dedicated patriot: DIGNITY was his country, MANHOOD was his government, and FREEDOM was his land."

(from AND THEN WE HEARD THE THUNDER,
by John Oliver Killens)

OUTLINE FOR PETITION TO THE UNITED NATIONS CHARGING GENOCIDE AGAINST 22 MILLION BLACK AMERICANS

We are engaged in America today in a momentous struggle for the freedom of 22 million of our people. A struggle which has, with much pain and courage, been a part of our life for three hundred years. A struggle which like a wave, containing all these years of oppression, has finally broken upon our shores, meeting thereon violent forces collecting themselves to hold back this wave of freedom—violent forces which are creating a clear and present danger to the nation as a whole and indeed, to the entire world. This wave of 22 million Americans who have so long suffered such violence certainly seeks no more, but it must, and will prevail.

We have appealed to the conscience of America, but her conscience slumbers. Her conscience, conceived and nourished in a soulless womb of material greed, slumbers in a darkness of hate and fear, permitting the violence to continue.

We gainsay nothing by turning our back on the fact that the wanton murder of thousands of black men and women, including little children, Birmingham, the murder of a young President, the murder of three young men in Mississippi and the recovery of two decapitated black bodies from a river in the same state, the bombings of churches and homes in the Southern part of the United States in retaliation against efforts by black Americans to exercise the constitutionally guaranteed right to vote, the gerrymandering of electoral districts in the Northern part of the United States in order to prevent effective political representation, the use of the electric cattle prods on human beings engaged in peaceful demonstrations, the presence of islands of culturally, educationally and economically disenfranchised black communities in most every city and state of this nation, have not penetrated the darkness nor aroused America's conscience. Instead, the majority population flits and skirts around these colonial islands as if they did not exist, carrying out the illusory functions of their lives, never really seeing the horror that marks our existence, never really hearing the painful groans nor the justifiable cries of anger that emit from eleven percent of this nation.

Since the wrongs committed against our person, our humanity and this nation of our birth are of long standing, and since the majority population has had in excess of three centuries to right these wrongs, we must conclude that America's conscience is not able to concede or affirm the rights of "life, liberty and pursuit of happiness" to human beings whose skin is not white, seeing them only as instruments of profit, be they black Americans, black Africans or colored Asians and Indians.

After three hundred years of slavery and caste oppression, unmitigated terror and torture, physical and otherwise—which continues today though opposed by every means possible of human conception—while all the time remaining faithful to this Government in time of war and peace, we feel the United Nations must give a hearing to the plight of 22 million black Americans.

After years and years of supplication, petitioning, pleading and agitation for affirmation of basic human rights, all to no avail, we see no recourse but to put our case to you the representatives and delegates to the United Nations. We come to you because we see in your deliberations and debates and the accords which often issue forth, where and how the conscience of mankind can be utilized as an invaluable aid in righting wrongs and securing peace, and understanding and well-being. We see the United Nations as the institution wherein world opinion and the conscience of mankind can be appealed to.

Our experiences in the United States have taught us beyond hope of doubt that nothing short of a massive assault of conscience will have any but the slightest effect upon the psyche of the majority population, so conditioned have they become to luxuriating in their ill-begotten gains at the expense of 22 million caste-locked citizens of color.

We address ourselves now to you, whose task it is to establish a universal climate wherein those rights set forth in the Universal Declaration of Human Rights, Resolution of the General Assembly, December 10, 1948, will finally and definitely be regarded as rights belonging to all men, legally, under International Law.*

We charge that the Government of the United States has violated, in the most gross manner, all of the aforementioned wise and just declarations which should and must fashion and mold the conduct and relations of governments to their citizenry, no less so than nations to each other.

We further charge that the nature and character of our Government's desecration of these declarations is genocidal, as defined by the 1948 Draft Convention on the Prevention and Punishment of the Crime of Genocide.

We shall document our assertion that a vast and systematic form of oppression does exist in this country based on color and race: that it is the nub of, that it is central to, and that it is the fulcrum of most all important social and political issues in this nation.

We shall prove, conclusively, that the charges contained in the above and all that shall follow are the result of governmental activity from the Federal level to the local, inclusive.

We shall point out those areas where the charge of genocide is most critical in the daily life of our people, and where the United Nations has competence to give consideration and to act.

Economic Genocide

There is a widespread evidence of economic genocide, which is illustrative of "deliberately inflicting on the group

* We refer to Articles 2, 5, 6 and 7 of the Declaration. Also, Article 16, Sections 1 & 3; Article 17 and Article 23, Sections 1 & 2.

conditons of life calculated to bring about its physical destruction in whole or in part." These conditions exist in contradiction to Article 2, Section 3 of the Genocide Convention.[2]

Mental Harm

Murder and brutalization is a source of terror, as it is intended to be, to the whole population of America's black nationals. As a result, our people exist in a constant fear that cannot fail to cause serious bodily and mental harm.

Another source of serious bodily and mental harm is the segregation which imprisons American black people in most every case, from birth to death, marking their status as inferior on the basis of race, cutting them off from adequate education, hospital facilities, medical treatment, and housing, forcing them to live in ghettos and depriving them of rights and privileges that other Americans are accorded as a matter of course.

Psychological and physical terror carried out by the KKK, the White Citizens Councils and other organizations and groups against Americans of color deters millions of them from voting or otherwise exercising their rights under the Constitution of the United States and the Charter of the United Nations. Thus many of our people, particularly in the South, live their lives in fear of violence for allegedly overstepping one of the many prohibitions in the extra-legal white supremacy code. If these people sometimes avoid physical violence, they never escape from "serious mental harm directed against the group." Such conditions violate Article 2 of the Genocide Convention.*

Emasculated role of the black male, with slave antecedents.†

---

* Relatively short, non-statistical explanatory statements on the following: EDUCATION, EMPLOYMENT, HOUSING, HOSPITAL FACILITIES, MEDICAL CARE, DISEASE AND INFANT AND ADULT LIFE EXPECTANCY AS COMPARED WITH THE REMAINDER OF THE POPULATION: INSURANCE and FINANCIAL AND LENDING INSTITUTIONS.

† Relatively short, non-statistical explanatory statement.

Triple oppression of black women, with slave antecedents.*
Adolescent traumas, all of which are destructive of the
family unit, and as such are violative of Article 16, Sec-
tion 3 of the Universal Declaration of Human Rights.*
Jim Crow laws defining and limiting the choice of marital
partner, also in violation of Article 16, Section 3 of
Declaration.*
Psychological tensions arising from ghetto existence.*
Numbers of black people in mental institutions as opposed
to the rest of the population.*
Distortion, if not complete deletion—as a weapon of oppression—of our proud history and its unique and central
relatedness to all of American history. This applies to
African history as well. Particular emphasis on how this
is carried out in the educational system.*
Public media used as weapon to distort existing conditions
and to twist out of focus all efforts on the part of black
people toward correction of these conditions.*
Mythology of "race" utilized as weapon of oppression.*

Killing Members of the Group

We cite killings by police, killings by incited gangs,
killings by the Ku Klux Klan and White Citizens Councils,
on the basis of "race." These atrocities, more often than
not, occur as a result of attempts to vote or otherwise
demand the legal and inalienable rights and privileges of
United States citizenship formally guaranteed all Americans by the Constitution of the United States but denied
to those whose color is not white, in violation of the
Constitution of the United States, the United Nations
Charter, Articles 3 and 22 of the Universal Declaration of
Human Rights, and Article 2, Section 1 of the Genocide
Convention, which declares that "killing members of the
group" is a crime under International Law.

ITEMS

Killings and/or serious injuries which result from attempts to vote or otherwise affirm legal and constitutionally guaranteed rights.*

* Relatively short, non-statistical explanatory statement.

Killings and/or serious injuries which may seem at first to be isolated and useless, but are indeed part of a broad design, particularly in the South, wherein Americans of color must be killed for being too "uppity," must be killed or hurt for being too "sassy," must be killed for any activity which might change or lead to changes aimed at destroying the inferior status of black Americans.*

Conspiracies, Attempts, Incitements and Complicity to Commit Genocide

Public officials, particularly in the South, are frequently guilty of murder on the basis of "race," of genocide, by direct and public incitement to genocide, by participating in actual violence on the basis of "race" as in the case of sheriffs and law enforcement officers, by the use of courts to kill innocent black Americans in order to sustain white supremacy, by approving and soliciting the murder or assault of black Americans who attempt to vote, by passing and enforcing laws providing for segregation in violation of the 14th Amendment to the Constitution of the United States, the Charter of the United Nations, and Article 3, Sections A, B, C and D of the Genocide Convention, which declare genocide, conspiracy to commit genocide, direct and public incitement to commit genocide, and complicity in genocide as punishable.

ITEMS

Federal and state police and judicial system—North.*
Federal and state police and judicial system—South.*
Genocide is possible because of negative or positive sanction of the Federal Government and its three departments.*
Division of three branches of government an aid to conspiracy against black Americans.
Monopoly capital prime mover in conspiracy.*
Government as a creature of monopoly capital.*

* Relatively short, non-statistical explanatory statement.

Key government posts in defense, war preparation, utilities, and transport held by representatives of Wall Street, who control the economic life of the nation.*
Incitements by judges, governors, senators, congressmen, police chiefs, etc., that are conspiratorial in nature.*
Role of the FBI. Statements by J. Edgar Hoover.*

The Law

How the Convention grew out of the Nuremberg trials of Nazi war criminals.*
The Convention's relevancy to the situation in the United States.*
The Convention and the United Nations Charter.*
The Charter and United States law.*
Statement to the effect that the genocide indicated above justifies inclusion of Articles 5-10 of the Convention, dealing with punishment and persons liable.*

History of Oppression

Constitutional background of civil rights.*
  A) What are civil rights in the United States?
  B) What does it mean to be a citizen of the United States?
The 1787-1808 Constitutional Compromise on slavery, which confirms the Constitution as basically an economic document favoring the Southern planter class.*
The Dred Scott Decision.*
The Fugitive Slave Act.*

Requirements of the Constitution

The 13th Amendment.*
The 14th Amendment.*
The 15th Amendment.*

The Civil War and Emancipation

Conservative and radical Republicans.*

* Relatively short, non-statistical explanatory statement.

Use of Civil War by Northern industrial capitalism to consolidate political power.*

Reconstruction

Lincoln's cautious policy in regard to the ex-slave following the Civil War.*
Andrew Johnson's conception of democracy, which did not include the black man.*
Republican passage of re-enslaving Black Codes as a means of cutting down potential Southern congressional representation and political power in order to further increase Northern industrial might.*
Establishment of the 14th Amendment through passage of 1866, 1870 and 1875 Civil Rights Bills.*
Military Rule.*
Hayes-Tilden Compromise.*
Southern planter's use of crisis produced by the Civil War and Reconstruction—centered around competition between the industrial North and the agrarian South and which put free black men into economic competition with poor whites—to bring into the open the conflict of class interests that had always existed in the South.*
Supreme Court decision of 1883, holding the Civil Rights Act of 1875 to be unconstitutional. Supreme Court decision of 1896, as progenitor of segregation laws as we have come to know them, declaring separate but equal to be constitutional.*
Agrarian discontent used by Southern planters to arouse race hatred which led to extensive violence and terror against black people. The institution of legislation throughout the South that divested the black citizen of all privileges and immunities of the 14th Amendment, including the right to vote.*
Growth of terror against black citizens and its relatedness to growth of monopoly capital in the United States and abroad, Hawaii, Puerto Rico, Cuba, Guam, and the Philippine Islands.*

* Relatively short, non-statistical explanatory statement.

Genocide Leads to War and Silencing
of Domestic Dissent

American slavery, the "killing of part of the group" led to two wars. The Mexican War in 1846, seeking to expand slave territory and the Civil War.*

Murder on the basis of race by police, courts, and bands of white supremacists has been widespread in the United States for a long time, and is currently on the upsurge. Crimes of murder are increasing because genocide, by its very nature, becomes more aggressive as the militancy of oppressed people grows and develops.*

Terrorism following Hayes–Tilden Compromise.*

Terrorism following First and Second World Wars.*

McCarthyism during and after Korean War.*

Furthermore, genocide has a clear and definite relationship to foreign affairs. The genocide of which we speak cannot be seen apart from America's engagement in an unpopular war in Vietnam, America's unpopular intervention in the Congo, America's unpopular accord with former Nazi militarists, or America's unpopular war of subversion against Cuba. Unpopular wars and interventions require a silencing of the people, a breaking of their will for resistance.*

Violence against American black citizens goes hand in hand with increased repression throughout American life: The McCarran Act, Subversive Activities Control Board, HUAC, Landrum-Griffin Labor Law.*

* Relatively short, non-statistical explanatory statement.

A SELECTED BIBLIOGRAPHY
OF BOOKS AND ARTICLES
RELATING TO THE LIFE OF
MALCOLM X

——————————— COMPILED BY *A. Peter Bailey*

Books

Baldwin, James. *The Fire Next Time*. New York: Dial Press, 1963.

Barbour, Floyd B. (ed.). *The Black Power Revolt*. Boston: Extending Horizon Books, 1968.

Bennett, Lerone, Jr. *The Negro Mood*. Chicago: Johnson Publications, 1965.

———. *Confrontation: Black and White*. Chicago: Johnson Publishing Co., 1965.

Bontemps, Arna, and Conroy, Jack, *Anyplace But Here*. New York: Hill and Wang, 1966.

Breitman, George. *Last Year of Malcolm X, The Evolution of a Revolutionary*. New York: Merit Publishers, 1967.

——— (ed.). *Malcolm X Speaks*. New York: Merit Publishers, 1965.

Broderick, Francis L., and Meier, August (eds.). *Negro Protest Thought in the Twentieth Century*. New York: Bobbs-Merrill Co., 1966.

Clark, Kenneth B. (ed.). *The Negro Protest: James Baldwin, Malcolm X, Martin Luther King Talk With Kenneth B. Clark*. Boston: Beacon Press, 1963.

Cleaver, Eldridge. *Soul on Ice*. New York: McGraw-Hill, 1968, pp. 50–61.

Cruse, Harold. *Crisis of the Negro Intellectual*. New York: William Morrow & Co., 1967, pp. 6, 242, 273, 355, 405, 408–9, 416, 421, 430, 441–43, 492, 548, 557–58, 563–64.

Drimmer, Melvin, (ed.). *Black History*. New York: Doubleday, 1968.

Ebony, Editors of. *The Negro Handbook.* Chicago: Johnson Publishing Co., 1966.

Epps, Archie (ed.). *The Speeches of Malcolm X at Harvard.* New York, William Morrow and Co., Inc., 1968.

Essien-Udom, E. U. *Black Nationalism: A Search for an Identity in America.* Chicago: University of Chicago Press, 1962.

Farmer, James. *Freedom—When?* New York: Random House, 1966.

Franklin, John Hope (ed.), with Isidor Starr. *The Negro in Twentieth-Century America.* New York: Vintage Books, 1967, pp. 15–16.

Hernton, Calvin C. *White Papers for White Americans.* New York: Doubleday, 1966.

Jones, LeRoi. *Home: Social Essays.* New York: William Morrow & Co., 1966.

Lincoln, C. Eric. *The Black Muslims in America.* Boston: Beacon Press, 1961.

———. *My Face Is Black.* Boston: Beacon Press, 1964.

Lomax, Louis E. *The Negro Revolt.* New York: Harper & Row, 1962.

———. *When the Word Is Given.* Cleveland: World Publishing Co., 1963.

Malcolm X (with the assistance of Alex Haley). *The Autobiography of Malcolm X.* New York: Grove Press, 1965.

Mitchell, Loften. *Black Drama.* New York: Hawthorn Books, 1967.

Randall, Dudley, and Burroughs, Margaret B. *For Malcolm.* Detroit: Broadside Press, 1966.

Warren, Robert Penn. *Who Speaks for the Negro?* New York: Random House, 1965.

Book Reviews

Bayard Rustin, in *Book Week,* November 14, 1965.

Emile Capouya, in *Saturday Review,* November 20, 1965.

Thomas Bretz, S.J., in *Christian Century,* December 8, 1965.

Truman Nelson, in *The Nation,* November 8, 1965.

Robert Bone, in *The New York Times Book Review,* September 11, 1966.

Nikki Giovanni, in *Negro Digest,* November 1968.

Pamphlets

Breitman, George (ed.). *Documents on the Negro Struggle.* New York: Pioneer Publishers, Document No. 4, 1939.
————. *Malcolm X: The Man and His Ideas.* New York: Pioneer Publishers, March 1965.
Malcolm X. *Two Speeches by Malcolm X.* New York: Pioneer Publishers, March 1965.
————. *Malcolm X Talks to Young People.* New York: Young Socialist Pamphlet, October 1965.
Mitchell, Sara. *Brother Malcolm.* New York: Malcolm X Memorial Committee, May 1965.

Articles

"Malcolm X Splits with Muhammad." *The New York Times* account of the split, March 9, 1964.
"Interview with Malcolm X." A. B. Spellman, *Monthly Review,* May 1964.
"Black Nationalism and Radical Unity." A. B. Spellman, *The Second Coming,* January 1965.
"Feud Within the Black Muslims." Gertrude Samuels, *The New York Times Magazine,* March 22, 1964.
"Malcolm X: Charismatic Demagogue." Albert Southwick, *Christian Century,* June 5, 1963.
"The Malcolm X Myth." Albert Cleage, Jr., *Liberator,* June 1967.
"Malcolm X." Laurence and Richard Henry, *Now,* March–April 1966.
"The Muslims' Decline." Eldridge Cleaver, *Ramparts,* February 1967.
"Mystery of Malcolm X." Hans J. Massaquoi, *Ebony,* September 1964.
"Malcolm the Martyr." Clarence Major, *Negro Digest,* December 1966.
"Malcolm X Lives." Laurence Henry, *Cavalier,* June 1966.
"The Life and Death of Malcolm X." William F. Warde, *International Socialist Review,* Vol. 26, Spring 1965.
"The Red Chinese American Negro." William Worthy, *Esquire,* October 1964.
"Playboy Interview: Malcolm X." *Playboy,* May 1963.
"Malcolm X: The Final Interview." Roland Miller, *Flamingo,* Ghana edition, June 1965.

"Interview With Malcolm X." *Young Socialist,* March–April 1965.

"Who Was Malcolm X?" Charles W. Wiley, *National Review,* March 23, 1965.

"Malcolm X: Prophet of Harlem." Cameron Duodu, *Drum Magazine,* Ghana edition, October 1964.

"Interview With Malcolm X." Interviewed by Jack Barnes and Barry Sheppard, *Young Socialist,* March–April 1965.

"The Meaning of Malcolm X." C. Eric Lincoln, *Christian Century,* April 7, 1965.

"The Pilgrimage of Malcolm X." R. A. Schrath, *Catholic World,* September 1967.

"Malcolm X Is Alive." R. A. Schrath, *America,* April 22, 1967.

"Malcolm X." Glanville, *New Statesman,* June 1964.

"Malcolm X." Murray Kempton, *Spectator* (London), February 26, 1965.

Malcolm X Obituary, *The New York Times,* February 22, 1965.

"Elijah in the Wilderness." Nat Hentoff, *Reporter,* August 4, 1960.

"Violent End of the Man Called Malcolm X." Gordon Parks, *Life,* March 5, 1965.

"Assassination of Malcolm X." *Illustrated London News,* February 27, 1965.

"Minister Malcolm: Orator Profundo." N. H. Boulware, *Negro History Bulletin,* 1967.

"Violence vs. Non-Violence." Editorial, *Ebony,* April 1965.

"Tragedy of Malcolm X." *America,* March 6, 1965.

"Journey Towards Truth." T. Kretz, *Christian Century,* December 8, 1965.

"Enter Muhammad." *National Review,* July 2, 1963.

"Malcolm X: Mission and Meaning." Robert P. Warren, *Yale Review,* December 1966.

"Odyssey of a Black Man." Nat Hentoff, *Commonweal,* January 28, 1966.

"Who Issued the Order?" *Newsweek,* March 21, 1966.

"Angry Spokesman Malcolm X Tells Off Whites." *Life,* May 31, 1963.

"Now It's a Negro Drive for Segregation." *U.S. News & World Report,* March 30, 1964.

"Malcolm's Brand X." *Newsweek,* March 23, 1964.

"Miami Notebook: Cassius Clay and Malcolm X." George Plimpton, *Harper's,* June 1964.

"Ominous Malcolm X Exits From the Muslims." Marc Crawford, *Life,* March 20, 1964.

"Pied Piper of Harlem." *Christian Century,* April 1, 1964.

"X on the Spot." *Newsweek,* December 16, 1963.

"Lesson of Malcolm X." Editorial, *Saturday Evening Post,* September 12, 1964.

"I'm Talking to You, White Man." Excerpts from *Autobiography, Saturday Evening Post,* September 12, 1964.

"Who Killed Malcolm X?" Eric Norden, *The Realist,* February 1967.

"Redd Foxx—Crown Prince of Clowns." Louie Robinson, *Ebony.* Famous comedian recalls past friendship with Malcolm X, April, 1967.

"Who Killed Malcolm X?" Allan Morrison, *Ebony,* October 1965.

"Malcolm X: Nothing But a Man." Wyatt T. Walker, *Negro Digest,* August 1965.

"Why I Eulogized Malcolm X." Ossie Davis, *Negro Digest,* February 1966.

"Brother Malcolm and the Black Revolution." W. Keorapetse Kgositsile, *Negro Digest,* November 1968.

"A Visit with the Widow of Malcolm X." Fletcher Knebel, *Look;* March 4, 1969.

"The Legacy of Malcolm X." Betty Shabazz, *Ebony,* June 1969.

ABOUT THE CONTRIBUTORS

JOHN HENRIK CLARKE, the editor of this volume, is a specialist in African history and his works include "Reclaiming the Lost African Heritage," published in *The American Negro Writer*. In addition, he edited *Harlem: A Community in Transition* and *Harlem U.S.A.* Since 1962 he has been Associate Editor of *Freedomways* magazine and since 1964 he has been Director of the Heritage Teaching Program of Harlem Youth Opportunities Unlimited—Associated Community Teams. He is also a lecturer of African history at the New School for Social Research and a teacher of African and Afro-American history with the Head Start Training Program at New York University.

C. ERIC LINCOLN, author of *The Black Muslims in America,* is currently Professor of Sociology and Religion at the Union Theological Seminary in New York City. His articles on race relations have appeared in *The Reporter, Phylon,* and the New York *Times.* He has authored several other books, including *Is Anybody Listening to Black America?* and *The Negro Pilgrimage in America.*

REVEREND ALBERT CLEAGE is currently Chairman of the Detroit Inner City Organizing Committee and is both author and minister. His articles appear in *Negro Digest* as well as other magazines.

CHARLES E. WILSON, an author from Brooklyn, New York, received a master's degree in psychology and has studied public administration as well. His articles have appeared in *Liberator* magazine, *Liberation, Negro Digest, Jewish Currents,* and others.

W. KEORAPETSE KGOSITSILE, a poet, was born in Johannesburg, South Africa. His essays and poems have been published both in the United States and abroad. He has studied at Lincoln University, Columbia University, the University of New Hampshire, and the New School for Social Research.

JAMES BOGGS is the author of *The American Revolution,* which has appeared in translation in Latin America, France, and Japan, He has also written articles on Black Power. He was born in Alabama and is a major revolutionary theoretician.

PATRICIA ROBINSON attended Simmons College and her graduate studies were taken at the Boston University School of Social Work. She has had a varied career in social work, private psychotherapy practice, and as staff correspondent for Afro-American newspapers. Her articles have appeared both in this country and in Italy.

WYATT TEE WALKER, a longtime associate of Dr. Martin Luther King, Jr., developed major projects for the Southern Christian Leadership Conference. Formerly Director of the Negro Heritage Library, he is now a practicing minister in Harlem.

ABDELWAHAB M. ELMESSIRI was born in the United Arab Republic (Egypt) in 1938 and had his early schooling in that country. He received his B.A. at Alexandria University in English literature and his M.A. at Columbia University. He is presently a Ph.D. candidate at Rutgers University. He has been the Editor of the *Arab Journal* and an anthology of nine studies of the Arab-Israeli conflict.

EARL GRANT has traveled extensively abroad and has lived and worked in a number of cities in West Africa, primarily in Ghana, as a student of Afro-American and African history. He became associated with Malcolm X in 1957 and remained so until Malcolm X's death. He currently resides in Queens, New York, where he produces visual material on African history.

ART SEARS, JR., a staff reporter for the *Wall Street Journal,* is a graduate of the University of Pennsylvania (journalism). He also attended the University of Wisconsin where he studied political science and criminology. He has been on the staff of the Johnson Publishing Company of Chicago, Illinois, as an Associate Editor, and has been the New York Editor of *Jet* magazine and an Associate Editor of *Ebony* magazine. For several years he served as a member of the Public Relations Committee of the Interracial Council for Business Opportunity, a voluntary organization to aid small black business enterprises.

MBURUMBA KERINA attended Lincoln University and the New School for Social Research and received his doctorate at the University of Djakarta in Indonesia. Presently he is Assistant Director of the South Bronx Educational Center and he is an adjunct Assistant Professor at the City University of New York, Brooklyn College.

GORDON PARKS, one of the outstanding and creative modern photographers, is on the staff of *Life* magazine. A film producer and author, his works have included *The Learning Tree* and other books.

SHIRLEY GRAHAM DUBOIS is the widow of the late W. E. B. Dubois. An internationally known author in her own right, her works include *There Was Once a Slave: The Story of Frederick Douglass, The Story of Phyllis Wheatly, Your Most Humble Servant* (the story of Benjamin Banneker), among others. She is a former Director of Ghana Television.

OSSIE DAVIS is an internationally known actor, producer, and playwright, and a civil rights activist. His roles have included the title role in *Purlie Victorious,* a major Broadway play.

BETTY SHABAZZ, widow of Malcolm X, formerly was a registered nurse and now lives in New Rochelle, New York, with her six daughters while she continues to work in the black struggle.

KENNETH B. CLARK is Director of the Metropolitan Applied Research Center in New York and a Professor of Psychology at City College in New York. He was one of the founders of Harlem Youth Opportunities Unlimited. His publications include *Dark Ghetto,* a study of the ghetto community with specific emphasis on Harlem, and *Prejudice and Your Child;* and he is editor of *The Negro Protest.*

LESLIE ALEXANDER LACY is co-author of "The Sekondi-Tacoradi Strike" in *Politics in Africa* and is currently completing an autobiographical book which Macmillan will publish early in 1970. He is a Professor of African Studies at Howard University in Washington, D.C.

LEBERT BETHUNE, currently working on a novel concerning Africa and the Caribbean and a new collection of poems, authored *Juju of My Own*. He worked for the Tanzanian Government as a film maker and his travels have taken him through East Africa, Europe, and the Middle East. He attended New York University and the Sorbonne in France.

RUBY M. ESSIEN-UDOM was formerly a public school teacher in New York City. She is presently teaching in Nigeria and is the wife of Professor E. U. Essien-Udom.

E. U. ESSIEN-UDOM is author of *Black Nationalism: A Search for an Identity in America*. His articles have appeared in *Freedomways*. He is presently Chairman of the Department of Political Science of the University of Abadan, Nigeria.

A. PETER BAILEY, Associate Editor of *Ebony* magazine, was born in Columbus, Georgia, and grew up in Tuskegee, Alabama. He attended Howard University. A founding member of the Organization of Afro-American Unity, he was also editor of the OAAU newsletter "Blacklash." In addition he served the NAACP Youth Group, CORE, and the Harlem Rent Strike Committee. His articles have appeared in *Negro Digest*.